The Business Analyst's Career Master Plan

Tools, techniques, and strategies for a thriving career in business analysis

Jamie Champagne

The Business Analyst's Career Master Plan

Portfolio Director: Pavan Ramchandani

Relationship Lead: Mohd Riyan Khan

Program Manager: Divij Kotian

Content Engineer: Akanksha Gupta

Technical Editor: Vidhisha Patidar

Copy Editor: Safis Editing

Proofreader: Akanksha Gupta

Indexer: Pratik Shirodkar

Production Designer: Vijay Kamble

Growth Lead: Priya Bhanushali

First published: September 2025

Production reference: 2010925

Published by Packt Publishing Ltd.
Grosvenor House
11 St Paul's Square
Birmingham
B3 1RB, UK

ISBN 978-1-83620-685-9

www.packtpub.com

To all of those who have let me collaborate with you on incredible ideas for a better world,
one business analyst at a time: thank you for letting me call you ohana (family)!

And for all those that read this, like my husband and daughter help to keep the stoke alive in me,
may the stoke for greater value always stay at the surface while the value swims deep!

—Jamie Champagne

Foreword

It's not every day you get asked to write the foreword for a book written by a friend, and not just any friend, but someone you've had the privilege of working alongside, learning from, and watching grow into a trusted voice in the business analysis community.

Writing this foreword isn't just a professional honor. It's a personal one, too.

Business analysis, at its best, is about more than just eliciting requirements or documenting processes. It's about creating clarity where there's confusion, building bridges between ideas and action, and uncovering the hidden value in the way things are done today, so we can make tomorrow better. This is where Jamie Champagne truly excels.

This book captures all of that and more. It's insightful, practical, and, maybe most importantly, rooted in the real-world experience of someone who has done (and continues to do!) the work, has faced the challenges, and has come out the other side with insights and lessons worth sharing.

One of the things I've always admired about Jamie is her ability to bring a thoughtful, human approach to the work, while finding the fun in even mundane tasks.

Business analysis can often feel like a technical or procedural discipline, but this book reminds us that at its heart, it's a people business. Whether it's uncovering stakeholder needs, guiding a team through change, or aligning a project with strategic goals, Jamie never loses sight of the human element.

We first crossed paths in a pub in Manhattan one Sunday night. We were both in town to speak at a conference over the next few days, and were the last to arrive. Being relegated to the end of a 20-person table, we became incredibly fast friends, which continued over the years and has only increased through our shared work as LinkedIn Learning instructors, where we are both active in creating courses to help professionals level up their skills and navigate an increasingly complex business world. This has even led to a collaborative course where we share our perspectives: Jamie's tactical slant and my strategic view of the business analysis profession.

Over the years, we've shared more than just a platform. We've shared ideas, feedback, support, and a lot of laughs. We even co-presented a keynote on having more fun at work…and yes, that is possible!

This book is a reflection of all the qualities that make Jamie not just a great business analyst but also a great teacher, communicator, and colleague. It's practical without being dry, deep without being dense, and personal without ever losing sight of the reader's journey. Whether you're new to the field or a seasoned analyst looking for a fresh perspective, you'll find something here to inspire, challenge, and guide you.

More than anything, I hope you read this book the way I know it was written: with a spirit of curiosity, generosity, and growth.

You're in good hands.

Vincent Mirabelli, CBAP, MBB, PMP

Principal Research Director, Info-Tech Research Group

President, IIBA® Toronto Chapter

LinkedIn Learning Instructor

`vincentmirabelli.com`

Contributors

About the author

Jamie Champagne, CSP, is a speaker, author, and trainer who is passionate about helping professionals find joy and success in their business analysis careers. With over 20 years of experience in business analysis, project management, and change leadership, she has authored *Seven Steps to Mastering Business Analysis, 2nd Edition*, and created popular courses on LinkedIn Learning and Pluralsight. Jamie is grateful for the support of her family, friends, and mentors, who have encouraged her to share her passion with the world. When not collaborating with teams, she can be found collaborating with her friends and family on a surfboard on the waters in Hawaii.

About the reviewers

Benjamin Yuan is a seasoned technology executive with over 20 years of experience in cloud transformation and strategic partnerships. Currently serving as Global Strategic Partnerships Leader at **Amazon Web Services (AWS)**, he leads initiatives driving cloud adoption and digital transformation across markets. Previously, as Chief Revenue Officer for a strategic consulting firm and Principal/CRO for a technology solutions company, he specialized in scaling operations and building high-value partnerships. His extensive background includes PMO leadership at Fortune 500 companies and major healthcare organizations. Ben is a faculty member at the University of Hawaii, serves on PMI's Global Board, and holds an MBA from Hawaii Pacific University.

I would like to thank my family for their unwavering support throughout this journey. Special appreciation goes to my colleagues at AWS and the global cloud community for their collaborative spirit and innovative mindset. I'm also grateful to the PMI community and my students at the University of Hawaii, who continue to inspire me to share knowledge and drive technological advancement.

Darrah Ruiz is a consultant based in Hawai'i, where she specializes in information technology and Medicaid systems for state government. With a background in business analysis and project process improvement, she has supported efforts in system modernization, user acceptance testing, and governance documentation. Darrah also co-leads professional communities of practice that foster learning and certification preparation for business analysts. Rooted in Hawai'i's spirit of collaboration and respect, her work emphasizes clarity in communication, cross-team partnerships, and translating complex requirements into actionable solutions.

I am deeply thankful to my husband for his unwavering support and encouragement to keep growing in my knowledge. I am also grateful to my peers, who remain a steady source of insight and inspiration in the ever-changing world of business analysis.

Christina Lovelock is a BA leader, consultant, coach, and author. She has over 20 years of experience in business analysis and digital transformation, and has built teams ranging in size from five to 120 BAs. She is active in the professional community, regularly speaking at events and global conferences. Committed to advancing the BA profession, she has introduced entry-level BA roles into her organizations and chaired the development of the UK National BA Apprenticeship Standard.

Christina loves writing about topics relevant to BAs and is a regular contributor to *ITNow* magazine, *BA Times*, and *BA Digest*. She is the author of two books, including *Delivering Business Analysis* and her latest release, *Careers in Tech, Data and Digital*.

Thank you to all the amazing BAs who share their knowledge and experience with the wider community through books, articles, webinars, conference presentations, and podcasts. There are so many brilliant ways to continually learn as a business analyst, and being part of this international professional community has always been an absolute pleasure.

Table of Contents

Part 1: Introduction to Business Analysis Work

1

2

3

Part 2: Building a Career in Business Analysis

4

5

Specializations within Business Analysis   89

6

Business Analysis Certifications and Training   111

Part 3: Being Successful in Business Analysis Work

7

8

9

Leadership and Mentorship in Business Analysis   173

Part 4: The Future of Your Business Analysis Work

10

Continuous Learning and Professional Development   197

11

Emerging Trends and the Future of Business Analysis   213

12

Assessments and Techniques for Career Success   239

13

Final Thoughts and Next Steps   253

Preface

This book is a practical and inspiring guide for business analysts, taking you from foundational skills to advanced strategies and empowering you to shape your career, embrace technology, and drive meaningful change.

Who this book is for

This book is written for **anyone doing, or aspiring to do, business analysis work**. That includes:

- **Early-career professionals** who are just discovering business analysis and looking for direction
- **Practicing business analysts** who want to sharpen their skills, expand into specializations, or pursue leadership opportunities
- **Project managers, process improvement specialists, change managers, and other professionals** who find themselves performing business analysis activities and want to formalize and grow their expertise
- **Senior professionals and leaders** who want to mentor others, understand the value of business analysis better, and maximize the contribution of their teams

If you're curious about advancing your career, exploring career paths, or simply finding new ways to **deliver value through analysis**, this book is for you.

What you should know before you start

A few essentials will help set the stage for your learning:

- **No prior experience is required.** If you've only just heard of business analysis, this book will guide you through the fundamentals, techniques, and career opportunities.
- **Bring your project and work experiences with you.** If you've ever found yourself working on projects, supporting change, or helping solve problems in your organization, those experiences will fuel your learning as you connect the dots with the ideas in this book.
- **An open mindset is essential.** The profession is evolving rapidly with new technologies, practices, and expectations. Success comes not from memorizing techniques but from learning how to adapt, apply, and grow.

This book is meant to be an action-focused career guide. And this means a few things you can do to make the most of this:

- *Action-focused* - this means that each chapter has activities for you to do while reading the content. Don't be afraid to pull out your favorite notebook, digital or otherwise, and pause to make notes and capture some ideas.

- *Guide* - this is not a cookbook, not an explicit checklist to mark off as complete and move on. It is a book of ideas, inspiration, and great questions for you to reflect on where you are in your journey. Each decision on your career path can be treated like business analysis – with the right input, you can charge forward with data-driven decision-making when it comes to your next career move.

- *Career* - business analysis takes many shapes and forms and will continue throughout your work experiences. This book can definitely help you in your immediate work – don't be afraid to flip to different sections depending on what you are working on – but also remember that it is designed to help you in the long run. Build out a plan for your career path but also know nothing is set in stone. Keep your mind, your career path, and your decision-making just as nimble as your daily analysis work.

What this book covers

Chapter 1, Unlocking Opportunities in Business Analysis, introduces the evolving world of business analysis, defining its purpose, roles, and skills while showing how it opens diverse and rewarding career paths across industries.

Chapter 2, Foundational Skills for Business Analysis Professionals, focuses on core competencies, practical tools and techniques, and the habits that create a solid base, laying the groundwork for effective business analysis.

Chapter 3, Advanced Business Analysis Techniques, explores advanced techniques that build on your core foundational analysis skills to help you tackle bigger challenges and more complex problems.

Chapter 4, Navigating Career Progression in Business Analysis, turns to applying those same analysis techniques to your own career by exploring career advancement opportunities, approaches to challenges you may face, and building a roadmap for your career success.

Chapter 5, Specializations within Business Analysis, helps you explore the specialization options available to business analysis professionals along with their benefits and challenges to help you consider your own career progression.

Chapter 6, Business Analysis Certifications and Training, explores certifications as one of the most powerful tools to advance your career. It highlights some of the most valuable options and techniques to help business analysis professionals successfully earn credentials that can propel their career forward.

Chapter 7, The Role of Technology in Business Analysis, explores some of the most powerful emerging technologies today and their impact on business analysis work. It discusses techniques you can use to integrate these technologies in your work while also staying abreast of technological trends and evolutions regardless of your career stage and specialization.

Chapter 8, Building Effective Stakeholder Relationships and Upholding Ethics, dives into the soft skills that transform your analysis work into meaningful impact. It emphasizes building successful relationships in your analysis work through collaboration, engagement, respect, and understanding, including maintaining your integrity when faced with ethical challenges.

Chapter 9, Leadership and Mentorship in Business Analysis, shows how business analysis professionals act as leaders in their roles, teams, organizations and communities. It explores how to measure and grow these valuable skills and introduces the power of mentorship and how it can be the secret to your career success.

Chapter 10, Continuous Learning and Professional Development, highlights how continuous learning is the hallmark of successful analysis professionals. This chapter helps you build a professional development plan to incorporate learning through various resources to ensure long-term career success.

Chapter 11, Emerging Trends and the Future of Business Analysis, explores the impact of technological innovations, evolving business models, and adaptive approaches and methodologies on your analysis work. It provides insights and direction while also forecasting the future environments that analysts may encounter.

Chapter 12, Assessments and Techniques for Career Success, gives you the tools to assess your own analysis career. It also equips you with techniques to incorporate feedback into your daily activities such that you continuously improve your performance and grow your skills with measurable results.

Chapter 13, Final Thoughts and Next Steps, summarizes the key takeaways and helps you build your actionable plan for immediate use. In this chapter, we encourage you to join the vast community of business analysis professionals and continuously grow the value you provide wherever your analysis career takes you.

To get the most out of this book

Approach each chapter with curiosity and a focus on your own professional journey. This is not just a reference, but a career guide designed to help you actively shape your path in business analysis. As you read, pause to reflect on how each idea relates to your experiences, and use the tools and assessments to capture insights you can apply immediately. By engaging with the content as a personal roadmap, you will transform the book from information into action.

As you work through the chapters:

- Pause and connect each idea to *your* work

- Note your own lessons and "aha" moments that relate

- Try the activities – they're meant to spark action!

- Let this only be the start – keep building your own career roadmap as you go

Conventions used

There are a couple of text conventions used throughout this book.

Bold: Indicates a new term, an important word, or words that you see onscreen. Here is an example: "**Data mining** and **data analysis** are additional techniques often used during your review of materials specifically related to the data."

> **Tips or important notes**
> Appear like this.

Get in touch

Feedback from our readers is always welcome.

General feedback: If you have questions about any aspect of this book, email us at customercare@packtpub.com and mention the book title in the subject of your message.

Errata: Although we have taken every care to ensure the accuracy of our content, mistakes do happen. If you have found a mistake in this book, we would be grateful if you would report this to us. Please visit www.packtpub.com/support/errata and fill in the form.

Piracy: If you come across any illegal copies of our works in any form on the internet, we would be grateful if you would provide us with the location address or website name. Please contact us at copyright@packt.com with a link to the material.

If you are interested in becoming an author: If there is a topic that you have expertise in and you are interested in either writing or contributing to a book, please visit authors.packtpub.com.

Share Your Thoughts

Once you've read *The Business Analyst's Career Master Plan*, we'd love to hear your thoughts! Scan the QR code below to go straight to the Amazon review page for this book and share your feedback.

https://packt.link/r/1-836-20685-2

Your review is important to us and the tech community and will help us make sure we're delivering excellent quality content.

Your Book Comes with Exclusive Perks – Here's How to Unlock Them

Unlock this book's exclusive benefits now

UNLOCK NOW

Scan this QR code or go to `packtpub.com/unlock`, then search this book by name. Ensure it's the correct edition.

Note: Have your purchase invoice ready before you start.

Figure 0.1: Next-Gen Reader, AI Assistant (Beta), and Free PDF access

Enhanced reading experience with our next-gen reader:

- **Multi-device progress sync**: Learn from any device with seamless progress sync.

- **Highlighting and notetaking**: Turn your reading into lasting knowledge.

- **Bookmarking**: Revisit your most important learnings anytime.

- **Dark mode**: Focus with minimal eye strain by switching to dark or sepia mode.

Learn smarter using our AI assistant (Beta):

- **Summarize it**: Summarize key sections or an entire chapter.

- **AI code explainers**: In the next-gen Packt Reader, click the **Explain** button above each code block for AI-powered code explanations.

> **Note:**
>
> *The AI assistant is part of the next-gen Packt Reader and is still in beta.*

Learn anytime, anywhere:

Access your content offline with DRM-free PDF and ePub versions—compatible with your favorite e-readers.

Unlock your Book's Exclusive Benefits

Your copy of this book comes with the following exclusive benefits:

- Next-gen Packt Reader

- AI assistant (beta)

- DRM-free PDF/ePub downloads

Use the following guide to unlock them if you haven't already. The process takes just a few minutes and needs to be done only once.

How to unlock these benefits in three easy steps

Step 1

Have your purchase invoice for this book ready, as you'll need it in *Step 3*. If you received a physical invoice, scan it on your phone and have it ready as either a PDF, JPG, or PNG.

For more help on finding your invoice, visit `https://www.packtpub.com/unlock-benefits/help`.

> **Note**
>
> Did you buy this book directly from Packt? You don't need an invoice. After completing *Step 2*, you can jump straight to your exclusive content.

Step 2

Scan this QR code or go to `packtpub.com/unlock`.

On the page that opens (which will look similar to *Figure 0.2* if you're on desktop), search for this book by name. Make sure you select the correct edition.

Figure 0.2: Packt landing page for unlocking the book on desktop

Step 3

Sign in to your Packt account or create a new one for free. Once you're logged in, upload your invoice. It can be in PDF, PNG, or JPG format and must be no larger than 10 MB. Follow the rest of the instructions on the screen to complete the process.

Need help?

If you get stuck and need help, visit `https://www.packtpub.com/ unlock-benefits/help` for a detailed FAQ on how to find your invoices and more. The following QR code will take you to the help page directly:

Note

If you are still facing issues, reach out to `customercare@packt.com`.

Part 1:
Introduction to Business Analysis Work

In this part, you will be introduced to the business analysis profession and the practice of business analysis work. You will explore the key activities common to all business analysis work followed by more advanced techniques as your comfort and your career grow in the field.

This part has the following chapters:

- *Chapter 1, Unlocking Opportunities in Business Analysis*
- *Chapter 2, Foundational Skills for Business Analysis Professionals*
- *Chapter 3, Advancing Your Business Analysis Techniques*

1

Unlocking Opportunities in Business Analysis

A *business analyst* is more than a job title: it is a role, a skill, and, most importantly, a great career path you can take to bring about impactful value. If you search business analysis job descriptions, however, you will find such variation in scope, size, responsibilities, and requirements that it can be hard to understand what exactly business analysis is and what it looks like to be a business analyst. And that is exactly where we will start – by defining business analysis and why the practice is not only evolving but becoming more critical to businesses. The skills of a business analyst overlap with that of many other professions, and understanding the relationships and differences can be key to helping you in your career planning.

Business analysis brings real value to organizations through the defined functions and responsibilities performed by those doing analysis work. Understanding these activities and what differentiates junior analysis professionals from senior analysis professionals can help you seek out organizations and industries that are actively investing in business analysis talent. These skill sets include competencies you probably already have and more that you can develop based on where you want to go. On your business analysis career journey, you'll find that not only are the opportunities vast and exciting but there is also an entire global community dedicated to enabling changes that deliver long-lasting value.

In this chapter, we're going to cover the following main topics:

- Defining business analysis
- The role and importance of business analysis in organizations
- Exploring career opportunities in business analysis
- Defining the essential skills for business analysis professionals

Defining business analysis

Business analysis is all about the delivery of value. As true as this definition is, it is quite vague and all-encompassing. However, if you not only define business analysis but, more importantly, clearly articulate the impact of great business analysis work on an organization, *you* are truly adding value! With this perspective of your business analysis work, the possibilities for your business analysis career are limitless – not only in terms of where you can take it but also in the success you can achieve by fully focusing on maximizing value in every endeavor.

So, what is business analysis?

Business analysis has been defined as follows:

> *"The practice of enabling change in the context of an enterprise by defining needs and recommending solutions that deliver value to stakeholders."*

> *International Institute of Business Analysis™ (IIBA®)*

This definition is great for many reasons.

First, it articulates *enabling change.*Business analysis is about change-based work. Whether you are enacting the change yourself or are responding to changes around you, change is the only constant. This is exactly the environment for business analysis and why its value shines.

Now, the work of business analysis professionals is all about two key actions:

- Defining needs
- Recommending solutions

Many stakeholders will tell you what they want or even simply their frustrations. The power of business analysis is in taking all these inputs and understanding them to identify what is truly needed to bring about the desired business value. Business analysis professionals seek to understand how to accomplish goals and act as unbiased parties in a conversation.

With that understanding, you can recommend solution options. The keyword here is *recommend*; you do not make the decisions. Making decisions is the job of your stakeholders, particularly sponsors and owners. Your job is to define the options in detail and make such a compelling business case that the best choice becomes obvious to the decision-makers. We'll highlight how to make these compelling business cases throughout the book. For now, approach this journey from a perspective of not only understanding what is needed but also recommending smart solutions that make it easy for your stakeholders to decide and act on.

Now, the last portion of this definition that we need to consider is the keyword *value*. Business analysis is all about delivering value. No matter what your position, department, organization, or even the industry your career grows into, always focus on adding value. How are you helping the project deliver, and therefore add, value? How are you helping your department get the most value out of their investments? And how are you helping to ensure products continue to be long-term solutions and never stop delivering value? That is the creed of a business analysis professional that will guide you in your career.

Understanding who is a business analyst

Now, one of the important things about the term *business analyst* is that the job role and title are often confused. This means that you can find that the same job title has very different job descriptions from company to company. This shows even in how the IIBA describes a business analyst as "*anyone who performs business analysis work.*"

Again, this is a very vague definition that suggests the role is all-encompassing. But understand that this role has evolved from its roots as a technical position whose focus was often on simply supporting company technical projects. These projects' customers were often internal staff. Take, for example, implementing a **customer relationship management** (**CRM**) system. The main installation work might be primarily done by the **information technology** (**IT**) team; however, the primary customer of the CRM system is the marketing department. The system is not meant for external customers. So then, IT staff have to try to understand marketing processes and requirements. This can be a challenge because you hired technical experts who are great at installing and maintaining software, but not necessarily knowledgeable in sales campaigns and customer relationships. There needs to be some translation of what the system does and can do for the marketing team, and how the software needs to perform to help accomplish the marketing goals. This is where the role of the business analyst comes in.

As the role of the *translator* melted away and business analysts found themselves working as key stakeholders on project teams, the business understanding became so valuable that technical **subject matter experts** (**SMEs**) were receiving training in various business areas to be able to do this translation work between technical and business areas. Thus, we began to see the rise of general business analysts who were not reporting to an IT department but rather to other areas of the organization. Analyst roles began to emerge in marketing, human resources, and security. And with even further growth, analysts were found in project office and even enterprise positions that looked across all departments.

Here's a question to stop and ask yourself right now

Do I enjoy learning technology, understanding how it works, and defining scenarios for the other areas of the business, including where and how they can take advantage of these capabilities? Or would I rather work in an area of the business focused on the non-technical business work outside the IT department?

Your answer may not only sway your career but also help you decide what types of analysis roles you are looking for. Just because the original careers began in technical positions does not mean you have to take a technical position to be a great business analysis professional. The position descriptions, and even the names of the positions themselves, are evolving and will continue to evolve. The key point is to recognize the analysis activities that are performed and ask yourself what is most important to you, remembering there is both a practice and profession of business analysis work.

The purpose of business analysis in organizations

With the focus on delivering value, business analysis has become a key component to those who are driving organizations forward. In general, business analysis is focused on the needs of the organization. Business analysis professionals are the unbiased parties that look holistically at every situation to see how the organization can gain the most value.

Going back to that definition we began with, *business analysis professionals use their analysis skills to understand needs*. These needs are not obvious but must be elicited, leveraging various techniques from document analysis to interactive facilitated stakeholder sessions, for example. Many end users tell you what they want, not what they need. They might say they need a new app when in fact, all they need is to know how the current system works and what buttons to push. How do you define the needs correctly when stakeholder demands can be contradictory? The answer is that you need someone who can analyze the situation and make recommendations on the best way to proceed.

That is the second part to think about: *business analysis professionals make recommendations*. They have to leverage their powers of influence coupled with technical analysis skills to present solid business cases of why one might choose one option over another.

Remember

A business analyst never actually makes a business decision. They *recommend* business decision options but ultimately must get stakeholders to make, and own, the business decision.

This is why interpersonal communication skills, and technical analysis to analyze options, alternatives, risks, and potential impacts are critical to your success in a business analysis role.

As you will see in the next section, there is a need for roles that are unbiased, removed from having any investment in the product, and focused on the organization as a whole. Too many areas of organizations today are function-oriented, compete for resources, or are focused on a singular internal or external success metric. These all have to be balanced before, during, and after project-based work. This means asking the great questions:

- Are we getting all the value we planned for?

- Are we still getting value?

- What can we do to maximize the return on all our investments in terms of both time and resources?

How business analysis professionals differ from project managers and technical roles

Business analysis skills have long overlapped with other position descriptions. In fact, you'll often come across many position descriptions that seem to describe a business analysis professional even though their titles may be of a program manager or a financial or risk analyst. These are all positions that use business analysis skills.

Take, for example, a project manager. This is a long-established position that has a very clear goal: the successful completion of a project. Their sole focus is on achieving the objectives set out by the project charter. They concentrate on scope, schedule, and budget. Their responsibility is not to do the work but to direct the creation, approval, and ongoing change work of executing the project plan (PMI®, 2024). Now, there is often a lot of work to define the specific tasks that must be completed to achieve the project outcomes. How do project managers know which tasks to complete? Well, the **requirements** for the project determine what has to be done. And where do those requirements come from? Good analysis work!

A lot of work goes into coordinating with stakeholders to elicit, define, verify, validate, and trace requirements through approvals and implementation. That is all business analysis work. Now, in a perfect world, a project has a project manager to ensure the work is carried out, as well as a business analyst who ensures the right work is done at the right time for the right reasons. It is a wonderful symbiotic relationship. The challenge is that not every project office is staffed this way. Actually, it can be quite hard to justify a second "coordinator" role on a project. So, the project manager is often responsible for not only managing the tasks to complete the work but also doing the analysis work.

The same goes for system analysts, solution architects, and other technical positions that have a general responsibility for day-to-day operations. While making sure the systems are up and running may seem like it needs more technical, application-specific skills, think about when things do not go as planned. The amount of analysis, research, testing, and exploration that goes into finding the root cause is a great example of the analysis skills required of every position that supports technical applications and equipment. Those analysis skills are then coupled with their subject area expertise to help deliver recommendations. No application owner wants to be told there is nothing they can do when an issue arises. They want options. Good analysis work, even in a specific subject matter area, is what helps define options for more informed decision-making.

Also, think about maximizing the investments of the technology you already own. Your process improvement and solution evaluation teams are filling the roles of business analysis professionals. Process improvement teams often seek to understand current situations to define potentially improved future processes. Auditors seek to understand what is and is not being captured in systems. Finance departments are always looking at budgets to see whether teams really need all the licensing or maintenance investments. Looking at what you already have and seeing whether there are better, more efficient, or more effective options, is a great analysis that often does not happen in project-based work. Yet, there needs to be dedicated analysis time for these kinds of efforts. So, if you do not have someone on your team who performs this function, then you, even as the SME, will need to equip your toolbox with analysis skills to help address all these situations. That is why it would be great if every technical team had a group of business analysis professionals who could easily help take a look at the current issue, situation, or opportunity with an unbiased eye focused on maximum value. So, as the title and the role of the business analysis professional continue to evolve in every industry, it is important to look at the value business analysis skills can bring to any organization. Think about both the work you have done and want to do in the future as we dive into defining the work of a business analysis professional.

Understanding the role and importance of business analysis in organizations

A business analyst is defined as anyone who performs business analysis work. No matter the technique, task, or context, their focus is on maximizing value (IIBA, 2024). Even if you choose not to focus solely on business analysis later in your career, the skills you gain now will benefit both you and your organization for years to come, regardless of technological or even industry changes.

Core functions and responsibilities of a business analysis professional

As you explore the various career paths for business analysis in the next sections, you'll see that while the work can sometimes feel vague or broad, there are core functions and responsibilities you can focus on, no matter what your position or the industry you work in.

The most common is being an SME on any **change-based work** (i.e., a project). Your responsibilities lie in defining the requirements of the solution and then validating that the solution does indeed meet your requirements. You might need to articulate to others how things do or do not work, producing some process models. Requirements will be traced to solution components and your test plans and results will need to be verified and validated.

Even if you are not the SME, you may need to elicit information from the stakeholders to define these requirements and detailed work. This is very common in project-based work. The business analyst is responsible for ensuring requirements are verified and validated throughout the entire change work. These are not just the technical requirements but rather all the requirements to deliver the goals of the project. Having a person not assigned to a particular line of business brings a more holistic approach to the team. This role can then focus on those non-functional requirements, including quality elements; transition requirements, such as training, communication, and data migrations; and potential opportunities to leverage the work for far greater gain than perhaps originally identified in the project charter. This comes through conducting interactive and facilitated workshops with stakeholders, engaging them in their workplaces with observations and interviews, and reading through the available documentation.

But business analysis resides well beyond the confines of a project or program. IIBA (2015) defines six knowledge areas of business analysis work, which includes both *strategy analysis* and *solution evaluation* that look beyond the scope of project-based work. Strategy analysis is the realm where senior professionals tend to migrate. This is where larger questions are asked about what is best for the organization. SWOT analysis, balanced scorecards, benchmarking, and market analysis are the techniques analysts use to look at what is happening both inside and outside the organization. Discussions range from reviewing and even defining the organizational mission and vision to exploring enterprise architecture and understanding what capability gaps the organization may possess.

But too often, the area of solution evaluation can quickly be overlooked with the day-to-day pressure to respond to current issues and market changes. Solution evaluation focuses on looking at what you already have and identifying whether it is still providing the maximum value for the organization. These are the operational improvement teams that plan for tomorrow by assessing what is and is not happening today. Those who love numbers will enjoy analyzing the statistics of metrics and **key performance indicators** (**KPIs**) of the organization and then crafting persuasive recommendations for business cases that will drive the greater value of the prior work. Regardless of whether this is an assigned position or simply rolled into the lessons-learned activities of the project, business analysis professionals will continuously identify areas of improvement and work to define the requirements that will enable the right changes to be quickly implemented.

Contributing to project outcomes and organizational efficiency

When business analysis skill sets are added to a project, the chances of success go up exponentially. Why? Because every decision point, which is a common risk area for a project manager, has extra support in analyzing the options and recommending solutions. Remember, business analysis professionals worry about what is best for the organization, not just a project. While a project manager may be trying to control the budget with design options, the long-term support models, integration capabilities, and options for future enhancements might be benefits that are worth paying more for. Someone must think beyond the project scope.

Remember, business analysis professionals are great change agents. All their work involves making changes for greater value. This is especially true when making organizational changes that impact the way stakeholders complete their work. Helping to articulate what is changing, what impact it has on the stakeholders, and how to make changes, as well as, most importantly, following up to help ensure the changes are firmly rooted in daily operations, is a big responsibility. You cannot simply throw a new application to the organization and just hope people use it. Defining the transition requirements that will turn your product into a solution is the key area where business analysis professionals justify their involvement in project-based work.

From start to finish, a commitment to understanding and natural curiosity drives continuous improvement in daily operations. For instance, a common activity might require you to understand a process to be able to identify the technical integration requirements. But in that same discussion with the stakeholder, you identify another process, related but out of the scope of the project, that needs improvement. You notice that a little training might be the answer to getting more users to use the system daily. You then use this insight to make a business case to justify some training time to help the organization get the most out of their investment. Despite it being outside the scope of the work of the project, you have identified an area where value can be added. That is because the business analysis professionals are always trying to understand the full context and see items more holistically.

So, with this understanding of what it takes for business analysis professionals to deliver value, let's explore the specific job titles and roles you can explore throughout your business analysis career.

Exploring career opportunities in business analysis

It can be challenging to define business analysis roles and work. However, the great news is that this creates a huge spectrum of career opportunities. The trick is to understand yourself and what motivations, desires, and hopes you have for your career.

Traditional business analysis career paths

When we think about the more traditional path of a business analysis career, we focus on starting in a **junior business analyst** position in a major corporation. Often, these roles are in technical teams, and they seem to take two types of starting points – either a role dedicated to business analysis or a system analyst position. Let's talk about the system analyst position first.

Starting as a system analyst

System analyst positions normally have you dedicated to a single system or application. You are expected to become an SME in this system. This makes you the perfect person to both troubleshoot when things go wrong and define opportunities for improvement. With this knowledge, though, you might find yourself doing more operational activities, such as supporting end users and performing maintenance tasks. However, with all this central focus on a single area, you are the perfect person to define any requirements for changes or analyze impacts from other project work for this system. Every one of these activities requires business analysis skills even if the position is not called a business analyst. But all of these roles and job titles are great areas for you to start building your skills and practicing analysis techniques. And these jobs that require analysis work are great places to begin building your experience in working with requirements and verification and validation activities.

Starting in a role such as this, typically your career path will then see you start to get offered analyst positions that focus on more **enterprise applications**. These are applications that often have more business-side end users. You will have to spend time understanding business requirements as much as technical requirements. This is often a great point for you to determine how technical of a position you want. Stepping beyond these types of roles can often go in two directions. Business analysis professionals are found in both: the lines of business of an organization and multiple areas of IT teams. You can continue to look more broadly at where and how your analysis skills can be used to help run the business. These roles are less technical and more focused on the *what* and *why* of change work. But you can also go deeper and become more technically focused on learning the *how* of the change work and help with detailed specifications and implementation and testing of changes.

For example, those who want to stay more technical often search for **solution architect** positions. These roles have more understanding of all the technical areas involved in an organization but are true analysts in that they analyze needs to determine the best solutions. There is more design work and focus on the optimization of technical assets and planning the future technical architecture. These are also great positions to push you to learn and understand all the facets of technology that both support and drive the business.

Another area that is great for senior technical analysts is management roles, from a single program area focus to a technical manager of teams. **Program managers** are great positions because you begin to balance both the operational and project-based work that leverages and exploits the value of a single program area. This could be an application, or it could be a functional area of the IT teams. This is where your leadership and interpersonal skills will be brought to the forefront. You will not only balance technical and business requirements but also the skill sets of your teams and look at capabilities coupled with long-term visions.

Starting as a junior business analyst

Now, the definition of the profession of business analysis by IIBA (2022) and the **Project Management Institute®(PMI®)** has led to the recognition of more and more business analysis-titled positions (Hass, 2005), so much so that there are many organizations that have junior and senior business analysts on a business analysis team in their companies today. These are often larger organizations with the business analysis teams found either in **project management offices** (**PMOs**), within the IT department itself, or even in enterprise areas of business development. These larger, more invested areas of business analysis work mean there is more dedication to a business analysis career path within the same company, if not the same organizational department (IIBA, 2023).

With some university-level schooling, often in a technology area, junior business analyst can be an entry-level job. Entry-level roles will be quite focused on understanding requirements and modeling business process and documentation. This is great as it will give you the opportunity to start both practicing business analysis techniques and learning about the organization and what drives this business. As you get comfortable working in project teams, learning to troubleshoot problems, and articulating clear requirements that can be easily developed and delivered, you can then move to a more in-depth-business analysis role.

Typically, we see the evolution of a business analysis professional in both the techniques and tasks they do, and the scope of the project work they are assigned. As they advance in their career, mid-level business analysts start to get assigned to larger projects. These are often for efforts that span beyond one department and require more coordination of both stakeholders and requirements. There will be recommendations requiring greater in-depth analysis of options as the decisions will require the collaboration of stakeholders and are not confined to a single domain. In these roles, you will find yourself learning more about different areas of the organization and will also start to develop your skills in repeated areas of work as an SME.

Once your project experience has you transitioning to enterprise, large-scale projects, this is often when you can grow into a senior business analysis role. Here, you are looked at as a guiding expert, able to be assigned to any project or initiative the organization identifies. You will have the experience to tailor your analysis approaches and leverage a greater number of in-depth techniques. You will start spending more time outside project work and having discussions with leadership about the strategic direction of the portfolios and even the organization. These discussions will shift over time to analyzing the current capabilities of both the internal workings of the organization and the external threats and opportunities the markets, competition, and even industry are presenting. Senior business analysis professionals often find themselves starting to mentor junior professionals who are beginning their careers in the same organization to help prepare them to grow and succeed in more advanced analysis positions.

Starting as a mid-to-senior-level business analyst

Individuals who have experience in business analysis, working on cross-functional projects, and collaborating with stakeholders on solutions are able to not only seek advanced business analysis positions that have a more strategic view in their change-based work but also shift to management roles.

In organizations where the profession and skill of business analysis are recognized, there is often a **business analysis manager** or team lead. Just like project managers have a PMO and a project management officer, organizations with a business analysis team will have a business analysis manager or lead. These roles shift the analysis work from focusing on being a project team lead to analyzing the business analysis skill sets and competencies employed at your organization. You do a lot of resource allocations to ensure the right projects get the right business analysis support. This can be as simple as assigning senior business analysts to more complex projects while ensuring junior business analysts work on simpler tasks.

At the same time, you may take on typical management duties, but again, will be leveraging your team's skill sets. You might assign that same junior analyst to assist the senior business analyst on a high visibility and high-risk enterprise project to not only provide support but also help mentor and train the junior analyst. You will be coordinating lessons learned and retrospectives and be responsible for the continuous improvement of the business analysis competencies at the organization. As a senior member of the team, you will be invited to take part in more strategic discussions around the portfolio of work the organization has as a whole.

Examples of the different levels of analysis work

Project-based business analysis work is one of the most common areas business analysis skills are applied to in organizations. But even within a project, there are different types of business analysis skillset demands and roles you can play. Consider the options listed as follows and think about what areas resonate with you. Where are you now? Where might you want to be?

- **Entry-level** and **junior business analysis roles** get assigned projects such as upgrading a server or building reports. These projects are technical in nature in that they require analysis support, but the roles are confined to either a single business unit or application in their scope of work. In these instances, analysts work directly with SMEs on project-based tasks that revolve around routine, day-to-day operations for the stakeholders involved. This routine nature makes the work easier to describe and understand. The tasks of the project are often known ahead of time or are easy to identify from prior experience.

- **Mid-level business analysis roles** involve tracing requirements on projects that are implementing new solutions for the organization. These are common digital transformations, such as implementing a CRM system or migrating to Microsoft Office Online. These projects will often introduce business analysts to change management topics and facilitate the delivery of systems such that the enterprise begins to leverage the solutions.

- **Senior-level business analysis roles** often get assigned before projects start, wherein business analysts are requested to help build out the potential business case. High-level goals of engaging in new markets or considering a merger or acquisition drive the change work that these professionals occupy themselves with.

All of these are project-based business analysis roles and activities. But just like the positions in an organization, the specific role you play on a project can vary. Even the role itself can evolve from a business analysis position to one that simply uses the business analysis skill set.

Transitioning to and from business analysis work

As described so far, there are a number of other roles that involve business analysis work but may not be titled business analyst roles. Project managers are a great example. Their jobs require a lot of analysis work to be successful, just like other common positions that are working to effect changes for greater value. Anyone doing business analysis work in these kinds of positions can easily pursue mid-level business analysis positions. They bring a great wealth of knowledge while having real-world experience. These transitions are relatively easy as mostly it is a shift in mindset to understanding the new area of work responsibilities. Often, these transitioning roles benefit from training in more specific analysis tasks and techniques.

Another popular role, especially with the rise of the agile methodologies and approaches, is the **product owner** role. Many business analysts on teams working with more agile and adaptive approaches find that they become pseudo or proxy product owners. They may not have ultimate control of the final decisions and priorities, but in the absence of a vested product owner, they begin to weigh in on the trade-offs with each decision by leveraging their experience and contextual understanding of the customer and solution spaces. Having worked on an agile team and understanding the information they need to run their development in an adaptive manner, sliding into official product owner roles comes quite naturally. They often work well with product teams, but they need to simply focus their perspective on what is best for the customer while still supporting the organization. Here, more in-depth knowledge of the business value of the product area and the alignment with the overall mission and vision of the organization will help the transitioning business analyst succeed in a product owner role.

Evolving business analysis career paths

While business analysis is not going away, keep in mind that these are just example career paths that are quite common with organizations that have established business analysis roles and capabilities. On the other hand, many business analysis professionals have never had a position titled *business analyst* and yet have performed business analysis work throughout their entire careers. This will continue to be the case for years to come. Business analysis is and will continue to be both a skill set and a profession. You can still dedicate yourself to business analysis roles as well as find success in pursuing positions, organizations, and even industries of interest to you where they need business analysis skill sets.

Take, for example, a **prompt engineer**. This is an exciting career path at the time of writing. The development of technology is exploding at an exponential rate. If you are enjoying learning about **artificial intelligence** (**AI**) and work on becoming an SME in the area, the position of a prompt engineer would leverage both skill sets. You would need the technical aptitude to understand the technology while leveraging your business analysis skill sets in the decision-making, design approaches and options, and value delivery propositions of solutions. This is a technical position that is only successful when it employs business analysis work. Many of the jobs of tomorrow have not even been created today, which is why having a transferable skill set such as business analysis will allow you to evolve your career path in sync with the industry. Again, as your career progresses, take note of what areas you enjoy working in and learn more about as this will be key to not only your success but also your career happiness!

Industries favoring business analysis professionals

While business analysis roles are evolving well beyond a technical SME, technology teams remain common areas where business analysis professionals focus on requirements and understanding how their respective areas, or even the IT equipment in general, operate. While rooted in technology, this does not mean you need to be working in the technology industry. Our world is becoming more digitally connected than ever before, and so IT teams across different industries are seeking business analysis positions from entry-level system analysts to seasoned professionals who analyze entire IT investments and enterprise architectures.

Industries that are big into research are great areas to seek out business analysis roles. Areas such as healthcare and finance continue to hire analysts on staff. They need the analysis skill sets for quality control, regulations, and an evolving technical landscape of requirements and building business cases for investments. Sales and marketing teams are always looking for analysis professionals to help understand customer sentiment and buying patterns, predict industry trends, and re-evaluate portfolios.

In addition, the consulting industry continues to seek qualified business analysis professionals who can jump into any project or industry and quickly identify the requirements that will fast-track quality deliverables. With the variety of industries and breadth and depth that contract work can take, it is easy to see the power in knowing not only your strengths and areas of work you enjoy, but also why it is so important. It is also necessary to not just learn new things but to learn them quickly to adapt to dynamic team working environments. With the essential skills that we will describe next, you will see just how exciting a career in business analysis you can have!

Essential skills for business analysis professionals

As challenging as defining business analysis work and role in the organizations of future can seem, the great news is that this means there is a huge spectrum of career opportunities for doing business analysis work. The trick is to understand yourself and what motivates and excites you in your career.

Skills and competencies for success

At the core of business analysis work is identifying the needs of stakeholders and organizations. This means requirements. Even if you prefer higher-level business focus areas over detailed technical implementations, being able to articulate what is required for the business to achieve its goals in a way that solution teams can build, test, and deliver is crucial to being a successful analyst in any environment. No matter what kind of analysis work you do, hold the definition of a requirement close at hand. Be able to recite the following throughout your career to keep you focused as this is truly what is required!

> **Requirement**
> Usable representation of a need (IIBA, 2015).

Knowing and applying this definition is a crucial skill for any analyst no matter where or what they are working on. So, much of the value-adding work we do is focused on understanding what is needed and capturing the information in the form of words, such as requirements traceability matrices; images, with process models and diagrams; and even products, such as prototypes. You must focus on the delivery of this work in various formats for different time zones, languages, backgrounds, education, and even cultures. Business analysis professionals are successful in so many areas due to their dedication to practice and improving both the art and science of business analysis work, primarily in the definition and management of requirements.

Technical business analysis skills

The science of business analysis is your analytical skills applied through business analysis tasks and techniques. Capturing, verifying, validating, and tracing requirements is a critical skillset to ensure that the solution delivers the intended value. You will find a number of roles responsible for planning and managing test plans and **user acceptance testing** (**UAT**) periods for this very reason – to ensure the requirements are not only delivered but delivered in a way that provides the intended value.

Defining these requirements requires an analytical eye and understanding of how work is carried out, where decisions are made, and what systems must integrate and share data to make the processes successful. To show their understanding and communicate their knowledge to others, business analysis professionals must be comfortable with visual models. Process modeling, data modeling, decision modeling, interface diagrams, and contextual visuals are key skills in a business analysis toolkit. But then you must also be able to layer on analysis skills. From building a business case, prioritization activities, and SWOT, PESTLE, and MoSCoW analysis techniques to lessons learned and retrospectives, the analytical focus on value is key to your success.

Communication and collaboration

Simply having technical analysis skills isn't enough as most of your analysis work will require you to work with people – stakeholders such as end users, decision-makers and sponsors, product owners, and SMEs. This is where the source of much of your information will lie. While there are many analysis positions that might solely focus on data analysis and technical areas, you will always have to communicate your analysis work. *This is why successful business analysis professionals are ones who can both effectively communicate and collaborate with their stakeholders.*

The emphasis here is on collaborating *WITH* your stakeholders. Most of your stakeholders will never report directly to you, from a management position. That means you are asking for them to take precious time away from their current work to help you understand the situation you are analyzing. You have to be able to communicate not only the work you are doing but also why the work is critical, especially to your stakeholders. You need to articulate your role and then effectively communicate the requirements, often from business needs down to technical details. This is why the technical skills of being able to not only carry out but also visualize and even demonstrate the analysis work are key competencies of senior business analysis positions. You have to understand the work as well as be able to communicate it to others.

The way you elicit the information, decisions, and group buy-in is often through engagement. You not only have to facilitate workshops and focus groups, but you will also need to get participation from stakeholders coming from various time zones and cultures, speaking different languages, and, especially, having varied personalities. While the technical skills of running a hybrid meeting are critical, the soft skills of getting people to participate in an online meeting with cameras on, actively give feedback, and frequently ask questions are almost more important. Many times, these people will not even report to you, and in fact, they may be senior-level staff at your organization. You will be tasked with bringing them together in a collaborative approach to analyze an opportunity or challenge to select a solution they all agree on. These interpersonal skills, required of many customer service and end user positions, are also required of business analysis professionals. That is why the role is so valued by organizations who understand business analysis work – they know the dual skill set that must be present in order to deliver value.

Strategies for continuous learning and keeping up with industry trends

So, how do you stay relevant in industries that are changing faster than sometimes the job market can keep up with? The answer lies in one of the most critical skillsets a business analysis professional must possess: continuous learning. When asked, many professionals give the same answer about one of the most valuable traits of successful business analysts, and that is to be a quick learner. You must have the tenacity to learn new domains, technologies, and ways of working. But then you must be able to quickly translate this into your work and apply it to your challenges. Whether it is trying a demo version of a new technology tool or watching webinars and attending conferences, there must be a desire in you to learn more. Continuously ask what else is going on in your topic area, organization, and industry. Learning new techniques and approaches from other organizations and your business analysis communities can be the insight you need to help bring new ideas into your own company and analysis teams. The world is going to change, and business analysis professionals prepare for these changes by being abreast of trends and ideas so that they can apply their skills when the given situation calls for them.

Conferences, both in-person and online, are great places to learn about industry trends. Seek out support from your organization to not only cover the costs but to also communicate to your leadership the topics and areas of interest that you want to bring back to your organization. Spending company resources (money and time) on learning will also hold you accountable for the value you will need to return to your organization. The same is the case with online training programs. Seek advanced coursework that explores topics deeply and gives a greater understanding of what, why, and how technological components are working and how organizations are pulling value out of their digital innovations. Hands-on practice will be central to developing your skill sets so that you are comfortable with applying them everywhere your business analysis career takes you!

Career development and networking tips

Central to your career in business analysis is working to develop your professional network. There is a whole worldwide community of business analysis professionals for you to connect, learn, and grow with. For business analysis, this network is the IIBA. This is *the* professional network of people dedicated to the practice and profession of business analysis. Joining this professional association will grow not only your network but also your career. Finding communities of practice with techniques and templates, examples and application scenarios, and especially other professionals you can reach out to for help as you build your experience will be incredibly valuable to your successful career growth.

This is also the place where you find out more about certifications and additional training that will elevate your experience to the next level. International professional organizations serve as certifying bodies and identify the criteria that describe successful professionals. This is exactly the information you can then use to articulate to your employers your added value when you pursue and achieve certifications. Certifications and concentrated studying are second to work experience in propelling your career forward, and being part of a community that nurtures the professional recognition of your skill sets is a key asset to leverage in your toolbox. You will learn more about these options and their impacts in later chapters.

This is also where you begin to build your personal network. Your career will move in a positive direction when you collaborate with others. First, there are the stakeholders you work with. Demonstrating your analysis skills but, more importantly, your facilitation and engagement skills to help projects succeed builds your credibility as a valuable team member. Referrals from those who have seen your work and the value it can add to an organization are your tickets to progressing in your career. From promotion to more senior analysis positions to referrals for transition to project manager or other roles, those stakeholders you impress with your analysis skills are incredible resources for your career growth. Then, when you couple this with your professional associations and meeting others doing similar work for other organizations and industries, you have a sounding board for articulating ideas and sharing challenges. You can get inspired and share ideas that improve your skill set and your drive to deliver more value.

Your career is a living thing that needs to be fed; it grows when treated well. Investing in your professional network, seeking mentors, and then ultimately mentoring future professionals is how you keep up the energy in your analysis work and continuously enjoy a long and prosperous business analysis career.

Summary

In this chapter, you were introduced to the foundational business analysis concepts and the profession of business analysis work. The business analysis role is all about adding value no matter what changes occur around you. While business analysis originally focused on technology application, the role can be found in multiple positions in organizations, including those that are not titled business analysts but require the key skill sets of business analysis to be successful. You have learned about the key actions core business analysis professionals focus on, including requirements analysis and management and a heavy emphasis on engaging and collaborating with stakeholders. Remember that business analysis is a career path with exponential growth opportunity as skills and experience can be transferred to other positions, markets, and even industries.

As you think about your career and what areas of the analysis work motivate you to connect and grow your passion, you will need to identify and focus on the foundational skills you want to ensure are rooted in all your analysis work, which we will cover in the next chapter. There, we will not only jump into the entry-level and junior business analysis job descriptions but also start to define what business analysis looks like in greater detail so you can reflect on your own efforts to deliver value.

Further reading

- Hass, K. B. (2005). *The Business Analyst: The Pivotal IT Role of the Future.* Paper presented at PMI® Global Congress 2005 – North America, Toronto, Ontario, Canada. Newtown Square, PA: Project Management Institute.

- International Institute for Business Analysis® (IIBA®). (2015). *The Business Analysis Body of Knowledge® (BABOK®) Guide.* International Institute of Business Analysis, Toronto, Ontario, Canada.

- International Institute for Business Analysis® (IIBA®). (2022). *The Business Analysis Standard.* International Institute of Business Analysis, Toronto, Ontario, Canada.

- International Institute for Business Analysis® (IIBA®). (2024). *The Global State of Business Analysis Report.* International Institute of Business Analysis, Toronto, Ontario, Canada.

- Project Management Institute® (PMI®). (2024). What is a Project Manager?.. Retrieved from `https://www.pmi.org/about/what-is-a-project-manager`

Unlock this book's exclusive benefits now

Scan this QR code or go to `packtpub.com/unlock`, then search for this book by name.

Note: Keep your purchase invoice ready before you start.

2

Foundational Skills for Business Analysis Professionals

This chapter delves into the foundational skills and competencies essential for success as a business analysis professional. Here, we're going to walk through the most common tools and techniques used in business analysis work. Understanding the elements of these foundational concepts and the value they provide sets the basis to layer on more advanced business analysis topics.

Referring back to the definition of business analysis in *Chapter 1*, you'll first focus on defining needs. In business analysis terms, these are called *requirements*. But these statements of need must always have a *usable* element, and so knowing how to communicate requirements, both in written and visual models, is an indispensable skill that leads to long-term value. Since business analysis work is all about value, you'll then look at how to articulate the value of any change effort by exploring how to build a solid business case. This is the rationale behind any effort, but it is also an especially foundational analysis skill to define return on investment and justify the hard work we put into positive change efforts.

In this chapter, we're going to cover the following main topics:

- Essential skills and competencies
- Fundamental tools and techniques
- Building a solid foundation

Essential skills and competencies

When considering what makes a successful business analysis professional, you'll need to look beyond analytical thinking and problem-solving and focus on communication and engagement skills. Business analysis work, first and foremost, is about analyzing the business for how to get the most value out of it. This is where understanding needs and recommending solutions come into play as the core of a business analysis professional. Achieving that value often requires extensive change work. This refers to not only the changes that have to be made to IT systems or processes but also the changes that must happen in the ways people work and interact with the solution. Being a leader with positive influence is critical to helping teams buy into the change work and collaborate to ensure the success of the solution. So, the most successful business analysis professionals are those that communicate well with their stakeholders.

The value of understanding needs

Requirements are often the root of almost any business analysis work. While the knowledge of how to elicit, capture, and trace requirements is critical to almost any solution with digital elements, understanding requirements and how to communicate them is a skill set needed in every area of every business. So, no matter where your career takes you, building requirements knowledge, practice, and expertise into your career path will define long-term success.

The challenge is that many stakeholders are often going to tell you *what they want*. As we realized in *Chapter 1*, just because they say they want something, or even that they need it, it doesn't mean it is truly a business need. Consider the following discussion to understand what I mean by this:

Stakeholder: I need a shiny new sports car.

Business analyst: What do you need it for?

Stakeholder: I need to drive to work.

Business analyst: How far do you live from the office?

Stakeholder: Less than 1 kilometer away.

Business analyst: Is there parking at the office?

Stakeholder: I'm not sure yet. I'll have to ask.

Now, what are your thoughts? Does the stakeholder really need a shiny new sports car? That's what they said, right? But is it what they truly need? Here, the stakeholder tried to give you a solution before you could understand the problem. In this case, it does not sound like a solution. It is one option, but you have to ask, is it the best option? And not only for this particular stakeholder, but is it the best option for their family and lifestyle? Does it fit with the workplace and organization? This is where we turn wants and desires into a description of what is *required* to make the solution a success. A requirement for this stakeholder may be "to get to work on time with ease and efficiency." This is quite different from demanding a shiny new sports car, as stated. But this is exactly what a good requirement looks like. It does not have the solution stated. Our requirement gives us many options to define a solution – a bicycle, bus pass, scooter, and more. Our requirement is more valuable because it focuses on *what* needs to be achieved, not *how* it will be achieved. This is where innovation and new ideas can emerge in the design, if we focus back on the business value. While a simple example, this is exactly the work you need to do to understand the needs that drive good business value. Take the same approach in all your work – every conversation, workshop, and elicitation session – and seek out the underlying business need, and ask what is best for the organization.

Analyzing the business

As you work to uncover the needs of the stakeholders involved in your change work, you must next ask how each need ties back to what the organization wants to achieve. Doing this helps you practice and grow your analytical thinking and problem-solving skills daily. While enterprise views of the business and strategic thinking are core requirements of senior business analysis professionals, even when you begin your analysis work, always ask what value the organization gets from the effort.

Start simple and think about the goal of a meeting. What do you need to achieve from a meeting with stakeholders? It could be as simple as defining the needs for a new application. Then, during the meeting, keep the focus on this goal, such as this goal. When a stakeholder starts talking about having to modify the business process or asks questions about compliance, stay interested yet focused. Note these items down as areas to follow up on, but for each one, ask what ideas or thoughts the stakeholders have and how these are going to affect the new application.

The current processes being modified because of a change in technology is quite common and so may end up being a requirement.

Complying with laws and regulations is often a requirement of most organizations. Even though neither item is a feature or functionality of the new app, each of these additional topics is of value to the business because it turns the application (or any product for that matter) into a solution that the business can get value from. You will hear needs appear in the discussions that, if addressed properly, can deliver great value to the organization. That's what you want to do constantly in your business analysis work.

Always come in from the perspective of an inquisitive treasure hunter. You are searching for the valuable treasures buried in the day-to-day chaos that, when leveraged, bring increased revenue, decreased costs, increased efficiency, and long-term customer and employee satisfaction. Even if your first projects are simple upgrade or replacement projects where most of the work is known or has been done before, ask questions about why things work the way they do. Ask what issues occurred in the past and what the team did to address them. Ask what happened after the last similar project. Were positive impacts recorded? How were those insights recorded? Great questions are the tools of choice in an analyst's toolbox for any effort as it helps you seek understanding. An analyst's favorite questions to ask are *"Why?"* and *"Why not?"* in this endeavor to understand. Then, you ask yourself *"What does this mean to the business?"*

Take, for example, an issue with an application not responding. It appears as a simple need to troubleshoot and fix a problem. Analysis work is required to diagnose the issue. What might be causing this problem? Even though the application is not working, it could be that the connectivity was interrupted or the server hosting the app is not responding. So, now you must work with different teams to find the source of the issue and then determine the best solution. The team uncovers that the issue is with the application and a simple reboot solves the problem; however, while the application fails to load, the team notices that the server is having trouble responding and a number of other jobs have failed. So, the real value comes in when you ask what the team can do to prevent this from happening again. Now you are putting the business back into focus and getting the most value out of the team's efforts.

Yes, some people do not want to hear that they need to replace an entire server; however, if you have done the analysis and started asking how many times the server had jobs that failed or, worse, impacted work by not supporting the business applications, your findings might be the insights the decision-makers need to seriously consider the business case for replacing the server. But the trick is to not just seek out an understanding of the current needs and issues. You need to also go further and ask what it means to the organization. Always relate the ideas to what is needed to achieve the business outcomes. That is how you build value into your solutions. That is exactly what you want to articulate as you work with your stakeholders.

Working with stakeholders

Business analysis professionals will often find themselves having to work with all kinds of stakeholders. No matter how technical your area of expertise is, there are people who fill all kinds of roles to add value to the organization. The role of a business analyst is one of support and empowerment. You do not own the end solution – a product manager or system administrator might be the *owner* in this case. You do not make product or business decisions – you analyze the options and recommend solution ideas. You might understand and help articulate the change work that must happen to get solutions implemented and working properly, but in a business analysis role, you are not necessarily doing the implementation work, nor are you using the end result daily; the users are. So, you not only need people to give you their valuable time to sit and define what needs to happen, but you also need to be able to influence them to buy into solutions and actually use them. Hence, in your role, you need to be seen as a team player and a true enabler of success.

You need to approach your stakeholders from the perspective that you are working with them, not for them (and certainly not against them); that is, you're enabling *them* to do the work. You want *them* to own the work. This is why you should be cautious about being an SME on a project where you are perceived to be someone who can perform the actual work. When facilitating discussions and problem-solving as a business analyst, try to avoid taking on the work yourself. The analysis work will always continue to remain your responsibility, but not the execution of the changes. Always ask the team who is best suited to complete the defined task. Your role is to help everyone think through the problem or opportunity.

Even with the requirements work itself, you may be responsible for the requirements, but those are business and stakeholder requirements. They are the needs of the business by fulfilling which it achieves the desired business value. So, while they may be your responsibility, you do not own them; your stakeholders do. Thus, your skills have to shine in not only helping them articulate their requirements but also helping them buy into, own, and work to deliver those requirements to achieve their objectives. Always ask why the team is looking at the work in the first place. What goal is the team trying to achieve? One of the greatest things you can do is offer an objective perspective. Sometimes the teams are too close to the product or revenue goals to step back and see the larger picture. Making smart investments today can yield even bigger profits later, but only if they see it and are not focused solely on the short term. This is what business analysis work is great for!

That end-customer view is critical to the success of most change work. Even with your discussions with your project stakeholders, you may not have the customers or end users in the room. You need to either be able to talk with them or get someone to articulate their needs on their behalf. Many times, you will have to ask your stakeholders to describe and envision their end customers. You seek understanding from their perspective. This is why you are not simply an "order taker" of requirements. You seek understanding so you can help your stakeholders uncover their own needs. You ask the good questions that get them thinking.

Remember that some stakeholders may never have had the privilege to work with a business analysis professional before. The first time you deliver them value by improving processes, helping to define great solutions, and solving problems, they'll want you back repeatedly. You help make their work easy. You help them be successful. Who wouldn't want someone like that on their team? This is because you are not working *for* them but *with* them. You take their input to help define the needs, then step back and think about the value to the organization. With a focus on value, you then work to enable your stakeholders to be successful because you know that the needs of the business and the stakeholders combine for ultimate value delivery. But to do this, you need some good tools in your toolbox. So now, let's look at some of the tools and techniques you want to ensure are part of your daily analysis work.

Fundamental tools and techniques

No matter where your business analysis adventures take you, you will find common business analysis tools and techniques valuable to any industry and almost any type of change work. With this in mind, foundational knowledge of how to elicit, track, and communicate what is required to make the change work a success is what you want to immediately focus on in your analysis work. Communication is going to be key to achieving your goals by going beyond simply articulating needs and being able to get everyone on the same page. Are your stakeholders picturing the same thing as you and your documented requirements? This is key to your working relationship with your stakeholders and supporting their buy-in for the change work and the end solution. Learn to elicit information and then successfully use, leverage, and communicate your findings. You will need various forms of communication that help paint a picture of how that success will become a reality. Creating visual models of both the business context and the solution space will not only help you describe the work but also help you get your stakeholders collaborating with each other to deliver value.

Elicitation and seeking understanding

Elicitation is the art of understanding. Elicit means to *draw out*. While doing analysis and change work, you will quickly find out that you will have to elicit a huge amount of information from your customers on what they both want and need. Learning how to pull out information from stakeholders who are unsure of what they need, have ideas all over the place of what they want, or may even have no idea what is best for them or the organization is going to be one of your superpowers as a business analysis professional. You want to practice asking good questions and mine for connections and patterns in the information and data. Always ask for more insights to understand the bigger picture, as well as verify and validate the assumptions identified. Business analysis professionals seek out greater levels of information and ideas to maximize the value of all the change work they do. So, you want to ensure that up front in your analysis work are the skills to draw out information, ask great questions, and seek an understanding of the true business needs that can be addressed to deliver long-term value.

Analyzing available information

To focus on understanding what is going on, it can be best and often simplest to start with a technique called **document analysis**. By definition, document analysis is just a fancy way of saying that you're going to read and analyze all the available materials related to the change effort. This is something you want to do right from the beginning of any engagement. Read as much about the subject matter, the company, the technology, and even the project team as possible. Most document analysis is as simple as reviewing what already exists. Just asking what information the company has on the challenge or opportunity can give you a quick insight into how much work you will have to do. For instance, if there is little to no documentation out there, then you know this is a more novel concept or idea and will require greater work on your part to help the team articulate their needs. Opposite to this, well-documented business processes and known industry technologies will (usually) make the work more straightforward with detailed specifications being easier to articulate. But that also means you will need to read a lot before getting started so you are up to speed with the rest of the team. Again, do not worry about having to do the work, but focus on being informed enough to understand the context and general discussion space. Just like reading a book, read documentation to understand the story of what is or is not happening.

Now, the best way to analyze information is to simply ask great questions. As you read, explore, and learn, what questions do you think of? What questions are not answered in your material? Do you know where or who can help you find answers? What sources are there to help you learn more? What you are doing is not only learning about the current state and past issues, ideas, and decisions but also preparing yourself for your conversations. Stakeholders do not like repeating content that is already documented in sources readily available to you. You want to value their time and prepare for interviews and meetings by coming up with a list of questions that you did not see answered in the available literature.

An easy approach to document analysis is to simply take notes of what you do and do not find as you review materials. Make notes of what points are important and details to remember. Now, this may seem hard at the beginning because everything may seem important. That is okay when getting started. Make enough notes or highlights to make it easy to come back to the information to read more. What key takeaways did you get from reading company documentation? What insights did you get by looking through the user guides and **standard operating procedures** (**SOPs**)? Where did you get confused or lost trying to navigate the corporate website and investor information? Any confusion can be a signal that there are gaps in the information. So, make note of this and simply keep going. With business analysis work, there are always verification and validation activities you will do to confirm the information, so simply capture information at this point. You are simply seeking contextual understanding to better understand the solution space.

Now, with the impact of technology today, this may mean more than just reviewing company documents. You will definitely want to do your due diligence; research using web searches and have AI tools summarize and find patterns. **Data mining** and **data analysis** are additional techniques often used during your review of materials specifically related to the data. These techniques can be used to further refine your skill set every time you work with data. Here, your questions are about what patterns and trends the data shows. You will have to work to get the datasets and characteristics that give you meaningful insights. Learn how to use data analysis tools to understand the data or even find out which stakeholders are data experts to help guide you through the data. So, just like document analysis, identifying potential sources of information and then reviewing those sources are great activities to begin to warm up your analysis skills. Once you start to get comfortable with concepts and begin to form an understanding of the context and environment of proposed changes, then you are ready to go directly to the biggest sources of requirements and understanding: your stakeholders.

Eliciting information directly from stakeholders

The art of conversation is what will help you elicit the understanding you need from your stakeholders. **Interviews** are one of the most used techniques in business analysis work as they are all about asking good questions to seek understanding.

When doing any kind of elicitation work, you always start with a goal. What information or answers are you seeking? Have you clearly stated and worked to communicate this goal? You need that to keep both you and your stakeholders focused during the conversation. Get in the good habit of always coming back to the goal to avoid talking too much about unrelated topics. What information do you need from the stakeholders? What are you going to do with the information? How will the information help your change effort? Be clear in your introduction rather than just barging in and demanding answers.

While images of a news reporter might come to mind, remember that elicitation is not a process of running through a checklist for data points. It is about seeking *understanding*. So, before every meeting, phone call, workshop, or other planned event, plan out a list of core questions. With your goal as your focal point, think about what questions can help you get to that goal. It is hard to just ask someone what is required. You will probably get answers about what they want, not necessarily what they need (if they answer at all). It is often easier for stakeholders to describe what is or is not currently happening. They can articulate the challenges and pain points they are having with current systems and processes. They will even find it easier to talk about their own business work and what they are trying to achieve daily. These are great items to ask about to seek understanding. Within the notes you collect will be the buried treasure of requirements to be defined and confirmed. But first, focus on the good questions that lead your stakeholders along a journey to your goals.

Now, as you go through the planned questions, go back to your goal to use the unplanned questions. These are thoughts such as *"That's interesting—tell me more please!"* or *"Why do you feel that way?"* or *"Why do you think that is so?"* Show genuine interest in your stakeholders and what is happening in their world. This will both foster trust in you and your skills and help the stakeholders buy into the work. Explore the topics together *with* your stakeholders. Often, they are learning just as much as you about what work has to be completed to make the proposed changes a success. So, encourage greater conversation and exploration with your questions. Open-ended questions are preferred at the initial elicitation stage to give you the space to explore. As long as you focus on your goal, you are not going off-topic. These types of questions help you better understand where your stakeholders are coming from. The more you can understand and connect with them on the change effort, the more they will build trust in you and help you be successful in your analysis work.

Now, these don't all have to be face-to-face conversations. Some of the best information can be as easy as an email or as simple as a chat, or text conversation. If you need to get to know the stakeholders better or it is your first time meeting them, then an in-person or virtual meeting can be preferred. Again, this should at least be the case for the first time. Once you have built rapport with your stakeholders and they understand not only what you're doing but also why, then it is much easier to communicate with them via email or text messages and voicemails. Now they have become valuable sources of information to analyze. You will find having an alternative source for data and information will make your verification and validation work even easier since you can compare what you found in your document analysis work with what your stakeholders are saying. Just know that the more you understand the answer or the reason for an answer, the more insight you will have. The more informed you are, the easier it is to make confident, data-driven recommendations for how to best deliver value.

Capturing the business case

As you seek to understand not only what the change work entails but also why the change is valued, you will want to collect the information in a **business case**.

Business cases *"provide a justification for a course of action based on the benefits to be realized by using the proposed solution, as compared to the cost, effort, and other considerations to acquire and live with that solution"* (IIBA®, 2015). Business cases, which often take the form of formal proposals or presentations in many organizations, provide you with a great template to think through the change effort to ensure decision-makers are picking a long-lasting solution. Initially, always use a template. Use the following template in *Figure 2.1* or a modified version from your organization on every initiative, even if the project or work has already been defined. You want to practice answering these questions for every effort you are spending valuable time on. These questions answer not only the *what* but also the *why*. They also articulate why now, why this option, why not others, and more to give the decision-makers greater confidence that, given the current environment and business context, they have the best recommendation to address their needs.

So, what exactly is in a business case? Well first, always start with the goal: *what value is to be achieved?* This is something every technique, task, meeting, workshop, and even daily activities you do should answer. This answers the why: it is the reason the team has dedicated time or resources to this effort in the first place. To go along with this, you then want to know what is or is not happening right now that is prompting this discussion. That is, why are we talking about this now? Why not before? Why not later? What has happened? What is happening? What we often call this is the *current state*. Do we know what we are or are not doing?

You then want to be clear about what the *future state* looks like. Remember, your analysis work helps changes to be implemented successfully. What does "done" look like to this team? How do we know we've achieved the goal? The more clearly you can define the desired future state, the easier it will be to focus not only on the team but also on the output. *Scope creep* – where the size, space, and complexity increase well beyond the initial and often approved ideas – is something to be avoided at all costs, and being focused on a specific goal and outcomes helps!

With this known, the next step is to brainstorm ideas. In a perfect world, any idea might be possible. Every idea should be analyzed; avoid limiting solution options when first discussing how to realize the desired future state. The challenge is often that the business has already chosen an option, and that's okay. Asking you to still build out a business case is valuable because you are answering all the questions that need to be asked. Make a habit of asking these questions every time no matter what effort or stage of the change work is presented as the answers will guide your business analysis work.

Once there is a high-level understanding of why we're doing what we're doing, we can start defining the recommended approach. Many stakeholders want to list the product or technology they want to buy, but remember, it's about achieving value. A new calendar app will not bring value by itself. But an app that you have had properly installed and configured by a vendor who then provided you with end user training will give you a lot more value in keeping track of your calendar. See the difference? We want to clearly define the approach to achieving the solution, not just the product.

Every approach needs to then define the costs involved. Think not just in hard dollar costs but in time and resources. Even *opportunity costs* of what other work is not being done while doing this effort need to be considered. You want to lay out as clear a picture as possible of the effort required to bring about this change. It is then, as you think through these investments, that you start identifying the *risks*. What risks are involved with this approach? A risk can be both positive and negative. Try to lay out as many as possible. When you are first starting out, state what you know and simply add in the risks of what you do not know. For example, a great risk for a mobile application could be that the company has never custom-developed a mobile app internally before. Having never done it before, you simply do not know what unknowns there are with this work. But that's exactly what you're articulating. Remember, the content of your business case is there to not only clarify options but also help your decision-makers truly understand the context in which they are making their decisions.

Then, you shift to the potential impacts. Here is where the analysis work is critical and something you should work on whenever decisions come up in discussions. Think about what positive impacts this approach could have on the organization. Help the stakeholders see beyond a single line of business. For example, a mobile app for the marketing team could bring in new customers, but it also lets the security team leverage newer technology to secure account access. But marketing may never think about that! Of course, any action has an equal and opposite reaction; so what are the potential negative impacts of the approach? Could it take more time to train staff to support the application than planned? Issues with integration could delay launch dates or selecting a vendor the organization has never worked with before could be challenging. There can be a lot of risks with changes being made, but there are also risks of not achieving the goals if no changes are made. You are not trying to scare anyone. Simply focus on giving all your stakeholders as clear an understanding as possible of what opportunities and challenges they could face in their approach.

Now, the real value of your analysis skills is in the ability to define options. You want to define as many alternative products, approaches, vendors, and solutions as possible to show that the team truly has selected the best fit for their desired goals given the current and future contexts. This is why brainstorming at the beginning is helpful. The team might select one option as the preferred approach, but all the other options should be explored to help the team include or eliminate the options from their decision-making. Just like the preferred approach, you will need to do a cost, risks, and impact analysis of *each* alternative approach. Every option needs its own analysis. It is not busy work but rather answering your stakeholders' questions before they are even asked. You're building confidence in the decision-making because the stakeholders understand the ramifications of their choices with your laid-out analysis. This is where you can even bring up the idea of *not* making the change. There is always the option to do nothing. Put this in your options so that people think through the rationale for their change effort. Organizations can devote a significant amount of resources to something that becomes obsolete a few months later. You want to prevent that by having the conversation now.

Then, finally, always restate the recommendation with an initial plan and evaluation criteria. Decision-makers need to know what the next steps are once they have made the decision. How do they get started? What's needed immediately to move toward the future state? These are just the initial steps. Do not worry about building a full project plan. But then what is often more valuable is articulating how to measure the actual progress of the change effort. How and when would you measure success? Even initial metrics and ideas are helpful. Again, you are showing not only the opportunity but also the full landscape of the change work so that your stakeholders can make as informed a decision as possible.

These business cases can be as simple as an email or more formal in the form of a presentation. *Figure 2.1* lays out the questions that you want to walk through in any format to help ensure you have provided a solid business case.

Business Case Template
Recommendation Structure

- **GOAL:** *What business strategy does this support?*

- **Current Situation:** *What is happening to make this need required at this point in time?*

- **Desired Situation or Outcome:** *What does the business hope to achieve?*

- **Recommended Approach:** *How can we solve this need?*
    - **Costs:** *What <u>potential</u> costs would it take to deliver on this approach?*
    - **Risks:** *What things are unknown that are associated with this approach?*
    - **Impacts:** *What <u>possible</u> positive/negative impacts are there to this approach?*

- **Alternative Approaches:** *What other options could be considered?*
    - *For EACH option include the:*
        - **Costs:**
        - **Risks:**
        - **Impacts:**
    - *Ensure to also include an option of DO NOTHING and its information*

Option	Costs	Risks	Impacts
Do Nothing			

- **Restate and Define Recommendation Approach:** *Be clear on what you are recommending.*
    - **Recommended plan**: *What is needed to get this started?*
    - **Evaluation plan**: *If selected, how would you measure success?*

Figure 2.1 – Business case template

So, if your organization does not use a template or other business case format as in *Figure 2.1* already, start to use this template daily. No matter the size or scope, these are the questions you need to ask. Whether you write it in a formal document that is reviewed and approved, or you simply state the elements in an email or even a verbal conversation, get comfortable with looking holistically at challenges and opportunities by building out business cases. Even a simple email request to your manager can be structured using a business case format. In the email, you can present a brief analysis of the options considered, outline the potential impact, and recommend a specific course of action. This demonstrates that you've thought through the decision and are suggesting a well-considered solution. Seeing the alternatives and impacts of potential decisions will not only help you build fluidity in your work and expand the number of solutions you can recommend, but you will also demonstrate the value you provide for an organization by ensuring they truly have an understanding of what the change work means to the organization.

Whether from reading documents or working with stakeholders directly to understand their situation, consider all this work as input and insight into what the organization needs to deliver value. What you have found is simply information. Business analysis professionals are treasure hunters seeking the paths and opportunities to organizational success. The more you get to practice and experience these within different organizations and environments, the more comfortable you will be with sifting through the information to find those focal elements of needs. As you get more comfortable, you'll also more easily be able to use other analysis techniques as they will build on these foundational skills. You will commonly use these techniques to prepare for more interactivity and facilitate workshops as your analysis work grows in both size and complexity. But while you might have elicited understanding using these techniques, the true value comes now in how you analyze the information to clearly articulate the business needs. Being able to capture, trace, and manage those needs as you analyze them and turn them into working requirements is where the value of your analysis skills will truly begin to emerge.

Capturing needs

As you dive into the vast amount of information available in your analysis work, you will discover the need to properly capture, track, and categorize the information you are receiving. In business analysis work, you will often get more information than is required for the current effort. The upside is that it might be great input for future work. Learning and understanding never waste time when you think about always tracing back to what the business can do with the insight gathered. Being able to not only keep track of the requirements identified and their status but also keep yourself focused and on task are key skill sets of successful business analysis professionals that you want to start learning right from the beginning. **Item tracking** is the official technique defined by IIBA (2015), and you want to do it daily for not just requirements work but all your work. The focus is simply on taking information and its related data pieces to support the change work throughout its lifecycle.

As you identify requirements, and even potential requirements or ideas, the first thing you want to do is simply capture them. This is as simple as starting a list of items to track. First, you articulate the need: what is required? These are the statements of functionality, which might be *the system should be able to compute the tax rate on goods purchased* or *a user must be logged in prior to accessing the timesheet.* The documents you read or the stakeholder interviews never state it directly this way. But you come across a need and then you translate it to what is required. That's it. Don't overthink this step as there's plenty of opportunity ahead to verify and validate what you have captured. For now, simply articulate the requirement and write it down.

Also, start simple. You don't need any fancy technology to begin with, though it is good to always ask whether there is a format, software, or template that you can use. If not, however, one of the best tools to use right from the beginning is a spreadsheet application. Now, the reason why starting with a spreadsheet and not a word-processing document is advised is that you are going to want to track information about each requirement. This is **metadata** on the requirements. What do I need to know about each requirement? What questions will I be asked about the requirements? What actions will I need stakeholders to take on the requirements? All these questions can be answered with some smart item tracking. And that tracking needs to trace all the details back to the requirement and down to the solution. So, I might put things such as the following:

- Description
- Source
- Verified?

  - By whom?
  - When?

- Validated?

  - By whom?
  - When?

- Acceptance criteria
- Dependency

Again, use a simple spreadsheet to start, such as the one in *Figure 2.2*.

Item #	Requirement	Description	Source	Verified By	Verified Date	Validated By	Validated Date	Acceptance Criteria	Dependency
1	Available 24/7	Application must be available 24/7	Marketing	Marketing	2-May			Can use after business hours	
2	Able to log in	Users need to be able to authenticate to see their own items	Technology	Technology	7-May	Security manager	12-May	Authenticated users enter correct user name and password and then can see their accounts Non-authenticated users see no account data	Accounts setup

Figure 2.2 – Example requirements traceability matrix

Q **Quick tip**: Need to see a high-resolution version of this image? Open this book in the next-gen Packt Reader or view it in the PDF/ePub copy.

The next-gen Packt Reader and a **free PDF/ePub copy** of this book are included with your purchase. Scan the QR code OR go to packtpub.com/unlock, then use the search bar to find this book by name. Double-check the edition shown to make sure you get the right one.

What you are doing is creating a **requirements traceability matrix (RTM)**. This is a common way to track requirements as it allows you to trace all the metadata for every requirement or item you find.

Here are two habits that you want to build right away:

- Capture the requirements
- Add more fields (metadata types) for every question or process using the requirements

Use an RTM instead of notes or a note-taking app as it will save you a ton of time moving forward. Remember the requirements are not about producing a presentable document to be read and then discarded. Picture this more as an active, living, breathing entity that grows as you continue to elicit, understand, learn, and evolve the change work. Things will be added and then changed, updated, and modified. Perhaps a good column to add is *Status* to know whether it was just an idea versus something approved to build and deliver. Simply start by putting everything on here as you learn but then continually update and add more information as you go. You want everything you are doing with your analysis work in one place. Think of this as all the information you might need to track as the change effort moves forward. Again, this is why spreadsheets or some sort of relational databases are helpful so that you can track, relate, and report on the status of all the requirements.

Now, there are a number of requirements software out there too. Find out what your organization is using. If they don't have something, start an RTM for your current work. Turn your lessons learned at the end of the project into a template for your next change effort. Each time you use your RTM template, evolve it to help you trace those requirements all the way to their delivery. Think about reusability here as much as possible. Sometimes requirements on one project are similar or even the same as the ones you need on the next project (if they are a business need, then remember they exist and must be present even after a project has concluded). Think again about how great it is to have requirements already documented and analyzed for you! All you have to do is maybe make some small modifications or add some new test cases. That is definitely business value!

Companies with robust requirement management systems are great at reusability as the requirements are stored into a system for continued reuse. While these solutions are not as common due to their high costs right now, even saving spreadsheets to a project space or collaboration area can help future business analysts review the work you did for a prior project. Always think about reuse with the requirements: Reuse the list constantly throughout the project to stay focused. Then, reuse the requirements, the template, and any of the metadata for future changes.

> **Tracking requirements in agile environments**
>
> The spreadsheet and tracking list approach described so far is generally geared toward planning-based project work, that is, where all the requirements are defined upfront and the team works to deliver the requirements as confirmed (verified and validated) in the solution. However, while teams using agile approaches to requirements and development work might use software tools such as Jira™ and want requirements to be written in the format of a user story, they still require the same traceability. User stories are broken down into tasks to build, test, and deliver the requirements. User stories are traced back up to their themes, features, and epics or other categorizations where they add the most value collectively. You still need to track metadata such as status, priority, and level of effort. Simply find out what format or tool your organization uses and try that while you get comfortable with the process. The format is not as important as getting the data together in a consistent and usable format that helps you validate that the change work is delivering the intended business value.

Back to the definition of requirements that we saw in the previous chapter:"—*a usable representation of a need*." Remember that what you produce in your analysis work still needs to be usable (IIBA, 2015). That is why a simple spreadsheet can be quite effective. If the team members can all pick it up and use it to find out the status or answer a question about the work, then that is the best format. It is usable. And if people are picturing the same thing when they do read the work, then it is a usable representation. The requirements tracking, while your responsibility, is not your product. You are creating artifacts that *enable* the team to be successful. The requirements need to facilitate the successful implementation of a solution that addresses the business need. So, ensure you share and communicate your requirements tracking lists frequently. Placing your spreadsheet in a collaboration space so that others can review and update it can save you valuable time while quickly giving other team members valuable information. Knowledge management is an area you can explore further that helps you consider information from this larger perspective of reuse and leveraging for future efforts. That is the whole goal of capturing and tracking what is needed to deliver business value. The value in capturing the needs is in helping your stakeholders understand the full view of the change effort, often using multiple communication vehicles, as you will see next.

Visualizing requirements

Requirements, as stated, have to be usable. You need to be able to communicate the requirement to different audiences and have everyone understand and picture the same end goal. This can be very hard for many people. Remember, especially with project teams, that people of different backgrounds will have different experiences and biases that they naturally bring to information and discussions. Every single stakeholder, including yourself, needs to be able to articulate, translate, and comprehend the requirement in the same way. This is why your visual skills are key tactical components of your analysis work.

One of the best ways to visualize requirements that arise is **process modeling**. Process modeling simply shows how work is carried out in a graphical form (IIBA, 2015). It defines a process and the steps it takes to complete that process using visual cues to articulate the actions happening. *Figure 2.3* is an example process model for a purchase order process. The oval shapes show the start and end points while the boxes define the actions or steps taken to complete the process.

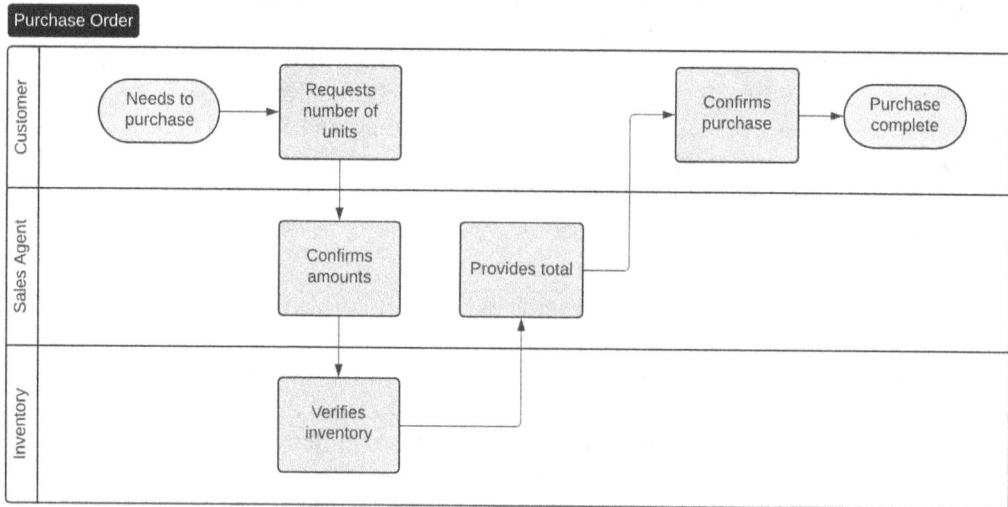

Figure 2.3 – Example process model

Process models are indispensable visuals that speak up to the business level and strategically look at how functions and capabilities are organized from the broader perspective. They can speak all the way down into the technical mappings of components and architectures at the tactical level. You will want to start getting comfortable with process modeling as part of your foundational skills. In your elicitation sessions, listen to what your stakeholders say are the steps that happen in a process. As soon as steps and actions are mentioned, start capturing them in a visual model. Stakeholders will appreciate the visual depiction of information as many stakeholders never see this kind of visual supporting their work. Business analysis is all about value, and that is exactly what process models do. Simply creating a process model during a discussion adds value in several key ways, including the following:

- Defining the current process
- Visualizing the future process
- Documenting elicitation results
- Drafting requirements
- Creating an artifact to verify and validate information
- Providing SOPs and user guides for staff

Wow! With just one visual, you can do all that! But you want to build these habits now. Get comfortable with creating visuals live during meetings. Then, walk through your visuals with your stakeholders before your meeting ends. This will help you quickly verify and validate any assumptions and ensure you heard them correctly. You can always clean up the diagram later (for example, align swim lanes, connect arrows, or explain acronyms), but capturing the ideas and information from your stakeholders while they are engaged and present is key.

Process modeling technologies and methodologies

To create some great process models, even if you feel you are not a technical analyst, you want to get comfortable with using some of the more powerful technologies early on. Microsoft Visio (2024) is one of the most popular modeling tools, especially if your organization uses Microsoft products. For Mac users, the tool of choice is Lucidchart (Lucid Software Inc, 2024). Either is a great option, so see whether your organization is already using them or you can get yourself a subscription. Remember, you are helping the business maximize the value you provide, so the better the tools you have, the easier you will find your analysis work.

As you learn more about how to use these powerful tools (check out my course on LinkedIn Learning here: `https://www.linkedin.com/learning/lucidchart-for-business-analysis/`), you will also learn that there are a lot of methodologies and nomenclatures out there. Learning what **Business Process Modeling Notation (BPMN)** is can be helpful, but do not feel pressured to push it on your stakeholders. Remember, the best technique is the one that works. Most stakeholders will never know what format your process model is in. They only care that their work is accurately captured. In the beginning, simply learn good process modeling standards, such as swim lanes and process steps. Ask your organization what formats they use and prefer. It is easiest to follow their standard or model. Then, focus on getting comfortable with drawing these live in your sessions. Start creating process models with applications you are comfortable with but know that an application whose purpose is process modeling will give you many more features and functionality that will streamline your work, especially with web-based applications such as Lucidchart that are adding more AI features to the application that greatly speed up and enhance your analysis work (Lucid Software Inc, 2024). While there are many free apps out there that can help you show visual steps, getting comfortable with these more advanced tools is what paves the way for more advanced diagramming in the future.

Building your foundational skill sets starts with seeking an understanding of the change effort, tracking the insights and results of analysis work, and then communicating them to your stakeholders. This will put you on the path to success no matter where your analysis work takes you. A business case or, more importantly, the questions that are asked when building a business case should constantly be considered by any organization to add value. Use these daily. Then, really take stock of where and how you track information. Getting comfortable with using and reusing templates and even sharing those templates with other analysts builds even greater value in your investment. But never lose sight of the fact that you are enabling others to succeed with their change work. You are providing the analysis to help them achieve the greatest value. That work is what builds the value of business analysis in an organization, but also in your career, as you will see next.

Building a solid foundation

As much as business analysis is flexible and thrives in agile environments, building a solid foundation of analysis skills is critical to ensuring growth in your career. The activities, techniques, and even the tools mentioned so far in this chapter are what you should be using daily wherever your analysis work takes you. Get comfortable with listening carefully to identify the needs, communicating ideas through documentation and visuals, and justifying decisions in your business activities so that they become healthy habits on your analysis journey. Build as much analysis work into your daily routines as possible. Seek a greater understanding of news stories. Ask family and friends for more details on their travels and their career paths. Be naturally inquisitive about why and how things work the way they do when going to the supermarket, store, or even medical appointments. You want to fire up those analysis synapses in your brain, so they are always firing while working.

As you gather information and greater understanding, you drive home the value of your analysis work with a focus on getting better business outcomes for your business cases. And the value becomes exponential when you enable teams to proactively make data-driven decisions with well-informed recommendations, especially when you integrate these skills and approaches into your daily habits.

Building the business analysis business case

When you work hard to deliver quality analysis work, you are helping to build the business case for more analysis positions and capabilities in your organization. The business case template in this chapter and the questions that it addresses is the approach to take with every single decision you and your teams face in your work. Business cases are more than just a project artifact—they're the alignment for the organization. They help decision makers make informed decisions. And a good business case can save an organization a lot of time and money.

But the analysis work is more than just the business case for the change work. The value comes in the complete package you provide. From building the business case and identifying options to defining and tracing the requirements all the way to the chosen end solution, the entire time you are keeping an eye on the business. You ask constantly throughout the effort whether the work being done or decisions that are being made are best for the business. Now, starting out, the scope is small. So, all you have to do is continuously ask teams whether the work is still supporting the goal. Bring up for discussion anything that does not appear to support the original goal. This will help the team, or even yourself, to align the work back to the reason you are all doing it in the first place. This keeps teams focused and on track. Any organization would be thrilled to know that their employees are working on the right things at the right time for the right reasons. But you have to ask the right questions to get the information that helps teams make those informed decisions.

When you keep this perspective, you are building the business case for business analysis. You are doing more than justifying your position; you are justifying the skill set that you bring to the table. Even with something as simple as creating a process model of the current and the future process, you need it to help get the changes in place. But then if you turn over the final validated process model to the help desk or applications team, you have just given them an artifact they can use long into the solution's life cycle.

Think about when you started your current position. Would you have appreciated it if every activity you needed to do for your work had been written down with step-by-step instructions? Or if you had a picture of the work or the process steps? That probably would have saved you a lot of time on even the smallest activities. Well, that is exactly what you do for the business when you do quality analysis work. You ask not just what is needed for the change, but also if the analysis work can be leveraged beyond the current project. It might be for cases such as this of supporting the operational teams. You can also help the team get ideas for future projects and changes through your research and analysis work. You have just saved the next team time and effort. This value only increases the more you look at what is best for the team, the organization, the community, and the business overall. Wear your business analysis "hat" for any work you do. Consider that you are justifying your position and the value you provide by always looking to deliver more than simply the tasks assigned to you. Think about how you can leverage the work you do for greater value in the future. When you shift your mindset to incorporating the tools and techniques of business analysis into daily work, you are truly building a business case for business analysis.

Recommending solutions

At a foundational level, a lot of your work is going to be very task-oriented, especially if the role is focused on requirements and project-related tasks such as specifying items, tracking and delivering documentation, and ensuring testing is completed successfully. But while you may be in a junior position when starting out, you are still the one to help analyze the situation to provide recommendations. You do this by seeking out understanding and uncovering needs. But the value truly comes when you offer a direction, grounded in facts and data, that offers the opportunity to achieve business goals. Getting comfortable with your analysis work is what will make you confident in approaching stakeholders with recommendations. That is what they are looking for from you: not the answer to every question but insights based on the information that you have acquired. They will see this value when you are focused on the business and not just a project or an application or technology.

An example change effort delivering business value

Let's look at an example that articulates how to immediately use the foundational skills while adding value. The IT department identifies that it is time to upgrade one of their servers. This is common and not unexpected as they do it often; however, they ask for a business analyst to help the team this time because it is a server that processes financial transactions, and they don't want any mishap. While this is not an official project on the overall company roadmap, you are assigned to the project team to help successfully complete it.

Now, you immediately dive into what information is available. What documentation do they have on the existing server? What documentation does the vendor have that explains the nature of the upgrade? Is there a project charter or work order that documents the expectations, timing, and any corporate requirements? Before the team meeting has even been set up to walk through the actual work, you are creating a clear picture of what needs to happen and why.

The next day is the team meeting, and you meet your primary stakeholders and SMEs to help you understand the change effort. While the team has been assigned the task with no deadline, one of the application managers informs everyone that they want to upgrade the application before the end of the month and do not want to have to switch servers mid-project. Now you have insight into the deadlines and dependencies. However, you ask a question during the meeting about what functions and processes the application runs on the server your team needs to upgrade. The application manager explains that this server is where their internal reporting happens. The main processing for their application is on a cloud-based server managed by an external vendor. This is a great insight as you helped the team see that there is a dependency, but the risk is low if there are any issues with the schedule as customer data and functions for the application are not being run via this server.

The team lead starts running through a checklist of tasks that they used when upgrading a different server last month. While there is some feedback from the team about differences and things they won't do every time, in general, it is a comprehensive list of tasks, making the meeting efficient. After the meeting, you ask the team lead where the checklist is located for you to review. They state that right now it is only on their desktop, but they'll email it to you. You ask whether it's okay if you review it and make it into a template for the next server upgrade, so other teams have something to follow as well. They love the idea and appreciate that you thought of it. They advise that you share the template with the server team manager and ask where it would be best to post it on the SharePoint site so the team can easily find it.

While setting up the test environment, you ask whether there is a checklist the server team follows. The main server administrator says no and that they just create it from scratch. They further explain that it was the same last time because they are never sure what exactly the applications teams want to test, so they just start with basic actions and adjust if there are any requests during the testing. You help to facilitate questions from the server administrator and project team in a short meeting later that day after you are CC'd into multiple emails going back and forth with test environment questions. The answers help build a more robust listing than what the server administrator started with.

While the team is feeling confident about the test environment, you ask how they will test in production. They say that in general, they don't. They just hope no one complains about anything being broken because they are scared to touch production data. You take the test environment checklist of test cases and validation checks to one of the IT managers and ask how the same functions can be validated in production. You explain that there is a risk to some other applications using the server for financial transactions. The IT manager shares that they actually have a set of "test accounts" that get zeroed out so as not to impact any reporting or compliance requests. The team just needs to request the data and can get some help with production validation when the server goes live. You share the good news with the project team. Many teammates mention that they have been working at the company for years and had no idea that that was possible. The team is fully prepared, and the migration goes well.

While the team wants to quickly move on to bigger projects, you request running a lessons-learned session to review the effort. While your personal reasons for this are to be a more helpful analyst on the next project, you find that giving the team members space to share their thoughts and feedback is welcomed and appreciated. They point out some of the great work each team member did, share some frustrations about deadlines and demands of internal users, and confirm some of the process improvements you had noted.

You request, as part of the final task, to sit with the server administrator and walk through their setup process and what requirements they needed to know to ensure the test environment supported the risk-averse- approach. You want to capture these requirements with both the idea to help create a template for future testing as well as to simply create a survey for future testing needs. This way, the server administrator can easily delegate the creation of new test environments by having a team member use the template structure. Then, any of the technical teams that are requesting the test environment can answer questions upfront regarding how, where, and when the test environment is configured to best support their testing requirements.

You leave this small project feeling more confident. While you almost created more work in making templates and checklists and communicating the outcomes of the lessons learned session than you did on the actual project, you were a continuously value-adding member. This example is quite common and a great way to think about how you can add value to future efforts, which in turn adds pure value to the organization. These recommendations and insights seen during the change effort do not have a huge scope; however, they can have a huge impact. While you may never be the person upgrading the server yourself, the insight you have on the process and the team that turns into actionable investments for future technical work is exponentially valuable to the company. You need to recognize not only the opportunities in your assigned work to make valuable recommendations but also the broader impact you can create by always asking: What delivers the greatest value to the organization?

Analyzing yourself

Carrying out analysis on yourself can be how you boost and continue a successful analysis career. What this means is to think about your goals and what you hope to achieve. Then, really take a hard look at where you are and where you need to be to achieve those goals. After that, start thinking of all the ways to go from your current state to your ideal future state. For each of these, analyze the pros and cons of the options. What kind of personal investment (time and money) do you have to make for each? What are the potential rewards and risks with each option? What if you make no changes and simply continue with your work as you do today (the "do nothing" option)? See? You're already doing a business case on your own career. This is a great activity to practice your analysis skills as it is on a topic you know best – you!

Treat your career the same way you treat your analysis work. Analyzing your career is the perfect practice for the conversations and analysis work you will be doing with stakeholders. When a new job opportunity presents itself, again, do a business case and consider your goals and what you can do to achieve the most value. Seek experienced stakeholders who know the business analysis career paths in your organization and even in other companies to give you insight into possible options. But you will be the one who takes the elicited information and analyzes it for its value to your career. What recommendations do you have for yourself and for your career? Have you really considered all the options and what they could mean for achieving your career goals and putting you on a path to success?

Practice daily in your work, asking, *"Why am I doing this?"* First, you want to ensure you are doing the right work to help the business achieve their desired change. You should not be wasting time on any work that does not deliver business value. This is a great habit to develop. Simply ask stakeholders for more information to seek understanding and insight whenever you are not sure why you were tasked with a specific activity. Again, do the same with your career. If you ever find yourself in a position that is not adding value to your future career goals, then stop and analyze the situation. For example, say you find yourself spending more time on just authenticating users and managing permissions on an application than actually troubleshooting existing issues or designing improvements and integrating new features. If this is what you like doing, then this is fine. Now, if you want to practice and apply those analysis skills of working with stakeholders, capturing their requirements, and presenting ideas, then you might want to inquire about getting some more project-based work. Actively ask and inquire how you can be on teams that need someone to analyze documents and define requirements that can be implemented. Now, you are not only putting your career at the forefront, but you are also showing the value you can add to the organization by growing your business analysis skills while helping change work be successfully implemented. Recommending that the organization (and you!) can get more value by including you in key change efforts can be one of the best recommendations you make in your business analysis work.

Summary

Business analysis work can start at any time, but building a foundation of essential skills and competencies will be valuable throughout your entire career. The emphasis throughout your work is to elicit and understand the business needs. These are the requirements for how the business creates, delivers, and receives value. But requirements are not just scattered on the floor waiting for you to pick them up. Your interpersonal skills to engage with stakeholders are going to be key in eliciting an understanding of context, challenges, and organizational needs. From there, you layer on the analysis skills to seek and mine the data not only for the requirements but to identify insights that help you make informed recommendations. When you can see business opportunities beyond the scope of the current change effort, you are demonstrating the power of business analysis skills.

Immediately, you can start practicing your document analysis skills and learning more about your team, processes, and what the value streams are for your organization. Then, practice asking questions to team members about what you discovered. Reshape your emails into mini business cases that clearly articulate the needs and goals daily but give options and think through all the ways to achieve your objectives. Start building task lists to think about what you are tracking and why. A spreadsheet of thoughts, ideas, and more is a great way to start visualizing traceability and helps you prepare for larger-scale requirements management. If you are not already doing so, start trying some visual models of the work you do. In meetings, try to draw out what is or is not happening. Even if at first you don't share it with others, start getting comfortable in both eliciting process steps as well as using technology to model out structures and more. The more you capture information that others can use for future work, the more valuable your analysis becomes to the organization.

Get comfortable with these core skills, practicing daily. You will see in the next chapter how powerful the ability to visualize the change work can be in working with your stakeholders and getting their buy-in. You also need to have that mindset shift of eliciting insights with the goal of recommending greater-value business solutions. This is the foundation for being more strategic and handling increasingly complex business scenarios with advanced techniques that you will learn more about in the next chapter.

Further reading

- Atlassian. (2024). *Jira*. Retrieved September 10, 2024, from `https://www.atlassian.com/software/jira`.

- International Institute for Business Analysis® (IIBA®). (2015). *The Business Analysis Body of Knowledge® (BABOK®) Guide*. International Institute of Business Analysis, Toronto, Ontario, Canada.

- Lucid Software Inc. (2024). *Lucidchart*. Retrieved September 10, 2024, from `https://www.lucidchart.com/`.

- Microsoft. (2024). *Visio*. Retrieved September 10, 2024, from `https://www.microsoft.com/en-us/microsoft-365/visio/flowchart-software`.

Unlock this book's exclusive benefits now

Scan this QR code or go to `packtpub.com/unlock`, then search for this book by name.

Note: Keep your purchase invoice ready before you start.

3
Advancing Your Business Analysis Techniques

As your business analysis skills grow and mature, you will find ever-expanding value that you can provide your teams, organizations, and environments. Now is the time to think beyond single change efforts and consider the bigger picture. What is happening before and after the change effort? What downstream effects might there be? What is or is not happening that created this situation in the first place? The way to start building this perspective in your analysis work is to use more advanced techniques that build on your foundational analysis skills.

The challenge begins with being comfortable with your foundational skills. Never lose sight of the true business need. What you are then doing is expanding the context of the change effort. With a larger context comes an ever-increasing number of stakeholders. This means that your communication and collaboration skills with your stakeholders are going to be even more important to your success. You are expanding in your scope and complexity and so should your business analysis techniques. Advanced techniques are what you need to consider now as you find success in your analysis career.

In this chapter, we're going to cover the following main topics:

- Exploring advanced analysis techniques
- Applying advanced techniques in real-world scenarios
- Best practices for implementation

Exploring advanced analysis techniques

The foundational elements of learning how to elicit requirements and then track and manage the requirements' details are only the starting point of what you will need as your career advances. Most analysts begin their careers in operations, maintaining and improving current systems, and then what is most common is project-based work. The challenge is that operations and project-based jobs have a very tunnel-focused view of the change effort, which in turn limits the analyst's value proposition. You need to start expanding your scope. And yes, with expanded scope come expanded complexities. But these more advanced techniques are how you can deftly handle the analysis of larger and more complex change work, all while keeping you focused on delivering value.

Let's begin with the more technical skills, which will help expand the ways in which you can collaborate with stakeholders to identify business needs in a larger context.

Advanced modeling techniques

Pictures are worth more than a thousand words in your analysis work. Getting stakeholders to all picture the same end goal, solution, and design ideas is both an art and a science. While your initial models are always going to center around basic process models, having the following models as part of your elicitation and analysis activities will not only help you build more robust and long-lasting solutions but also build strength and dexterity in your analysis work.

Context diagrams

Context is king for all your solutions. What I mean by this is that understanding the context in which changes are happening is what turns a product into a solution. One of the easiest ways to understand the context is with a diagram of what is happening. *Figure 3.1* is an example of a simple context diagram for a sales application upgrade effort. The context diagram allows you to centralize your work and articulate all the other elements of the project, environment, and organization that may or may not impact the resulting solutions in a visual format.

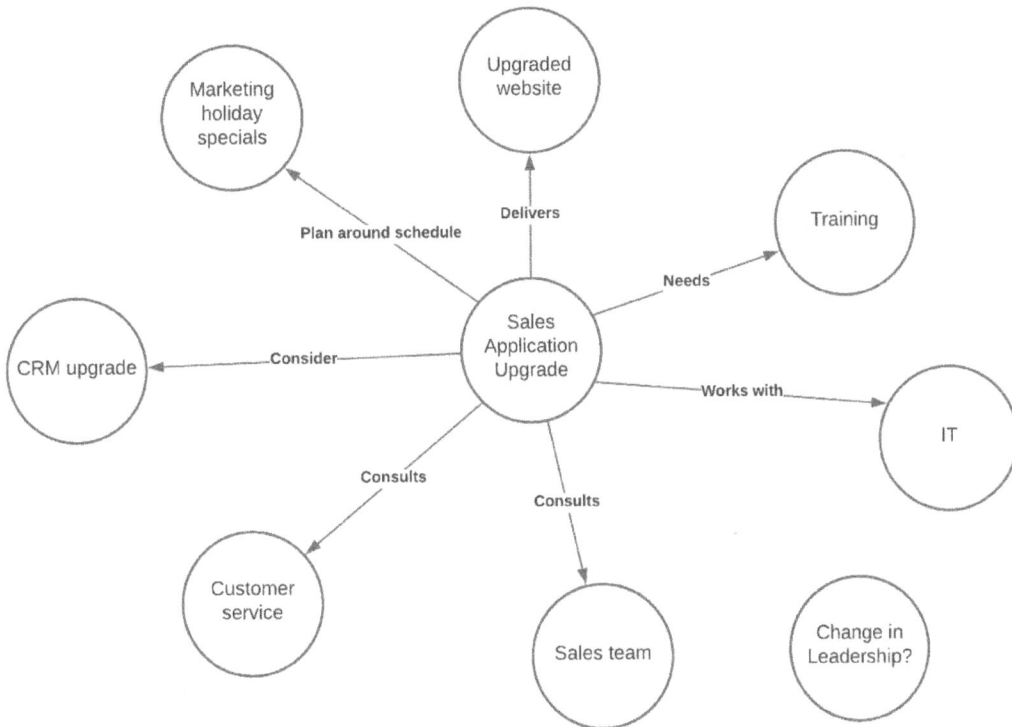

Figure 3.1 – Example context diagram for a sales application upgrade

Start with whatever is being discussed in the middle of your diagram. In *Figure 3.2*, as you can see, our work in this scenario is the upgrade of a sales application.

Figure 3.2 – Enter the focus of the change work in a circle in the center of the page

With this focus of our project, then, as you can see in *Figure 3.3*, we start listing out, around the focal concept, all the thoughts, activities, stakeholders, systems, and more that are being discussed through our elicitation work.

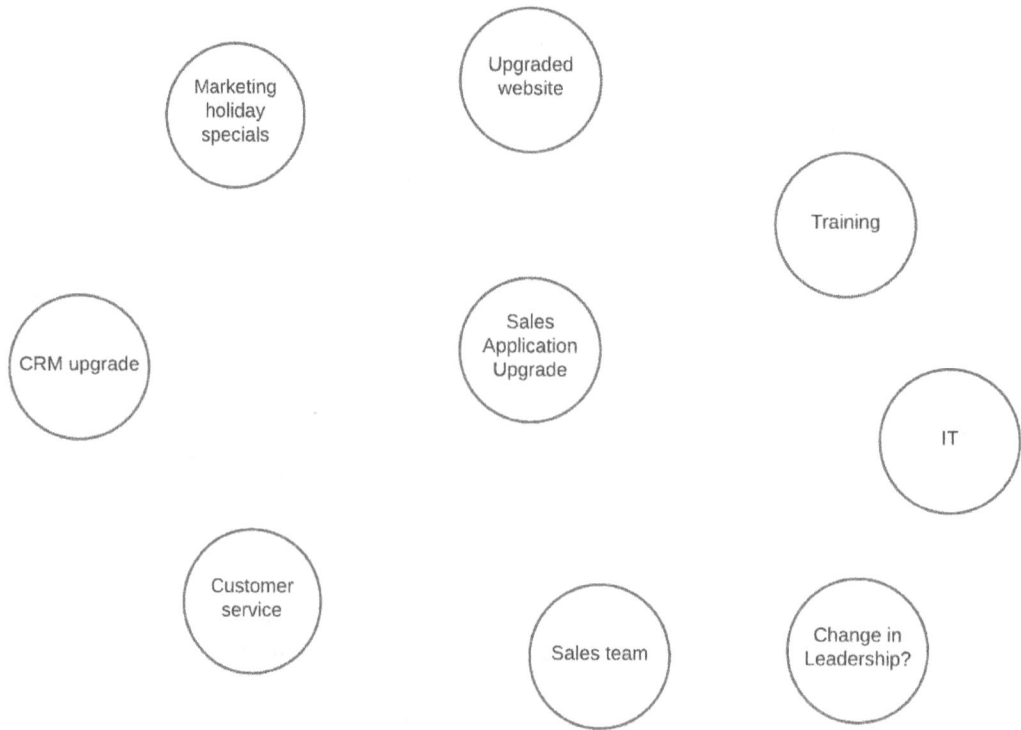

Figure 3.3 – Brainstorm related items around the central concept

This is a great brainstorming exercise at the start of any initiative to help people share what they are thinking and visualizing for the end result. Add anything that the group is unsure about as well. You want to create a space for and encourage your stakeholders to explore. Once you have identified the items in context (the circles in *Figure 3.3*), add lines that go from your topic in the middle to each concept around it. On each line you draw, articulate the relationship. How is each concept related to your effort in the center? Why is each concept important? Why does the team want to keep that concept in mind? If a concept is added but the team is not sure how or even whether that concept is related to the effort, then simply do not draw a line at this point.

What you have just produced is a workable model to leverage throughout your effort. The items without a connecting line are ones where you want to confirm whether they are related and therefore within scope. But what the team identifies at the beginning of any effort may not hold as the team learns more with the change work. Keep referring to this diagram, and as you discover and learn throughout the change effort, add, update, and delete items to help the team visualize the effort. An easy technique is to color-code the elements. In the example in *Figure 3.4*, the items the team knows are in scope have been colored in green. The elements the team thinks might be impacted but are unknown are in yellow.

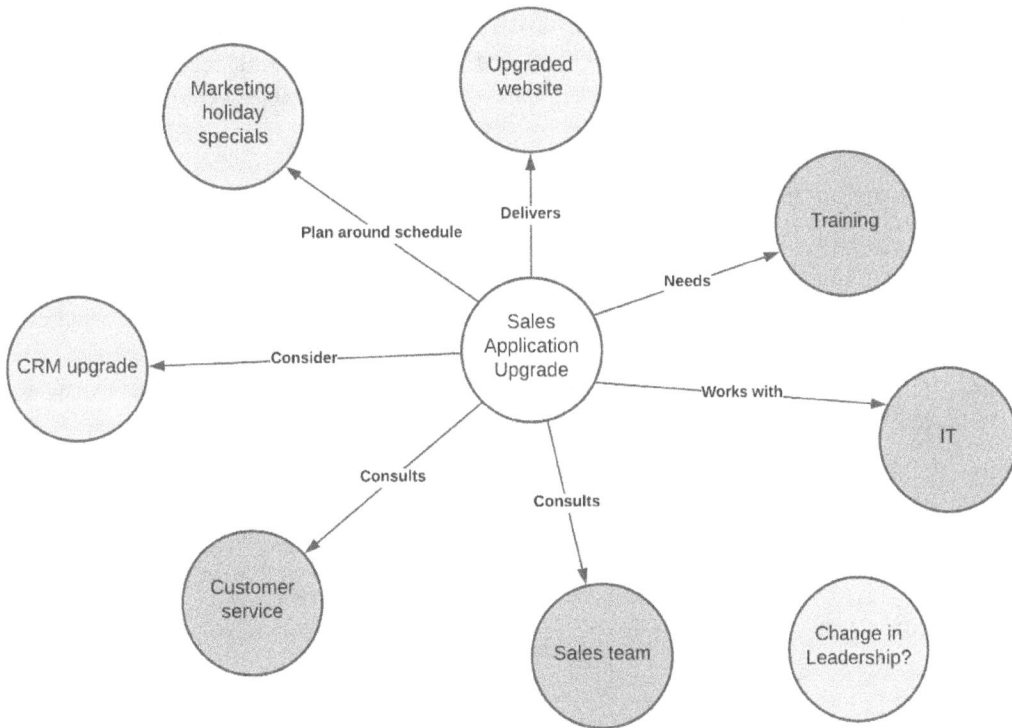

Figure 3.4 – Context diagram with coloring to identify scope or verified context items

As the project progresses, items are either turned green, or the relationship is removed and turned white so that there is always a clear picture of the context. This proves incredibly valuable to the team and helps them realize the complexity of the effort from the sheer size and scope of the work that is being generated.

These diagrams are simple to create, and it is a good habit to start one with every effort. Simply remember that the goal is not the diagram itself. The goal is to use tools and techniques that enable your team to be successful and drive the results. You use the technique that works for your team and enables them to achieve their goals. The hard work of getting stakeholders on the same page will always have a high **return on investment** (**ROI**), empowering them to be successful in their change work.

Data modeling

Helping information flow between systems is critical to enable the success of a solution. Understanding not just what but how the information is able to transition throughout the business processes is critical to designing solutions that enable data-informed and data-driven decision-making, which is key to business success. There are two general data diagrams you might find valuable in your analysis work, especially if you work on technical solutions.

Entity-relationship diagram (ERD)

First, there is the **Entity-relationship diagram** (**ERD**), as seen in *Figure 3.5*. This is a type of data model that lists entities and their related attributes along with their relationship to other entities (IIBA®, 2015). People who design relational databases or work with people managing related data will find these diagrams common to help organize and structure data. They list the data points, or *entities*, that are used and their related attributes, such as **Customer** in *Figure 3.5*. The models also help articulate the relationships of entities to other entities.

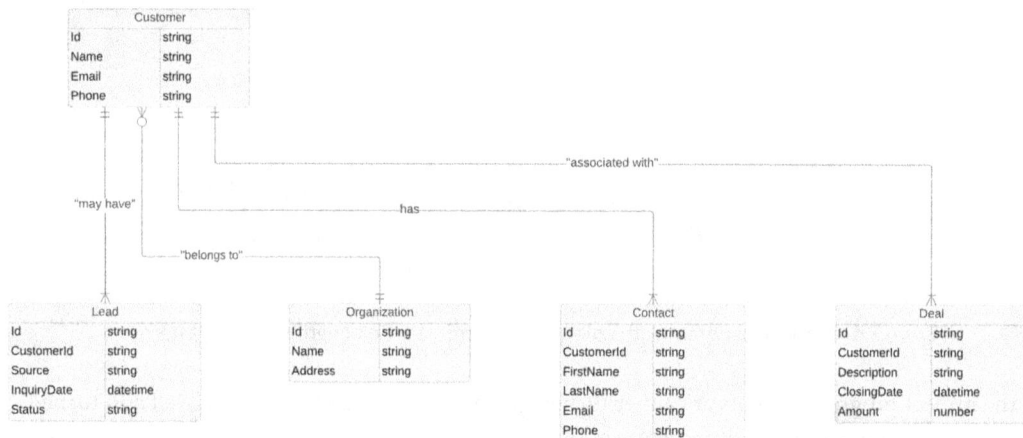

Figure 3.5 – Example ERD for a Customer Relationship Management (CRM) system

Many diagramming tools have ERDs or similar formats as base templates and shapes to leverage. There are also a number of import options and even **artificial intelligence** (**AI**) tools that can take the data requirements or information you already have and help you generate the models, such as Lucidchart (`https://www.lucidchart.com/pages/landing/er-diagram-software`). For each data point, you simply need the name and then a unique identifier. From there, the attributes are everything about that data point or entity. In our example in *Figure 3.6*, **Customer** is an entity that has a unique identifier, or **Id**. Then, for each customer is a **Name**, **Email**, and **Phone** value.

Figure 3.6 – Example entity and the attributes for the entity

After you have identified each element used by the solution or required in the end result, you will want to draw the relationships. ERDs use cardinality nomenclature to identify the type of relationship, such as one to one, one to many, zero to many, and zero to one (IIBA, 2015). In *Figure 3.7*, the cardinality is indicated by the connector on each entity. The example shows that a customer may have one or more leads.

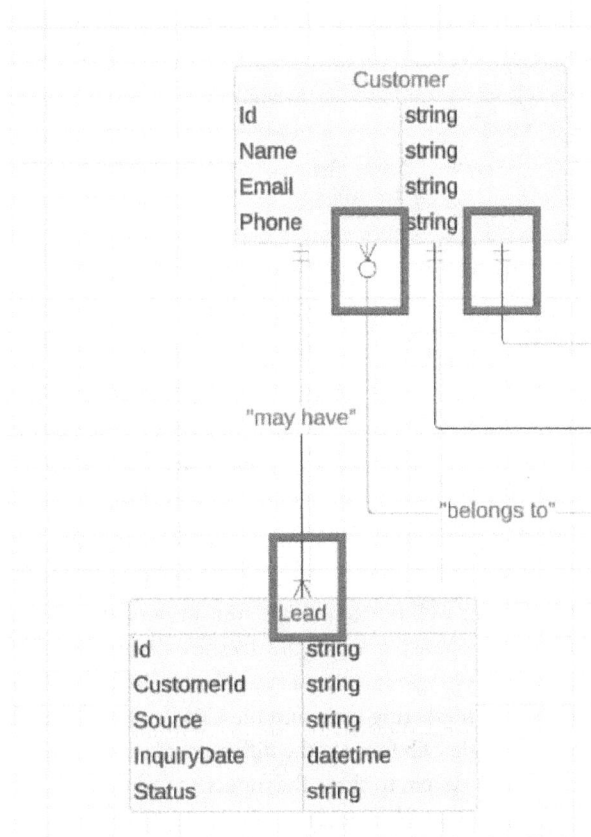

Figure 3.7 – The cardinality points indicating the type or relationships between entities

They are simple in concept, but the sheer volume of data elements can quickly expand the scope of your effort as you think about how many types of data or entities may be in your end solution. Always remember to ask stakeholders what is defined. Reuse prior projects' work and build upon existing diagrams to facilitate your work. Many solutions leverage existing or prior work. You could also check whether the organization has a repository of visuals and what standards they use. Even if you have to start from scratch with defining ERDs, the visuals can quickly help with articulating requirements and the solution scope for the entire team.

Data flow diagram (DFD)

Another helpful diagram to use in your analysis work, especially when working with multiple technical systems, is the **Data flow diagram** (**DFD**). *Figure 3.8* shows the concept of focusing on a central topic or component and laying out the external entities and data stores.

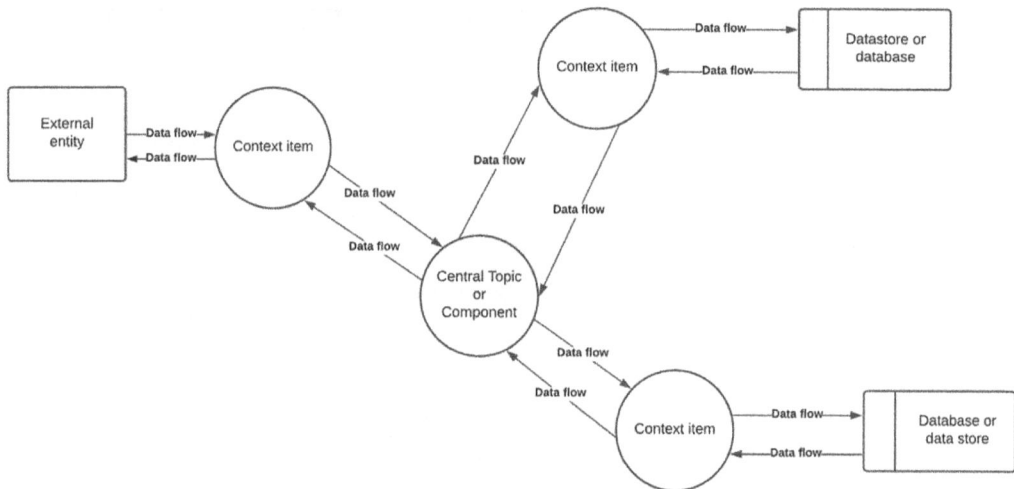

Figure 3.8 – The format of a DFD

DFDs help show the movement of data through a system or other technical component. There is normally data input and output from one part of a technical solution to another. For example, if you were going to work on the customer web portal feature your organization has, you would analyze where information comes from and where it goes. *Figure 3.9* shows an example DFD. In this example, your analysis reveals that there is a Google form that is used to collect customer information. That information is then sent to both the marketing team and the CRM system. You ask what types of data are collected from the external Google web form to the different solutions. Each type or piece of data can be labeled as a new arrow in the system to show the inputs and outputs. This helps articulate that while there is a CRM application, the actual data elements are stored in the CRM's database.

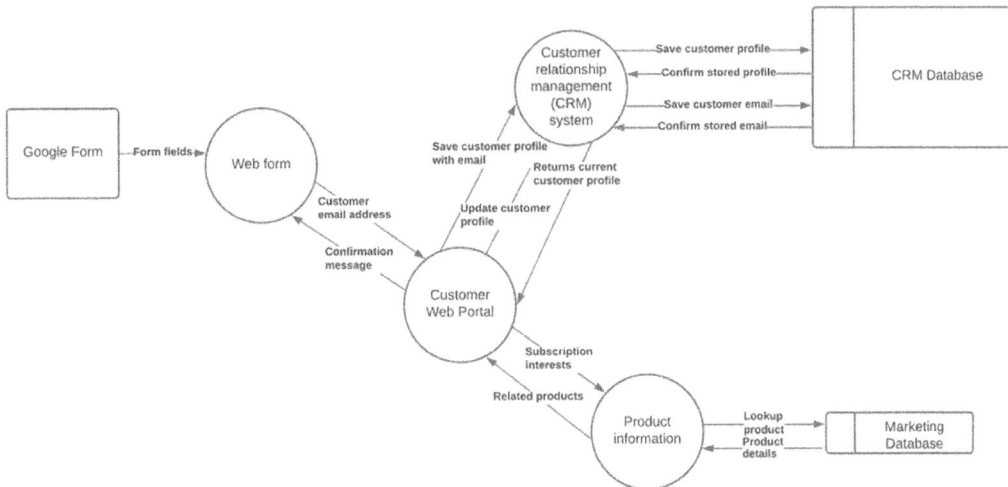

Figure 3.9 – An example DFD to show the data coming from a Google
form into various databases of internal solutions

Each of the steps (the circles in *Figure 3.9*) in your DFD would be a great place to get data requirements from. Asking technical SMEs how the data is transformed and integrated to be saved in the various databases will be key to solutions that may not be realized without understanding how and where data flows between solution components. That question of transformation and locations might introduce you to even more data models, such as an interface model or diagram to better show the information flow across and between different elements (IIBA, 2015). These are very helpful when you have multiple technical components working together to build a single solution.

There are a number of modeling methodologies and formats available to design visuals for your data, and it is worth understanding how powerful these data models can be to the organization. Data models, while helpful to project teams, are also great artifacts for operations and supporting the end solution. The exact format to use will depend on the owner of the final diagram. For instance, the database team may have a format for ERDs, and so it is best to start with their template even if you are simply exploring the possible requirements when you start. I always ask for the template the team uses or prefers and start there. But if none exists, you can create a template from the format you use and communicate both how you created the diagram and how you leveraged it. All the work you do should add value to both the change effort and the end solution.

Value stream mapping

An additional technique you want to include, particularly in any effort that aims to improve processes and how work is performed, is called **value stream mapping**. By definition, value stream mapping is *"A complete, fact-based, time-series representation of the stream of activities required to deliver a product or service"* (IIBA, 2015). This simply means listing out the steps in order as done today to achieve a result, then reviewing the process steps to ensure every step performed adds value to the overall goal. The best approach is to see this as a collaborative technique with your stakeholders. This is why you want to start doing this once you feel comfortable talking the process through with stakeholders. Once you are comfortable with the process steps and have elicited full details from your stakeholders, you can show your value by applying the value stream.

To build out a value stream map, you will first want clarity on the goal of the process or function in question. This is not the goal of the project or change effort but the business goal this process helps deliver. By doing this, you are getting your stakeholders to focus on value.

Then, name the process in question. Make it a good verb-noun description to show the action. "Customer service complaint" does not describe the process. You need a description of the action. Ensure your stakeholders state the process in action terms, such as "Receive customer service complaint" or "Track and record actions taken on customer service complaint." The more detail on the goals and the names of the specific process, the more successful the next steps will be.

Start with steps. Articulate the steps of the process as they currently are. This is the *as-is* process, not what stakeholders want the process to be. It is also what generally happens, not the one-off instances or random times when supplies were out, somebody was out sick, or there was a power outage. What happens 80-90 percent of the time? Just carry out simple steps with a focus on what action is taken. An easy way of doing this is to use sticky notes (which could be virtual) to articulate what is happening. *Figure 3.10* shows the layout where the goal is clearly displayed at the top. Then, each step is on its own sticky note laid out horizontally to denote the process actions.

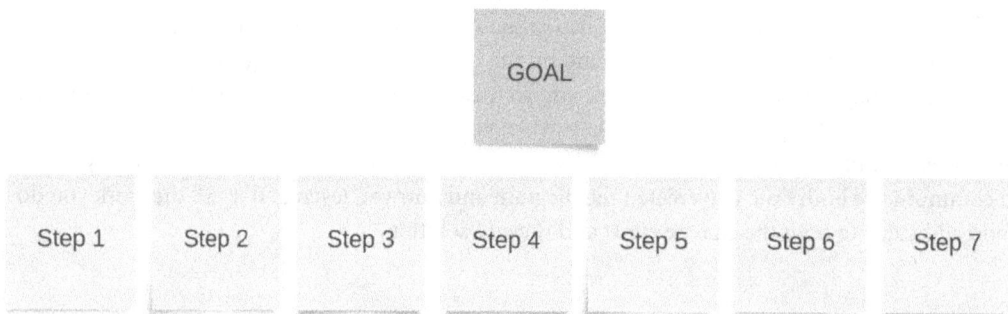

GOAL

Step 1   Step 2   Step 3   Step 4   Step 5   Step 6   Step 7

Figure 3.10 – Sticky notes laid out to start defining the value stream of a process

Now, for each step, you want to get the *cost* of that step. The easiest approach to quantify a step is often time. Simply ask how long (again, on average, the "what usually happens" definition) each step takes to complete. Go through and then add up the value of time at the end. In *Figure 3.11*, the sticky notes in the bottom row are the "time costs" for each step with a total at the end.

GOAL: Submit application

Create account	Wait for account confirmation	Login with account	Fill out application	Submit application	Wait for confirmation received	Receive confirmation of successful submission	
3 minutes	65 minutes	1 minute	10 minutes	1 minute	65 minutes	1 minute	146 minutes

Figure 3.11 – Example process for submitting an application

Then, for each step, ask whether the step helps to accomplish the defined goal. If it does, then you want to keep that value-adding step and so move the process step below the time amount. If it does not help accomplish the goal, then leave it as non-value-adding. "Waiting" is a common example where you find non-value-adding steps. You then add up the cost of the value-adding steps. *Figure 3.12* shows the value-adding tasks moved to the bottom, where the new total time would be just 16 minutes if the team removed the waiting time process steps.

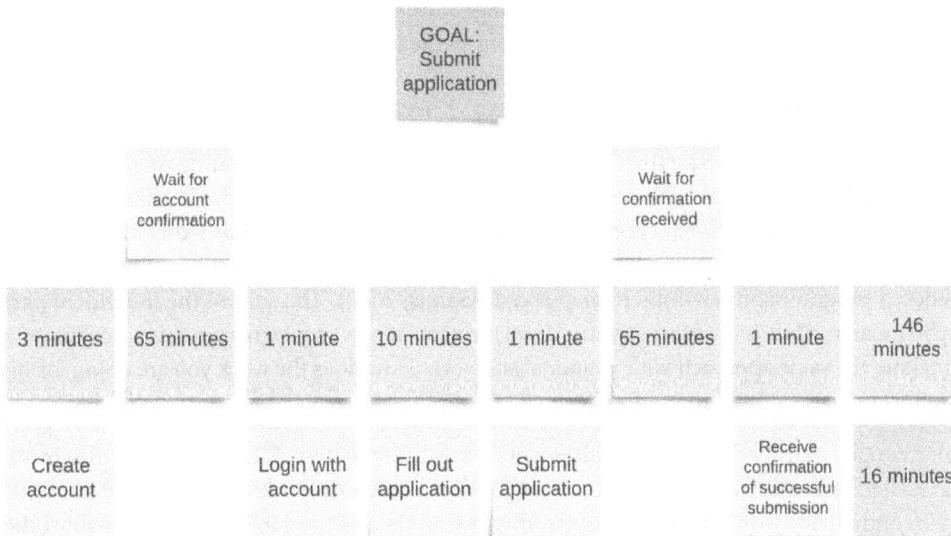

GOAL: Submit application

	Wait for account confirmation				Wait for confirmation received		
3 minutes	65 minutes	1 minute	10 minutes	1 minute	65 minutes	1 minute	146 minutes
Create account		Login with account	Fill out application	Submit application		Receive confirmation of successful submission	16 minutes

Figure 3.12 – Example process for submitting an application with only the value-adding steps measured

With this, the team gets a great visual to ask about what can be done to remove the "waiting" steps from the process. There is a clear measurement of 130 minutes of potential savings for each time the process is repeated. But until the process is broken down in a way where only the steps that help to accomplish the goal are analyzed, the team can find it challenging to see the opportunity. This is why having visuals to accomplish your analysis work can deliver not only faster results but also more effective, value-adding results for all your analysis goals.

Now that you can begin to visualize the larger scope of impact your change work can and should have, you want to layer on the skill sets that complement your learning of advanced techniques such that you are truly delivering value. The major difference between junior and senior business analysis professionals is their perspectives. Advanced business analysis work involves thinking more strategically about the upstream and downstream effects of changes. So, adding strategic techniques to your analysis work will help you advance your solutions and your career into more advanced value-adding spaces.

Thinking more strategically

Looking at your change work with a more strategic perspective will help you elevate your career path from tactical executioner to strategic partner. The way you do this is to start considering the bigger picture of every change effort. Consider each project or change initiative as a single building block helping to construct a larger structure for your organization. Where and how each block fits is determined by the overall picture and desired outcomes. Asking what these are is the best way to start moving in a strategic direction.

Since project-based work is often a very central point of business analysis work, understanding what a project is and the value of coordinating multiple projects together will help you expand your analysis perspective. You can simply start by asking what other projects are being worked on or planned. Just like your context diagrams; by considering these change efforts within the larger scope of the enterprise, you can start to look for the connections and relations to the overall value streams of the organization.

Programs and portfolios

Just like project managers who go from managing a single project to coordinating multiple projects, business analysis professionals will see their scope of work expand from single change efforts to larger integrated transformational efforts as they find success in their analysis work. When a group of projects is managed in a coordinated effort for greater results than individually managed ones, this is considered program and portfolio management (Gareis, 2000). The sum of the individual parts adds up to greater value than each individual item, project, and even program in this case. You want to start taking the same approach with your analysis work. How does the work you are doing for one change effort benefit many change efforts?

Take, for example, your diagrams or a **requirements traceability matrix** (RTM). There are the obvious lessons learned and creating templates for reuse for future analysis work. But then what about the data and requirements within each of those products? Can they be used to support and enable other projects? To understand this better, let's see an example: consider a discussion to learn how refunds are processed. There is quite a bit of talk about how the original request for a refund comes to the company. While your project is not focused on the customer service center or the store cashiers, you capture much of the discussion to understand the upstream processes and assist you with scenario questions relating to refunds. But even prior to this discussion, you know that there have been other questions and desires from the customer service center to review the metrics of how many calls they address each hour, separated by call type. The customer service manager has been considering this as a separate project, not related to the work you are doing. But knowing this desire, you encourage the team to walk through what they know about the customer service process, though still focused on the refund scenarios. Knowing more about how work is happening in the organization, you give the process information to the customer service manager to ask more questions about their concerns about the current metrics. The insight you get from the current refund process turns out to be just the information the customer service manager needs to start building a more thorough business case to review and hopefully improve many of their customer service processes. So, you were able to use the analysis work of one change effort to support and facilitate other work! But this value only comes when you are thinking more strategically by looking beyond the confines of a single project.

Even the simple activity of building a test plan traces back to requirements. The more you can set up the test plan and all the test cases in a well-documented and organized way, the easier you make the regression testing for all future work (Katalon, 2024). Do not limit the scope of the value you can provide with single initiatives. Always look to see where the work you are doing can benefit beyond the current change effort. The more you broaden your view and see the bigger picture, the more you can see how many business needs are connected.

Systems thinking

When you start stepping back and taking a holistic view of the scope of your work, you should begin to notice how interconnected and related your work is with other efforts. The value stream in organizations often extends well beyond where the work actually takes place. Looking at how people, processes, and technology are interrelated and connected is the foundation of **systems thinking**.

Systems thinking is about the relationships and how they come together to make whole concepts, not the individual pieces (Anderson & Johnson, 1997). Take, for example, the customer service department. Most organizations have a team whose focus is on supporting the customer. How they do that is through customer follow-up, responding to inquiries, complaints, and concerns, and possibly even outreach to see whether there are more products the organization can add to the customer portfolio. Now, a traditional approach would be to dissect the departments by each of the functions they perform. Handling a customer complaint is a business process. Following up on a recent purchase is another business process. Outbound sales to see whether the customer would like to buy more products are unique business processes that you could define with clear start and end points. Now, a more strategic approach is to consider customer service as a whole. What does customer service mean? Most organizations do not want it to be labeled as just troubleshooting. Customer service should be a positive value addition to any relationship. So, how does the organization add value to its relationship with customers via its customer service team and department?

Now you're thinking strategically. A customer complaint is an opportunity to sell more of a product. A customer inquiry is an opportunity to survey for questions and ideas for future products. Turning the customer service department into a customer relationship organization could have much longer-lasting business value than a simple product purchase.

But what systems are in place now to enable this relationship? Is the CRM system set up so that the customer service representative has a clear picture of the customer they are talking to? How do they quickly find as well as log information about every interaction the customer has with the company? Is social media and website or mobile app usage integrated into this customer portfolio view? Where and how are the customer service representatives empowered and enabled to make judgment calls as to how to best service the customer? Are the SOPs too rigid to enable the customer service rep to handle the call themselves? Or are there metrics on how many calls have to be escalated? Is the organization culturally averse to transferring phone calls and making the customer wait? How are customer service representatives compensated or encouraged to provide the highest quality service possible? And what is that metric and how is it recorded?

Just asking some great questions about the environment, context, and larger picture begins to uncover a hidden spider web of interrelated elements that can all impact, both positively and negatively, the environment in which customer service is provided. You cannot change one element without considering all the pieces of the web that are interrelated. That is both the power and challenge of taking a systems approach to your work. You understand the interrelated elements a business needs to include in solutions. This makes it easier to define the scope of work, even if you are now focused on an infinitely greater complexity of the work itself. You see all the touchpoints that are required for success. Think of all the related elements and what requirements would enable your change work to be a success. This broader view is how you change from delivering a product to rolling out and enabling a long-term solution. So, now that you have explored advanced techniques to help you tackle these more complex issues, let's move on to the applications beyond just a project scope to more strategic and solution-focused efforts.

Applying advanced techniques in real-world scenarios

The knowledge of techniques and their purpose and design is the first thing to focus on to build your analysis skills. The practice and application are the experience that boosts your career from entry-level to senior analyst. Additionally, transitioning from project-based work, focused primarily on requirements and delivering a specific, measured change, to strategically defining the projects in the first place is a different skill, founded in good business analysis work. Being able to look beyond just the project or iteration and analyzing processes and existing products for continuous improvements is where your business analysis skills are applied in your quest for career growth.

The two areas where you want to seek opportunities are the frontend, or the precursor to your current work, and the backend, the post-change efforts. These are where you strategize and help organizations pick the right directions for the right reasons, whether it is a specific project or product or even a change in service and branding. But also, do not be too quick to leave project-based work and time-bounded initiatives. Taking the time to measure the impact and asking what else can be done is the value-adding iteration many organizations do not take the time to analyze. So, when you do walk through the solutions and implementations to explore where more value can be added, you are truly adding analysis value to the organization with the right application of your analysis skill set to the right value-adding efforts.

Getting strategic with advanced techniques

Just like a project requires a lot of process analysis to understand how things work, strategic analysis looks at understanding how the organization works. While knowing that the processes, systems, and even people are often interrelated and layered with dependencies, taking a structured approach to analyzing the business can give you both the insights and the confidence to have value-adding conversations with leadership and decision-makers.

Using the business model canvas

The **business model canvas** is a way to articulate the business. It breaks down the business into nine key areas:

- Key partners
- Key activities
- Key resources
- Value propositions
- Customer relationships
- Customer segments
- Channels
- Cost structure
- Revenue streams

But rather than treat this as a simple checklist of items, laying out the elements in a visual model, such as in *Figure 3.13*, helps you facilitate discussions that explore opportunities and understand interrelationships and dependencies (Osterwalder, A., & Pigneur, Y. (2010)).

Key Partners	Key Activities	Value Propositions	Customer Relationships	Customer Segments
	Key Resources		Channels	

Cost Structure	Revenue Streams

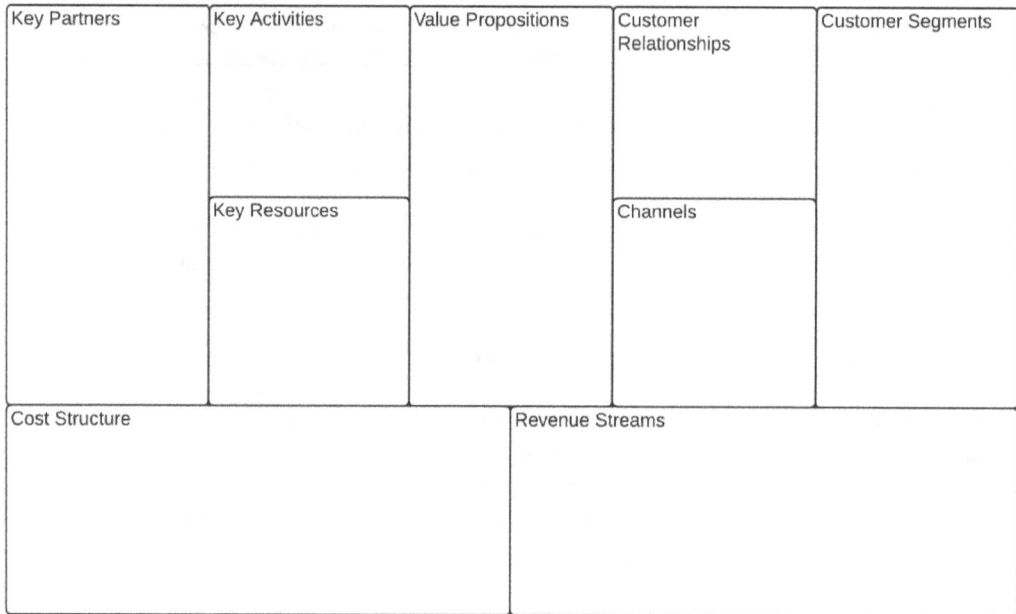

Figure 3.13 – The business model canvas visual layout

A good example of the use of *Figure 3.13* is thinking through the key partners for a company's annual employee engagement event. There are a number of activities the marketing team is focused on. They are doing a great job at leveraging existing customers to help support and be part of the exciting event. But when thinking about the partners, we start asking about who the suppliers are. The organization feels they are the suppliers. But then we might ask, who is making the T-shirts? Who is making the customized packaged desserts? We might also ask about the supplies for the activities that are planned. That is when marketing starts identifying who their preferred suppliers are. We ask whether these suppliers are customers (the organization is a financial institution). Most are. But that leads to a great discussion about the value of customer relationships where the organization could support their customers and the customers support the organization. The marketing team had never articulated this as one of the value propositions relating to a customer of the organization. Then, the customer segments which are missing are brought up. Why are these missing? Is it because there are limited channels the company is using to reach new customers? And what could that mean for the revenue streams?

This circular discussion is exactly the power of the business model canvas. The interrelated elements are simply a reflection of how businesses operate. One area of the business cannot be analyzed in isolation. Yet, the power of using this as a facilitated discussion tool is what elevates your analysis skills. The visual can be a guide for your stakeholders, and it helps you ask those good questions that get your stakeholders thinking. Senior analysts are not worried about finding the best solution. They are focused on enabling the stakeholders and organization to find the best solution that works for them. By combining your ability to see the organization through a holistic, interconnected lens with thoughtful questioning, you can help teams make more strategic, informed decisions.

Seeing the balanced scorecard in action

The analysis work at the strategic level often includes quite a bit of balancing both current needs with future desires, as well as past performance with industry trends and cutting-edge technology. Organizations want to invest in the future but balance that with the risks of today. Seeing when the organization is positioned to be unbalanced can be the strategic conversation that elevates your role from analyst to strategic advisor.

The **balanced scorecard** is a helpful technique for this. *Figure 3.14* lays out the concepts of the balanced scorecard to help you consider the strategic organizational value change efforts can have for an organization, especially when looking across multiple efforts (IIBA, 2015).

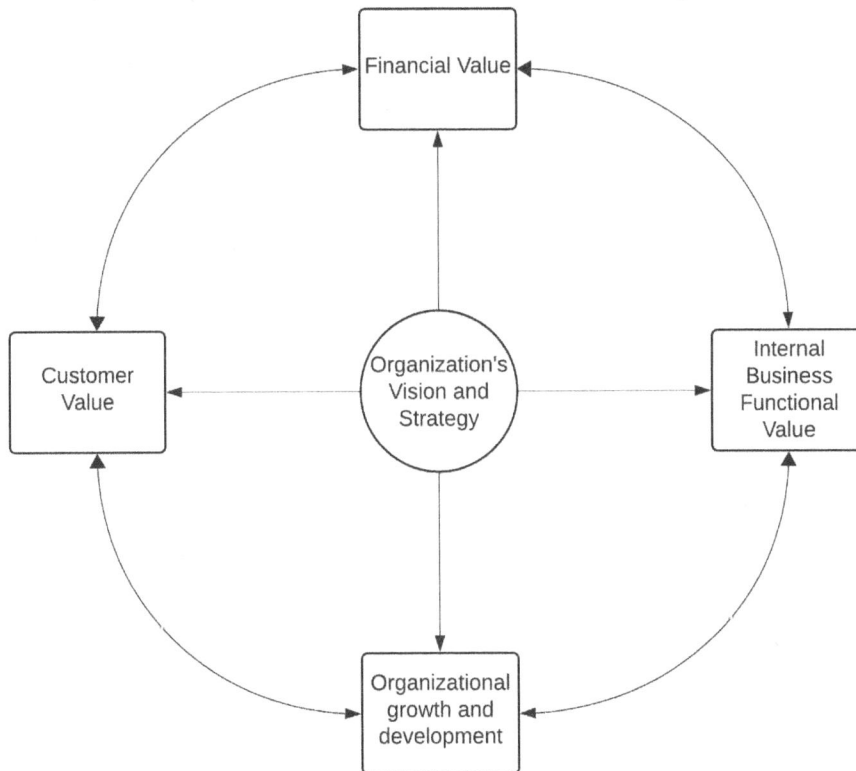

Figure 3.14 – The balanced scorecard elements

Let's take a look at this technique from the lens of an example IT project that is quite common in many organizations. Leadership decides to implement some new technology. The stated project charter defines great business applications and articulates the value the software itself should deliver. In the initial analysis of the effort, you, as the assigned business analyst, along with the assigned project manager are reviewing the information that was used to justify the project itself. Discussions with the technical team define the technical capabilities that they see value in and why they are excited about the solution.

So, in our analysis, we are seeing the internal business functional value – the benefits the IT team could get from advanced features and capabilities to manage the system. There is absolute value in investing in the capabilities of the organization to better manage data, services, and long-term future management. The challenge is that the technical benefits don't seem to benefit the end customer in any manner. It is not providing faster service to the end customer, even though the IT teams have more capabilities than ever before. Even when asked directly what changes the end customer would see with the solution in place, the technical team does not really have a good answer. The solution appears to be fully valued in the IT department only. And without the end customer being impacted, it is difficult to assess the financial value. The original business case stated that there would be greater access for the customers, which would be a benefit over the competition, leading to greater revenue. We are trying to look at this effort from the enterprise value stated in the business case, but the result appears unbalanced.

Referring *Figure 3.14* to analyze our situation, the internal business functional value is very clear for the IT teams, and it also enables them to be ready for greater growth and development. But those elements of development are more in supporting capabilities, so we feel the line is very light (if at all even existent) in terms of the customer value this is providing. While we have acknowledged the organization's vision of wanting to be a technology leader in the community, there is no correlation with financial value as even the support costs increase due to adding more technology.

We use the balanced scorecard model to have a discussion with senior leadership about the project's definition. Again, not devaluing the technical capabilities the project would deliver, we question the enterprise level of scope the business case originally pitched. Leadership agrees and scopes the project down to an IT investment project within the portfolio. This does not have a big impact on the project work itself as IT SMEs still get the support and schedule to implement the change. The bigger impact is on the overall portfolio and the discussions that follow to now rebalance the portfolio to consider where they are positively impacting both customer value and the financial bottom line. Having the view of the balanced scorecard in the selection of approved projects helps the organization to stay focused on both internal and external efforts that yield value to the organization's goals.

We just applied this model to a singular project here. But you could use the same thought process in any discussion, particularly if you find yourself as part of program and portfolio analysis. Using this technique can help the team see whether they truly have a balanced mix of change efforts that will drive the overall vision and strategy of the organization. Too often, organizations will learn the hard way that they need to focus on the change efforts' impact and delivered value rather than simply the type of changes being proposed.

Lessons learned

Lessons learned is a technique you will want to, have to, and without even knowing sometimes, leverage in every effort you put your analysis skills to work. It is all about learning from your experience. This refers to both good and bad experiences. Most often, you will remember those "not so successful" sessions or the meetings that "did not go as planned" in your journey and be determined to never repeat them again. The trick here is to move them from "lessons identified," where you realized what happened, to "lessons learned." The way to do this is to identify the action that will prevent that mistake in future efforts, or the actions you need to take to ensure that every future effort is just as successful as what you experienced in this past effort. Once you shift your mindset to the action-focused learning perspective, you just need to look at the work you do with your stakeholders and what that learning means for your career.

Lessons learned from your stakeholders

First, your stakeholders are going to give you the most lessons learned. Think about the fact that as an analyst, you will often work with people whom you are not in charge of. Yet, you will have the responsibility of helping those stakeholders successfully implement valued changes. Just reading this situation can feel like a lesson learned in itself! As long as you act on the learning elements, you will be wildly successful! Let's take a look at an opportunity to consider how best to run a successful lessons-learned session, or retrospective as they can be called in agile teams, that elicits learning and input for the next iteration.

Too often, stakeholders will use the "after action" time, the post-launch meeting, or some other post-implementation review to complain about all the things that went wrong on a project. This is common in organizations where many project managers often struggle to get support to have even a wrap-up meeting (too many are already burdened with more projects that are demanding their attention). You can be a facilitator to help ensure that while there were many learning points throughout the most recent effort, these pains do not need to be repeated or endured by others. Remember, like most of your analysis work, your job is to seek out value in both current and future efforts. So, when people start sharing how many changes and issues happened on the most recent project, first acknowledge it. Remember, feedback is a gift. In your role, you are always seeking input, ideas, and more. Feedback becomes that gift of information and more. Apathy will always be the obstacle to overcome because you will get little to no input. But feedback, even negative, is still feedback. So, your stakeholders should first be appreciated for simply taking the time to give feedback. Then, layer on your analysis superpowers and encourage them to share what would be useful or could have helped to avoid one of the issues in the first place. Not having a user guide can be very frustrating for any team, as a great example. So, now that you know the root of the issue, ask one more (most critical!) question – what can be done to prevent this issue from happening again? In this case, it can be as simple as creating a user guide. The team actually documented quite a bit of what they learned, so an action item to have the learning and development SME finalize a user guide for the new system can be assigned with a due date that is 30 days from now. *Remember that due dates always drive results!* Now we are getting proactive with the work on this application.

In a facilitated workshop session, the stakeholders will quickly get used to this idea of sharing feedback and then searching for ideas on how to solve issues, followed by an assigned action item. Once the stakeholders get rolling with ideas, layer in the positive outcomes as well. For example, in one project I was assigned as the analyst, which was a simple server upgrade, I coordinated the testing and troubleshooted all the issues to help be ready for production according to the schedule. It went so smoothly, and I documented things so well that the next year, when the server needed to be upgraded, the organization did not assign a business analyst. After the server upgrade was eventually completed, one of the engineers told me that they did not realize how much work I did in the testing phase to help keep things on schedule. The team really struggled without an analyst assigned and the schedule was severely impacted.

Together, the SME and I went to the technology leadership team and shared this information. We asked whether we could implement some scoping questions when projects are being resourced to identify testing requirements, or even the possibility of testing requirements earlier to help ensure the alignment of resources. In this case, we were hoping to set it as a policy to have more analysts, or those with analysis skills, added to projects where testing was a major component of implementation. In sharing the experience and leveraging some data, our work resulted in a policy that helped get more analysts assigned to critical projects. But this only came about by defining and following through an action to ensure the lessons identified became actual lessons learned.

Lessons learned from your experience

The second part is now to apply these same skills back to your business analysis career. With every effort you make in your business analysis work, always plan time to analyze your experience. Set a "retrospective" meeting with yourself on your calendar after you wrap up each effort, no matter how small. In this self-session, ask yourself the following questions:

- What did you like doing in the effort? Why?
- What elements of the work did you *not* enjoy? Why?
- What portions of the work challenged you? Do you know why it felt challenging?
- What portions of the work were too easy? Were there parts of your work that felt like they were a waste of your talent?
- Was there any area where there was more opportunity for greater business analysis work?

You can see these are very similar to the questions you would ask of any project or work effort retrospective. But now the tricky part is in actioning your career.

For each element you enjoyed, create an action item that addresses how you can get more initiatives that include these topics and techniques. For example, did you enjoy learning about other areas of the business and how they operate? If so, ensure you are assigned to projects that are cross-departmental or require cross-functional teams to be successful.

For each element then that was not enjoyable, take a hard look at why. Was it because of a lack of skill or experience? These are easily addressed sometimes with more training or by shadowing other analysts on larger projects. Was the content itself not of interest to you? Again, seeking out more diverse work or even shifting from project-focused to strategic analysis or process improvement efforts can switch up the change focus enough to reignite excitement in your analysis work. The trick is, just like with your stakeholders, asking yourself what you are going to do with these insights. Assign tasks with clear due dates and hold yourself accountable. In fact, share these with your management and put them into your development plans so that there is a logical connection to your own growth. When you do so, you are doing true business analysis work on the business value of your past actions for future success. This approach then benefits both your organization and your career for many years to come.

With the knowledge of advanced techniques and greater scope and insight into where business analysis work can be performed, let's now talk about how you can apply business analysis skills throughout your analysis work.

Best practices for implementation

The biggest differentiator in junior and senior business analysis professionals will often be not in what they do or even when and where, but in *how* they perform their analysis work. Business analysts empower teams to be wildly successful. They seek maximum business value and help organizations achieve greater good. No one person benefits. There is always a greater value delivery impact that even applies to the team's own learning and growth. An analysis professional who can positively impact individuals, teams, and organizational culture in addition to financial impacts and customer service is a person any organization would compete to hire.

As you work to implement successful changes in your organization, it helps to remember that the analysis professional does not own the end product. The analysis professional owns the *process* to enable the team to achieve their outcomes. The team owns the end solution and product. Your role is to facilitate success, both now and in the future. Facilitation is all about making things easy.

Facilitating workshops

To begin adding a higher level of service to your analysis work, you need to focus on facilitating the change efforts. You are no longer simply a task completer or order taker. You are the motivation and focus the team needs to achieve results. You do this through your facilitation skills.

> **Facilitation**
> Facilitation's root word is *facil* which means "to make easy."

Your job is to make it easy for others to be wildly successful. This can be hard to swallow for new analysts, and this is why it is an advanced concept. Senior analysts know that when the team is successful, it means they were successful. But you need to build confidence in that. The easiest way to experience this sensation of value delivery beyond just an assigned project is to facilitate collaborative experiences. Stakeholders may not understand what facilitation means to them until they experience the ease of accomplishing goals through a helpful guide.

A facilitated workshop simply means you will host a session to achieve some outcome. The outcome is normally business driven and you will have to have input from a wide variety of stakeholders with diverse backgrounds and experience. Being a facilitator means you bring everyone together and focus them on this singular goal. You set up the structure that you then walk everyone through to reach their intended end goal. Rather than worrying about an agenda, you focus on participation and outcomes. While you have your own goals in wanting to get everyone participating and contributing equally toward the desired outcome, helping the team achieve their desired business need is how you end a successful facilitated session.

Prioritization in action

A common practice is to bring teams together to brainstorm ideas. Building a mobile application is often very exciting for integrating technological advancements into the business model. With an enthusiastic group, it takes little effort to get them to throw in all kinds of ideas. Through some good questions and encouraging elaboration, your team will come up with a large number of ideas.

However, almost as immediately as these ideas are voiced, feelings of doubt will creep into team members' minds. Comments of "too expensive," "that'd never happen here," or "not in our organization" will begin to fill the sidebar conversations of your previously enthusiastic participants. You will need to quickly step in and reflect on how great the number of ideas is as that is exactly what you wanted – a large swath of ideas, regardless of their status, possibility, or popularity. Now, it is time to prioritize features that have the most value to pursue first. Again, to emphasize, it is far easier to prioritize from a longer list than to be stuck with only two or three ideas.

So, to prioritize where to start, before the first negative comment can even be shared, explain that you will do three rounds of voting. Each person will vote once each round. But what you do next is the special part. This is what makes it easy for the team to be unbiased in their personal opinions and focus on business outcomes. You tell everyone they are to vote first on the idea that is the most feasible. What would be the easiest to implement? You then give them only 15 seconds to choose before going on to the second vote. Now you ask everyone to vote for the idea that would be the most innovative. What would set the organization apart from your competition? Again, after a quick review, within 15 seconds the second vote is cast. Now that your team is warmed up, you ask them to vote for the idea that is the best. It is okay that each person has their own idea of what *best* means. After two rounds of voting, everyone will be quick to vote, and you will not even need the timer. Stepping back, everyone will be surprised that there are three ideas that have gotten more votes than anything else. In less than a couple of minutes, you have helped the team objectively and even strategically identify the first-priority ideas to start analyzing for implementation. The team finds it fun and is very optimistic and eager to start. The negative comments have disappeared, and the team is excited as the meeting now ends earlier than planned, leaving them to get back to their duties.

A shift in focus, coupled with some tight timelines, and you are left with a prioritized list of features. You had no input into what a "good" or "bad" idea was. In fact, the outcome is purely stakeholder-driven. You enabled *THEM* to look at *THEIR* ideas from an actionable perspective to move efforts forward. Those skills, the ones that help elicit the work that needs detailed analysis support, are the valued ones that turn good teams into highly successful partners.

Collaboration tools

As workplaces and the world in general continue to evolve and are pushed to deliver results at an incessant speed due to innovation in technology, getting people to collaborate on outcomes is as much a technical skill as it is a people skill. Your analysis work needs space – space to brainstorm and prioritize. These spaces are often created with the help of technology as teams are more spread out and remote than ever before. Your facilitation skills help with handling stakeholders and their ideas. Using collaboration tools to create the work environment, capture the inputs, and visualize data for tracking changes into solutions is how you enable your own success.

Collaboration tools are becoming more common in the workplace, so learning to navigate these technologies is going to be critical for your career. These are tools such as Microsoft SharePoint (`https://www.microsoft.com/en-us/microsoft-365/sharepoint/collaboration`), Google's Workspace (`https://workspace.google.com/essentials/`), and collaborative spaces such as Mural (`https://mural.co/`) and Miro (`https://miro.com/`), as just some examples of the more popular tools. These go beyond online meeting tools (although do get comfortable with having meetings in-person, online, and a mixture of both!). These tools are where the work happens. Get out of the habit of keeping your own notes and even emails and start ensuring anything worth knowing for a change effort is in a shared location. You should never be the sole source of information. Remember, it's not your information. It's the business's information. It's their ideas, decisions, and priorities. Even if you wrote the test cases, are they in a shared space for assignment, troubleshooting, and reporting status? This is the mentality you need for the work you do.

Setting up spaces for the stakeholders to work *with each other* is what creates that buy-in and focus back to business goals. Collaboration tools give you space to articulate team standards and expectations. Many use anonymous features so that people can share ideas freely without analysis. And more importantly, it shows what the group thinks and wants overall without the heavy weight of strong personalities. Everyone can participate equally.

If you have not used many of these tools yet, give them a go now. Start small and run simple meetings from the collaboration space. Try not to write down any notes outside that space. If someone emails you something, put it in the collaboration space and share the link until that person is available for some training (so they can post in the shared space and share next time!). Build in the behavior that to help changes get implemented, collective input is required. The more you can create a space for people to come together, the more buy-in you will see from the team, leading to more successful outcomes.

Measures of success

Now, with the work to help others to succeed, measures of success are critical. Knowing where you are at and what other measures there are helps you define the actions that take your analysis work from basic to deeper breadths and depths of work. Any good analyst will seek acceptance criteria for all efforts. Know what the acceptance criteria are for the success of the change work you are doing. How does the team know they are doing well? What value would be produced? Practice articulating this with your stakeholders to help them stay focused on goals and drive the discussions and decision-making toward clear outcomes.

You want to do the same with your own analysis work. When facilitating meetings, success metrics are derived from thinking about how the session went. Was everyone there who needed to be there (and *only who you needed...*)? Were effective collaboration spaces set up and enabled for participants? Did everyone contribute equally? Was there buy-in and acceptance for what the team produced during the session? Facilitation goals are almost more important than the meeting goals because the impact of good facilitation is felt long after the meeting concludes. Do this regularly on all your analysis work. Assess your results. Then, action each item just like a lesson learned.

As you begin to build metrics of your analysis work, be strategic in thinking about your career. What does success look like to you? What measures would be indicative of career progression at your organization? What is needed to grow your career beyond project-based work? Work to define these measures of success as then it becomes much easier to analyze the options to get you there. When on a path, if you have no destination, then any direction is correct. When you have well-measured success criteria, then the necessary action steps for your career are simply placed in front of you to own.

Summary

Your analysis work will grow with complexity and size as your skills progress. In the same manner, so should your techniques and perspectives. Helping teams articulate their needs and then visualize them as they work through change efforts are the technical skills you never want to stop growing.

Modeling software is one of the best technical tools in your toolbox that, regardless of the option, can help you get comfortable with articulating change work and value in visual ways. The more you can step back and see the bigger picture, the more you can guide teams to think more strategically. That shift in focus from a task-based effort to a strategic view of how the organization gets value from any efforts is how you grow your skills and your analysis career. When coupled with key measures of what success means for you, it can become easier to plan your value-adding actions.

Often, you will have to face your own decisions about where and how to take your career. By focusing on and articulating what valuable business analysis means to you, you'll be able to find success in a sea of change – whether in the industry or technology. Just as you want to enable stakeholders to own the change work and integrate the end solution, you need to own your career and work to overcome adversity to reap the rewards of satisfying value delivery. To establish that path to success, next, you will look at how to build a career roadmap so that you can continue to advance your analysis career and overcome hurdles in your goal to deliver value.

Further reading

- Anderson & Johnson (1997). *Systems Thinking Basics: From Concepts to Causal Loops*. Waltham, Mass: Pegasus Comm., Inc.

- Osterwalder & Pigneur (2010). Business Model Generation. John Wiley & Sons.

- Champagne (2022, August). *Lucidchart for Business Analysis*. LinkedIn Learning, CA. `https://www.linkedin.com/learning/lucidchart-for-business-analysis`.

- Gareis (2000). Program Management and Project Portfolio Management: New Competencies of Project-Oriented Organizations. Paper presented at Project Management Institute Annual Seminars & Symposium, Houston, TX. Newtown Square, PA: Project Management Institute.

- International Institute for Business Analysis® (IIBA®). (2015). *The Business Analysis Body of Knowledge® (BABOK®) Guide. International Institute of Business Analysis*, Toronto, Ontario, Canada.

- Katalon. (2024). *What is Regression Testing? Definition, Tools and Examples*. Retrieved September 20, 2024, from `https://katalon.com/resources-center/blog/regression-testing`.

Part 2:
Building a Career in
Business Analysis

In this part, you will dive into building a career in business analysis through a career roadmap that strategically links your decisions to your long-term goals. You will explore how to tailor the types of business analysis work you pursue based on your passions while ensuring alignment with your career roadmap. You will also be introduced to business analysis certifications – not only the available options but also what they can mean for your career growth and how they support your roadmap.

This part has the following chapters:

- *Chapter 4, Navigating Career Progression in Business Analysis*
- *Chapter 5, Specializations within Business Analysis*
- *Chapter 6, Business Analysis Certifications and Training*

4

Navigating Career Progression in Business Analysis

This chapter focuses on strategies for advancing your career in business analysis. From setting career goals to overcoming common challenges, you will learn how to navigate your career progression effectively. Many of the most valuable tools and techniques to do so are already in your analysis toolbox. Performing business analysis and learning more about the techniques and advancements in technology are core to a forward-moving career. However, the techniques to analyze the successes and challenges of your career are the same ones you use with stakeholders in your analysis work. When you start analyzing your own progress with the same passion and fervor you bring to your professional assignments, you can overcome any career plateau and continue to seek greater value in both your career and you.

In this chapter, we're going to cover the following main topics:

- Strategies for career advancement
- Developing a career roadmap
- Overcoming common career challenges

Strategies for career advancement

The foundational elements of learning how to elicit requirements and then track and manage the details of the requirements are only the starting point of what you will need as your career advances. Just like tasks in a project that move a change from the current state to a future state, you will need to take action to advance your career from entry-level to seasoned professional. This action can be on your assignments and what you do as a business analysis professional. You should also take your career into your own hands by considering certifications and seeking communities and resources of other business analysis professionals to engage and learn from. Let's begin with the more technical skills now to start expanding your offerings.

Experience

When starting out, much of your analysis work may be delegated or assigned to you. This can be great as it allows you to dive into the assignments and focus on tactical outputs that are more discrete and build a strong foundation of experience. The more assignments you complete successfully with high standards, the more your skill set will be recognized. Once this happens, it is time to shift from simply completing the work to seeking out the work. Identify the needs of your own business analysis work experience and seek out solutions that deliver value for your career.

Getting more strategic

Business analysis professionals who have started to prove themselves through a positive track record of great analysis deliverables coupled with positive interactions with stakeholders start to place themselves in a position of demand. As demand for your skills grows, it is time to start asking yourself what kind of work you both want and need. Yes, when employed by a company, you still need to do the assigned work and deliver the highest quality possible. However, as you start to notice the type of work you are often assigned, you need to ask yourself whether there are other kinds of analysis work you could be doing (or, more importantly, should be learning about) that are beneficial to where you want to take your analysis career.

As you do with your stakeholders, get in the habit of asking good questions, but start doing it on your business analysis work. Try some of these questions to expand your horizons:

- If you work on the same types of projects (for instance, IT or HR), then ask "*Are there projects in other areas or lines of business that I could be assigned?*"

- If most of your projects are short in duration, then ask "*Are there larger projects or efforts that might take six months or longer that I could be a part of?*"

- If you are often brought in after the project starts, then ask "*Is it possible to be included in the initial project kickoff to understand more of the business needs and desired outcomes?*"

- If you deliver analysis work and leave a project before it is completed, then ask "*Is it possible to follow up with end users after the changes or solutions have been in place for a little while to get their feedback and insight?*"

Try asking these questions to expand your business analysis horizons. Then, take note of what you enjoy with each different type of work and where you feel challenged. While those more challenging efforts might be made easier with more experience or professional development, enjoyable work can be key to designing your career roadmap. Focus on analysis work that aligns with the tasks you enjoy and challenges you to develop new skills. This approach is a valuable investment in your career growth.

Getting a non-technical position

Business analysis work is rooted in IT. The need to tie business goals to technical solutions is what created the business analyst role in the first place. With this foundation, many business analysis professionals start their careers working on IT teams or in IT departments. The challenge is that business analysis is not only an IT skill set, but is also good for business, drives better decision-making, and improves overall business performance.

So, how do you move out of the IT space or get assigned a more non-technical role? First, do your own analysis work on your organization. Are there *analyst* positions in other departments? They might be labeled as *marketing analyst* or *risk analyst* positions. If you begin to notice these, then you know there are opportunities for business analysis work in those areas. Many times, you can easily transition to another area of the business in an analyst role because you are bringing the analysis skill set. You may need to learn the terminology and processes of a different area of the business but, as a business analysis professional, your passion for learning will make this an exciting opportunity. Many analysts thrive on exploring new environments and contexts. This is why your foundational skills are so important – because they can transition to any environment and still provide value very quickly.

Another avenue to consider that is quite natural for many analysts is a *project manager* position. This is often a relatively easy transition for some analysts who have been assigned to projects, and it's even easier to quickly dive into if you have been doing requirements work. The reason is that requirements are what define the necessary work to deliver a change. This work is called *tasks,* and a project is simply all the tasks required to go from the current state to the future state. All these project elements and more require analysis work to deliver that requested change.

What's great about project management roles is that they are often not tied to a single department, especially larger ones. This means you will get to learn more about other areas of your organization by working in different spaces. The skills you develop as a project manager are also just as transferable as your business analysis skills. So, even if your future positions are not titled "project manager," getting experience in managing projects gives you transferable skills for any job, just like your business analysis skills. Getting experience in both these competencies will then enable you to seek out a wide array of positions throughout your career, especially as you get professional recognition for this experience.

Getting a technical analysis position

While many analysis professionals may start in technical positions, the opposite can also be true. You may be thinking that you are doing analysis work but find yourself in non-technical positions or roles outside the IT department. This is great as it shows the value of business analysis work and its application beyond just requirements work. For you, a shift to a more technical position can be a great career move to give you a different perspective on where you can add value with your analysis skills. Technical work can feel more detailed and specific, tracing discrete requirements through testing and into implementation. Often, roles can involve lots of troubleshooting that will require you to flex your problem-solving skills.

Just like our non-IT roles, look for *analyst* positions inside your technical teams. If you feel like you do not have a lot of technology experience, junior positions are great ways to learn both the technology and analysis skills focused on a specific program or technology type. Start simple and use the junior position to focus on learning the technology. Leverage your analysis skills and constantly ask good questions so you start to identify relationships between components and technical areas.

And a note here – you can leverage your analysis skills and relationships to get technical understanding without having to take a fully technical position. If you are worried about not having enough technical experience, gain some technological knowledge. A great way to do this is to ask technical team members if you can shadow them while they demonstrate the features of an application or ask to observe an IT team member when they are troubleshooting a problem. This is a great way to learn about technical topics as well as share your analysis skills and bring a unique, unbiased perspective to the work they are doing.

Certification

One of the best steps you can take for your career right now, whether you plan to stay in your current role or pursue a career in business analysis, is to explore relevant certifications. Certifications are becoming the biggest factor in hiring and promoting professionals today. Professional certifications mean a third-party entity will validate that you understand the activities and have demonstrated the skill set of that professional organization. They present a standard that organizations can use to assess your level of expertise. In your search for senior positions, you will notice that certifications are quickly becoming a requirement to even be considered for the position. However, the choice of certification should be made using strong business analysis skills and should align strategically with your career goals.

Certified Business Analysis Professional®

When searching for business analysis certifications, **Certified Business Analysis Professional®** (**CBAP®**) from the **International Institute of Business Analysis®** (**IIBA®**) is *the* certification to demonstrate and display your professionalism in this field. This certification requires an application documenting 7,500 hours of business analysis work experience, along with letters of recommendation, and then you must pass a test that is over three hours long. While this can sound daunting, this is exactly why the certification will quickly set you apart from others. And, actually, if you have been doing business analysis work (you do not need to be called a business analyst or have that job title!) for at least five years, you probably already have the qualifications. You have to be a good business analyst and do thorough document analysis and interview yourself to ensure your work experience addresses all the requirements. Anyone who understands what is required to earn your CBAP® certification knows that if you hold this, you are committed to analysis work, both in your career and in your activities.

Specialized business analysis certifications

In your career, you can go from a generalist to a specialist. Similarly, with business analysis certifications, there are also specialist certifications that you might consider. IIBA has certifications for analysis work in agile analysis, business data analytics, cybersecurity, and product ownership (`https://www.iiba.org/business-analysis-certifications/iiba-certifications/`). Each of these focuses on an area where you can do business analysis. Now, if you are enjoying project-based work, then looking into the **Project Management Institute's (PMI®) Professional Business Analysis (PMI-PBA®)** certification might be worthwhile (`https://www.pmi.org/certifications/business-analysis-pba`). This certification emphasizes requirements' traceability and change management work (PMI, 2024). There are also Agile and Scrum certifications including facilitation and more from the Scrum Alliance (`https://www.scrumalliance.org/get-certified`).

> **Tip**
>
> After reading the rest of the chapters, come back to consider certifications by developing a career roadmap to guide your decisions about certifications. The key is to choose certifications that directly support your career goals. This is what it means to be strategic in your career; just because you can pursue a certification doesn't mean you should. Focus on the choices that will move your career in the direction you want, ensuring your certifications align with your long-term objectives.

Continuous learning and professional development

Now, as powerful as certifications can be on a resume, continuous learning and professional development are key indicators of advancing professionals. Demonstrating your dedication to learning and mastering new concepts and techniques through training and growth opportunities shows others your commitment to delivering the highest value in your work. Training can involve online courses or in-person workshops but even listening to podcasts and webinars are great ways to learn new approaches and hear from industry experts who actively apply analysis skills. These are also areas you want to make healthy habits out of because when you get professional certifications, you often have to maintain them with a certain amount of professional development activity. Training then becomes a huge ROI when it is on both topics to support certification as well as immediately applicable to the work you are doing daily.

Know that your business analysis work will take you to many areas in your own organization and even to different organizations across a wide variety of industries. Each opportunity is a place for you to learn. Good business analysis professionals do not simply study business analysis, though. Instead, they often complement their depth of knowledge in analysis tools and techniques with a breadth of knowledge of business topics. The most successful business analysis professionals are the ones we see as "T-shaped," as identified in *Figure 4.1*. This is from going wide and knowing something about a lot of topics (breadth of knowledge) and then concentrating on a particular topic and going deep into learning the specifics of a subject matter (depth of knowledge).

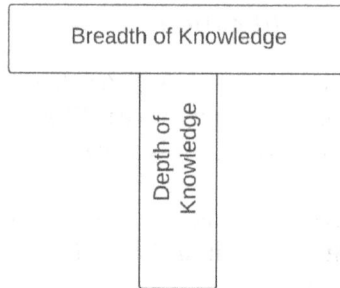

Figure 4.1 – T-shaped perspective of knowledge areas

For example, as you learn more about the profession of business analysis work, you can take courses on the following:

- Process modeling and analysis

- Requirements traceability and analysis work

- People skills, such as facilitation and scoping

- Change management practices

These will boost your analysis skills and capabilities to deliver value. Imagine you are an analyst at a financial organization. Perhaps your organization does general training on financial practices, or compliance has a vendor on site to share updates to federal compliance regulations. These may not seem to have many ties to business analysis work; however, they can help you understand the context in which your analysis work will take place. Understanding your client's world will only enhance the value delivery of your analysis since you will not be hindered by unfamiliar acronyms or unaware of core functions and concepts your stakeholders are more intimately aware of. Business concepts are always worth learning about as they will become valuable in the future work you do to analyze the business.

Networking, mentorship, and coaching

Hand in hand with seeking professional development opportunities is the ability to network with fellow business analysis professionals. The largest and most valuable business analysis organization is the IIBA. Although they are a global organization, they have local chapters and events all around the world. Finding out about the events and groups where you live can be a valuable resource for your continued development. Many offer support and study groups for various certifications, and you can meet business analysis professionals doing both similar and different work from you. You can get new ideas on techniques and approaches to be successful in your analysis work. You can also get inspired and learn about other ways analysis work is getting valued. When you need to search for your next business analysis position, your local IIBA chapter is often a great resource. Not to mention, your membership can keep you engaged with a fun and exciting community that enjoys its work and can simply be the motivation on tough days when your work may not seem like the most glorious job.

But just like with training, do not limit yourself to just business analysis organizations. Finding other professionals working in your local area or even remotely around the world can give you access to experts and insights, resources for facilitation and stakeholder engagement, and new and emerging technologies. Groups such as the **Association for Talent Development** (**ATD**®) (`https://www.td.org/`) and the **Society for Human Resource Management** (**SHRM**®) (`https://www.shrm.org/home`) can be great places to learn ways to engage with teams and define capabilities. Their topics and values might be the skills you need to add to your own toolbox that will help you grow your analysis career.

Seeking out multiple organizations to join can help you discover more resources for your growth. Finding a mentor as you build your professional network can be the guiding compass to help you as you encounter obstacles. Mentoring can take different shapes, from formal agreements and structures to more informal professional friendships. Either way, the role of a mentor to a mentee is to provide ideas and insights. Having someone you can reach out to ask questions or share experiences can be the sounding board to help you stay focused and successful. We'll dive deeper into mentorship in *Chapter 9*.

Besides mentors, you may even find a great coach! Mentors are often people you have a relationship with whom you can seek out and confide in throughout your career journey. A coach, on the other hand, can be targeted for more specific, direct business outcomes. They ask you the hard questions that help you navigate where you want to go and what you want to achieve. Now, don't think that coaching is limited to only when you might be struggling. Coaching can be an excellent way to help you move from good to great. Getting a business coach who is focused on business analysis work and the delivery of value can help you solve problems, ideate, and consider approaches that you had never thought of before, as they bring in their own experience. They can be great when defining or redefining your career approach to what you want to do and where you want to go. Just like a mentor, though, coaches do not do the work for you nor tell you what to do. Great coaches ask you good questions. Yes, they're often great business analysts themselves! They seek to understand your needs and then help you find your own path that works for you. But a guiding light on an unknown journey can be invaluable.

As you gain experience, strategically thinking about the work you do continues to shape your thoughts for the work that you *want* to do. Obtaining certifications and taking professional development courses helps you explore topics and broaden and deepen your knowledge so that you can explore more career opportunities. When coupled with a mentor or coach, these can help you define the direction you want your career to go in. Now is the time to develop a career roadmap where you can use some great business analysis techniques on your own career for the path to long-term success.

Developing a career roadmap

As you begin to think about what you want in your business analysis career, you will want to codify it with more structure to help you build accountability while keeping a larger, long-term vision. Creating and maintaining a comprehensive career roadmap can give you that focus. In this section, we'll explore how you can use SWOT analysis to understand your strengths and weaknesses and use that to build your career roadmap.

Using SWOT analysis to understand yourself

The last thing you may want to do at the end of your day is to do more business analysis work; however, performing business analysis on both you and your career is the trick to making a value-adding roadmap that drives long-term success. This is why business analysis is a skill set that is valued no matter where your career ventures. It seeks value from every effort, both in the workplace and beyond. Those same techniques you use to analyze a business opportunity or need are the ones you use to analyze your career.

A great strategic tool to keep in your business analysis toolbox is SWOT analysis. **SWOT** stands for **strengths**, **weaknesses**, **opportunities**, and **threats**. While it is very valuable in helping with strategic decision-making, this can be just as vital to consider your own analysis work from a strategic perspective. Just like the technique, though, you need to ensure you do the analysis work and not merely record the SWOT part. Here's what you need to consider.

Like all good strategic discussions, a brainstorming session on what your strengths and weaknesses are can be helpful to paint a current situation picture. You can do this by answering the following questions.

For strengths, ask the following:

- What do I do well?

- What do I enjoy doing?

- What do my stakeholders compliment me on when I do business analysis work?

For weaknesses, ask the following:

- What do I feel uncomfortable doing?

- What things have I never done before?

- What items (tasks, techniques, etc.) am I uncomfortable doing without assistance?

The answers to these questions should span a wide range of topics. Think about techniques, approaches, methodologies, and even different technologies. But then go beyond technical and think about the number of stakeholders, their positions, and experience; your types of business analysis work; and the *where*, *when*, and *how* of the project assignments. This is a very internal reflection with no right or wrong answer, but worth spending time analyzing.

Then, you have to look at the external forces. These are the opportunities and threats. In the same manner as your strengths and weaknesses, brainstorm the opportunities you know of or that might exist as well as things that could derail your success as a business analyst. Write down answers to the following questions.

For opportunities, consider the following:

- What new projects or initiatives are happening at your workplaces?
- What training is available?
- What events are bringing together people who are passionate about business value?

For threats, consider these questions:

- What are the job requirements or defined metrics that must be met?
- What organizational changes are happening?
- What industry trends are evolving?

This is by no means an exhaustive list, but it is enough to have you thinking and brainstorming ideas.

And that's all you have done so far – brainstormed ideas. Now, you have to do the SWOT *analysis* portion and consider these elements together. SWOT analysis takes this list of four items and considers the *2 x 2* matrix approach to analyze the options, as laid out in *Table 4.1*:

	OPPORTUNITIES	**THREATS**
STRENGTHS	What strengths do you have to take advantage of the opportunities presented?	What strengths do you have that can minimize the risks and impacts of the possible threats?
WEAKNESSES	What opportunities are out there that can help you turn your weakness into a strength?	What threats are out there that would exploit your weakness, and so should they be avoided at all costs?

Table 4.1 – SWOT analysis structure

Some examples of where the awareness of your strengths and weaknesses could be used to leverage opportunities or mitigate threats might include the following:

- There is a new project that has yet to define the solution option (i.e., nothing has been chosen yet). Getting assigned as the business analyst would allow you to practice and improve your business case skills, which you have currently identified as a weakness for not having had to create many business cases in your work to date.
- The marketing team wants to improve the efficiency and effectiveness of the growing team, and your experience facilitating process improvement workshops with diverse groups would be a strength to help them be successful in their endeavors.

- While you do not have a technical background, which is a weakness you are concerned about, you know several of the software developers who might be on the custom app project as you networked with them at local project management association events, which is a great opportunity to leverage.

- The larger projects require advanced PMP® certifications that you do not have, so you request not to be assigned as a senior project manager at this time.

A detailed analysis of your experiences, both past and present, alongside what is and is not happening in your professional environment, is key to generating the insights needed to chart a course for success. You will need these ideas and elements to build a roadmap of explicit steps that can move your career from the current state to your desired future state.

Building a career roadmap

A roadmap is a path to success. Without a direction, even simply a next step, you could be wasting time or missing opportunities that would excite and delight you in your analysis work, not to mention see you well compensated for your efforts. A career roadmap that lays out steps that go in the direction you want your professional work to go can be an essential tool in any business analysis professional's toolbox.

The agility tools that are used to manage user stories and product roadmaps are the very same tools you can use to manage your career goals and keep you focused yet flexible. The one constant you will notice in all your work (besides the value that business analysis can bring to any change effort) is that things will always continue to change. And so, a successful career roadmap in today's world requires that agility be built into the design. What this means to you is using a structure that allows changes to happen yet prioritizes the highest-value activities. Lay out a structure as in *Table 4.2* for your initial roadmap.

Start simple, and ask: *what are the most important things to your career right now?* Put these items in the **Now** column, as shown in *Table 4.2*. Perhaps you want to focus on the current job assignments and get an official business analysis certification. You notice how you want to do more of the testing plans and validation of solutions on a future project to expand your skills in traceability. You can add that to the **Next** column. You would like to work on a non-IT project at some point and think that while ECBA™ certification at this point is good, in the future, you should consider the CBAP® certification as well. Add these to the **Later** column. The **Not Now** column is a great parking lot to put items that come up but you're not sure are applicable. We do not want to delete any good ideas just in case we need them in the future, so we can use the **Not Now** column. The idea of PMP® certification could go there for now.

Now	Next	Later	Not Now
Define requirements for IT project	Create test plans and coordinate user acceptance testing (UAT) on a project	Analysis position on a non-IT project	
ECBA™ certification		CBAP® certification	PMP® certification

Table 4.2 – Example roadmap structure

Now, agility demands a flexible structure. Notice there are no concrete deadlines or timelines for these items. The **Now** column should have whatever is of most value to your career at this point in time. Prioritize the ideas based on their value to you and your current context, environment, and whatever else is going on in your work and even personal life. The trick is to think of your career roadmap as a living, breathing thing. While it looks to the future, it should be constantly reviewed and updated based on what is (or is not) happening today. As you learn, experience, and connect with others, take your insights and reflect them in your roadmap. That means moving things around and reconsidering priorities. Do not overload the **Now** and **Next** columns but fill up the ideas in the **Later** columns. Then, come back and reprioritize the options as you complete something in the **Now** column.

Roadmaps are a great space to practice rolling wave planning. Very common in agile projects, rolling wave planning focuses on planning those items that are closest to today with the greatest detail. Farther-out items and goals have less planning because things are likely to change between now and then. As the future gets closer and items are more likely to occur, then more detail is put into them. So, plan the specific actions or tasks required to complete those goals in the **Now** column. Build out mini-project plans to complete them. Do not worry about the details of items in the **Next**, **Later**, and **Not Now** columns. You will plan the details for those when they become of the highest priority to delivering value to your career. Until then, they are simply ideas on the roadmap. And know that there is always value in completing activities along your development roadmap – the ROI is that you will get more work opportunities, more pay and benefits, and will often enjoy your work so that it turns from a paid activity to a sought-after passion. After analyzing your career and working to identify how to capitalize on opportunities and minimize threats, a solid career roadmap equips you with the tools necessary to overcome any obstacles that may hinder your continued success.

Overcoming common career challenges

While a plan is a great way to move you forward, not everything will always go as planned. Even those who plan out a great journey in their business analysis careers can get complacent or restricted without knowing it. You have to constantly review your current state and desired future state. As you do that, you want to make course corrections to keep you on track to a valued career. Failing to identify these common challenges with business analysis careers is often the reason people stop enjoying the analysis work and seek other employment opportunities. Business analysis work can be very fun and rewarding, but only if you stay aware of your own work and constantly reflect on an active and evolving career roadmap.

Getting a different type of analysis work

The downside of getting known for your requirements work is that you can get known for *only* doing requirements work. Business analysis skills, techniques, and approaches are valued in so many areas of business that it actually can hurt the organization by only assigning you to elicit and trace requirements.

When you do requirements work, think of all the tasks and techniques you must use to leverage the value of great requirements work. You do interviews and hold focus groups to elicit information. You verify with document analysis and track and manage the requirements with item tracking. You conduct interactive and collaborative workshops to validate requirements for solution designs. These skills are not the easiest things to teach junior professionals and often have to be learned. As you get good at identifying needs, you do not want to wait for the project to be defined and the initial solution to be approved.

Eliciting information and getting stakeholders on the same view of a project are key change activities that business analysis professionals are great at. The launch of a new project needs clarity and focus on articulating what business value the project aims to deliver. Just like requirements, the business need or opportunity needs to be defined. Then, it has to be traced through the implementation of the solution. You are doing similar tasks and techniques to your requirements, but you are expanding to the larger project effort and focused on business value. If you only take project work where you are responsible for the requirements, you may have a hard time seeing the solution in your work. Getting experience with stakeholders throughout a project can help you learn the communication skills you need to ensure the requirements are not just defined and implemented but also understood and supported even beyond the implementation of the solution. Just like business analysis professionals can analyze more than requirements, they can analyze well beyond the scope of a single project.

Switching from project-based work

In project-based work, it is easy to see the analysis skill set. Business analysis professionals analyze the requirements that can define the task required to drive a change to implementation. But who asked why we were doing this project in the first place? Why now? Why not later? Or why not another solution or approach? Some of the most valued business analysis work is in deciding not only which projects to do but also whether the organization should even do the project in the first place. This switches your analysis work to a more strategic focus. In doing so, you get the opportunity to not only do more strategic tasks but also practice more strategic techniques.

Strategy analysis work involves looking at the current and future states of the business, not just the processes of a project. You analyze risks and recommend approaches that are input to the actual project work. You then apply more advanced techniques in this analysis work that utilize the balanced scorecard and business model canvases.

Then there is the operational perspective: analyzing how things are operating in the organization today. While you might do basic techniques of interviews and process models to understand what is happening, using some metrics and **key performance indicators** (**KPIs**) may expose opportunities for improvement. Measuring out revised processes with techniques such as value stream mapping and discussing evaluation criteria helps you ensure the organization is getting the most value out of their already invested people, processes, and technologies. This can be done well after the project has been completed and the solution has been in use for many months or even years. But like strategic analysis work, this kind of analysis perspective helps to determine the next most valuable project work to do to keep the organization moving forward. However, similar to how you can get trapped solely working on projects, you can get stuck with only being associated with technology work, which, again, does not leverage the maximum value of your incredible analysis skills.

Progressing beyond tech-based analysis

Many business analysis professionals begin their careers in the technology department, though this is happening less and less as the role evolves to be more of a strategic partner than simply a requirements role. However, those who begin jobs in the IT department or are responsible for technical implementations and management efforts may find challenges in expanding their scope. It is easy to seek IT-related work but even on IT projects, several business needs emerge, and opportunities are defined well outside the confines of both the project and the technology.

A case study on business value

Take, for example, a Microsoft SharePoint program manager. While the server upgrades, command-line coding, and JavaScript activities were supported by a developer, the young SharePoint program manager was ultimately responsible for the valuable use of the SharePoint system. Basic operational job responsibilities included ensuring the program stayed available for end users and troubleshooting any service interruption. But even in these activities, the program manager often would connect with end users to understand what they were trying to do when the issue was reported. The program manager would meet users who were only using the system for a single process as well as power users who were trying to do complex business applications in the program. This also revealed several employees who did not even use the system at all. However, the young SharePoint program manager was building some valuable relationships with these employees as they got to learn more about the processes the other departments were responsible for and how they completed their work. A lot of the troubleshooting would see the program manager sit with the developer to help walk through the issues to resolve the problems. The developer would often point out ideas on how to improve the system's performance and show off some of the cool features that could really help users.

With this background, as the program manager learned more about the business processes, they saw opportunities to do some educational training. They did basic training that was more informational and shared the capabilities of the program, but they also did more hands-on training for end users on how to walk through and use the program. The more time the program manager spent with the end users, the more opportunities and ideas for process improvement emerged. They worked to coordinate with the developer to determine which suggestions warranted custom development versus those that could be addressed through business process reengineering. This program manager was providing valuable business analysis work for years to come.

This example is a great way to see where and how business analysis activities can grow and add value to an organization. Review this case study and note the following business analysis tasks and techniques and the potential value they all offer:

- Troubleshooting issues with root cause analysis

- Interviews and focus groups with end users to define business needs and processes

- Process mapping and analysis of current and future statement processes

- Solution and business capabilities analysis and evaluation

- Acceptance and evaluation criteria

- Design options and solution approaches

- Stakeholder communication and collaboration

All these value-adding analysis activities were done not because they were assigned, but because those are the activities of someone with a business analysis perspective and goal to deliver the most value to an organization. These activities would not be possible if you only worked on projects. Project-based work can limit your perspective and reduce your chance for strategic analysis and solution evaluation experience. With a business focus comes the realization that your career can easily go well beyond the IT department, but only after you identify these potential roadblocks can you move your career forward on the path to success.

Summary

Just like you analyze business problems in your work, analyzing your career is how you can continuously deliver value in a prosperous business analysis profession. As you build your analysis experience and expand it to more areas of application, consider supplementing your growth with certifications, networking opportunities, and mentorship programs. These can be valuable resources to expand your toolkit for greater career success.

That path to success often comes from a defined map that lists the steps to help you go from the current state to a future state. You have to remember to be a good business analyst on yourself and leverage techniques such as SWOT analysis as your professional context continues to evolve. When you see the opportunities and your strengths, then building a career plan that is founded on agility and value-adding activities can give you the focus to take your career to the next level, while also exploring opportunities. Just like the variation in the types of work you take, consider our model of a "T-shaped" approach to analysis work. The examples in this chapter help you take a *breadth* approach to exploring analysis work. In the next chapter, let us explore the specializations you can dive deep into your career and deliver even more value.

Further reading

- Hermes, M. (2014, May 4). *The World's Theory – The History of Business Analysis & Evolution of the Business Analyst*. BA Times. Retrieved from `https://www.batimes.com/articles/the-world-s-theory-the-history-of-business-analysis-evolution-of-the-business-analyst/`

- Weissman, S. (2024, April 11). *Degrees Earned Fall Again, Certificates Rise. Inside Higher Ed*. Retrieved from `https://www.insidehighered.com/news/students/academics/2024/04/11/degrees-earned-fall-again-certificates-rise`

5

Specializations within Business Analysis

While business analysis professionals are encouraged to have a very broad knowledge of business processes and value delivery streams, specializing in a particular area can lead to a successful long-term analysis career. In this chapter, you will explore the various areas and approaches in which you can specialize in your business analysis work. Throughout the exploration of these areas and what the tasks and techniques might look like in day-to-day analysis work, you will need to go back and analyze your career in more depth using valuable analysis techniques. When you have analyzed the advantages and challenges of specialization, you can make a strategic, informed, and data-driven decision about where you want to take your analysis career.

In this chapter, we're going to cover the following main topics:

- Different areas of specialization
- How to choose the right specialization
- Benefits and challenges of specialization

Different areas of specialization

Business analysis is both a role and a skill set. With this in mind, you can choose to focus your analysis work within a specific specialization or area of work. Specialization simply means concentrating within an area or industry to the point you are both a subject matter expert on the topic and a business analysis professional. The need for deep expertise in specific areas is becoming increasingly important as businesses seek more support to navigate evolving trends. Technology is a driving factor in the need to specialize and understand how work is evolving. But just like your career, specialization does not require you to pursue purely technical positions or job titles.

Analyzing data

With the explosion of not just data, but the amount of data that is now available to end users, the ability to extract insights from an overwhelming amount of data is critical for supporting effective decision-making. Data analysis, data analytics, and business data analytics are growing areas of need for organizations to maintain a competitive advantage in the market. Working with data can take many forms – from developing business cases based on data, to creating diagrams that model where, how, and why data is created and consumed within an organization, to writing complex algorithms that extract insights from vast datasets. Any of these areas is like a treasure hunt to sift through all the information to find out what "secrets" it might have to help the business make smart decisions. If you like these treasure hunts but at a very tactical level, this can be a great specialization area to explore. If you are naturally curious about what data insights mean to your organization's direction, then an analysis position centered around data might be just what your career needs.

The power of business analysis when it comes to data is that the value is beyond just understanding what data is out there. The business analysis perspective considers what data is needed, where to get it from, how to organize it, and especially how to use the data to drive data-driven decision-making. Smartly organized data means that the insights and causative factors are more apt to be grounded in truth and, therefore, forecasts and simulations will hold true. What will set your career apart, though, from, say, the career of a data scientist is your ability to focus on asking what impact those data analysis activities and insights have on the organization's decision-making. For example, some data analysis scenarios might include things such as the following:

- Given the influential factors of the market's geography, where and when should the organization open another store?

- Given the causal relationship between the efforts to promote mobile technology and connect to new customers on social media, what does the product catalog look like when tailored to a younger generation of customers?

- Given the seasonal trends in credit card fraud and cybersecurity incidents, how should our organization assess and evaluate our current and future IT infrastructure?

Taking data, uncovering insights, and then driving decision-making within the context of the enterprise while seeking strategic alignment is the bigger picture and value description of a business analysis professional who specializes in business data analytics. But before you start researching what kind of technical language you need to know for data analysis work, remember that business analysis activities are about delivering business value, not how to analyze datasets. Let's now consider some aspects of specializing in data in your business analysis work (in a BA position) as opposed to taking a data position that requires you to do technical data analysis work (such as in a data scientist position).

Data flow diagrams

If you enjoy making visual models of how work is carried out and love data, then consider exploring data flow diagrams in more detail. Similar to process models that show how work is carried out, data flow diagrams show the flows of data: where they come from, what actions or activities happen with the data, and where the data gets stored or even utilized by other activities (IIBA®, 2015). This is a great example of the need to understand general business analysis topics and how to think about processes and systems. But there is also a deeper focus on the details. *Figure 5.1* is an example data flow diagram that was created for the process of ordering flowers.

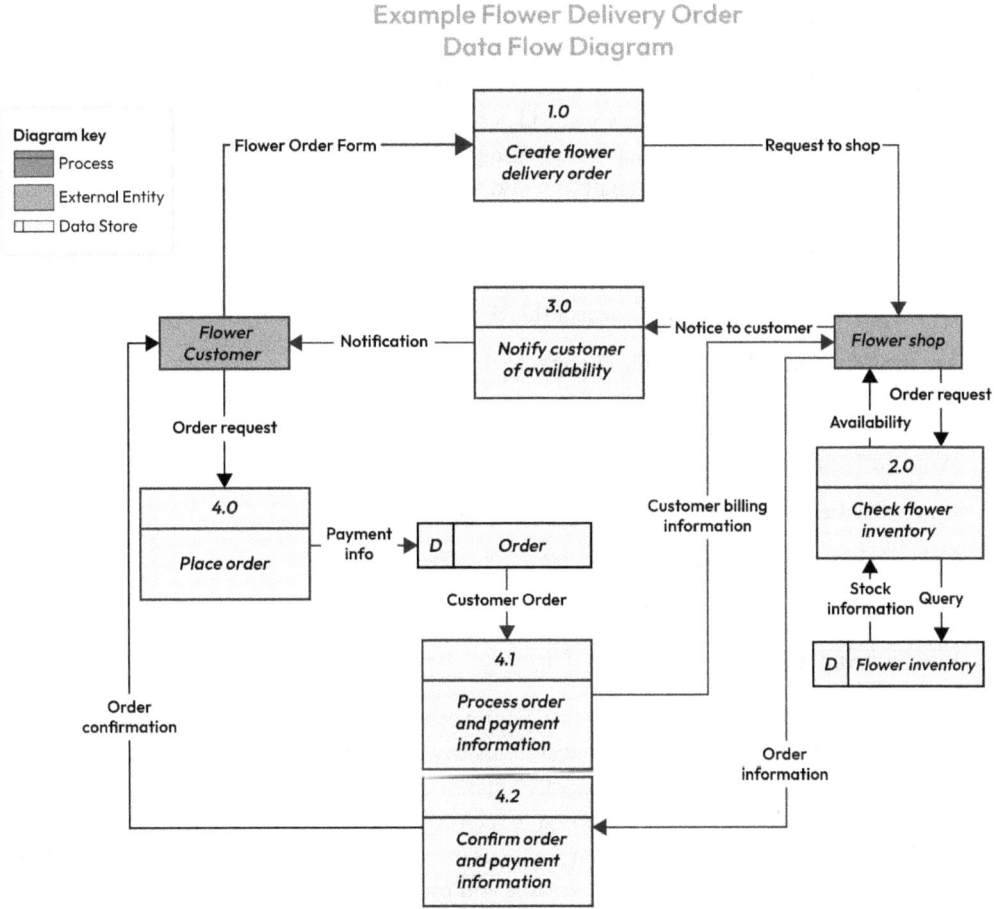

Figure 5.1 – Data flow diagram

Creating visual models

The model in *Figure 5.1* was created with **Lucidchart** (https://www.lucidchart.com/), a great visual modeling tool for Mac users. Microsoft users will find the same features and value in Microsoft Visio (https://www.microsoft.com/en-us/microsoft-365/visio/). Getting comfortable creating visual models with any software, even collaboration software such as Mural (https://mural.co/) and Miro (https://miro.com/) is a key skill set to add to your business analysis career. Models like these will be found throughout this book to help give you an idea of the variations even your analysis products can take.

Data models are often created with the same approach you might use with process models – asking what is happening, when, where, and even why. And then these models are often complementary because you can use the process model to ask about what data is stored where and what happens with it. This is what creates data models. While you will need to do the same elicitation work as you do for any process analysis to understand what is happening, as a data specialist, you will then analyze the data elements uncovered during your analysis work. You do not need to worry about building data stores, but you might uncover data management and technical infrastructure requirements when you dive into the details and ask questions such as the following:

- How are the data stores set up to accept this data and quickly mine it for insights?
- Are the data stores able to handle changes to the data flows?
- Is duplicate data going to separate systems and data stores?
- What other processes need this data?
- Is this data being used by other people/areas/departments?
- How is the data getting into the systems?
- How does the data get out of the system?
- What is being tracked on each piece of data?

These questions might require you to dive into your analysis training and do more work, such as interface analysis (what happens that allows systems to communicate and share data), advanced modeling (visuals of the enterprise architecture that makes things work), and business rules work (the policies that govern what is and is not supposed to happen); but you come from a data perspective. You bring the business value goals into a sharper focus on the data, and specializing in your analysis career can be a great way to demonstrate the value you provide for an organization. Exploring the where, how, and what of the data an organization uses is often a great area for business analysis professionals to move to in their careers, and if you like this area of data, where you not only want to uncover data insights but also visualize results and drive the business decisions at an organization, then specialization in **business intelligence** (**BI**) might be a consideration.

BI analysis

A specialty area that focuses on both data and business analysis skills is BI. Just like business analysis professionals, BI analysts use data to help with organizational decision-making. However, BI positions often require deep technical knowledge with a focus on understanding the data the organization already has and how to integrate it further for even more validated decision-making. BI analysts can often spend a lot of time focusing on building models for the decision-making process rather than asking why the insight would be helpful in the first place. If you like exploring what data is available and seeking more data sources to integrate for greater insights, BI roles are great ways to go beyond simple data analysis positions and leverage your strong business analysis skills because the insights are gathered to drive the organization's decision-making.

This is another place where you need to ask yourself what you like to do in your work. If you like using Excel to make PivotTables and pulling in multiple sources of data to analyze them together, then pursuing BI training and getting more proficient in BI tools might prove more valuable to both your interest and your career. The technical demands of these positions often require knowledge of tools such as Tableau and Power BI, and even programming languages like Python and R (Coursera, 2024). General business analysis work does not need programming experience. It can definitely help to have some knowledge of technical processes on technical projects; however, it is normally not required. For BI analysis positions, though, you will need deeper technical skills. The work shifts to you owning the responsibility for getting the data to display the insights rather than simply asking what the data means to the organization. This can be a great area to transition into if you have started your analysis career in a technical role or within technical departments. It was said many years ago that data is the currency of our world, and so those who learn to harness data and wield it to the benefit of their business goals are the ones who will be able to out-compete and withstand market trends and competition (Vavra, 2016). However, the management of data can easily feel overwhelming. So, let's look at an example to demonstrate the value of being able to go deep into the data of an organization with a powerful business analysis technique – a data dictionary.

Data dictionary

If you are wondering about how to differentiate between those who dive into data as their life's work versus those who use data as part of their business analysis work, let's take a look at a great business analysis technique: the **data dictionary**. While it sounds simple at first or may even get confused with a glossary, it is about standardization and getting everyone on the same page with what a particular piece of data is and what it means in context (IIBA, 2015). I love the example you can use to demonstrate its power. At any organization, ask your stakeholders to define who a *customer* is. Who a customer is to the marketing team is not the same as to a teller in the bank, nor is it the same to a help-desk technician. It is the same word, and everyone thinks they know who you are referring to, but in each context, it represents a completely different person. The real confusion arises when you dig into the details of how and where the term *customer* is used.

At the data level, a customer is made up of multiple components and is a composite term. It also can have different names depending on the context. When you start asking questions about where the term is used in different data stores and what elements of data are flowing between systems, concerns around data consistency and interpretation start to arise. Look at *Table 5.1* and see that a customer has multiple data elements – some are required, some are optional – and depending on which system you are in, they have completely different names.

Primitive Data Element	Data Element 1	Data Element 2	Data Element 3
	First Name	Middle Name	Last Name
Alternatives	Given Name	Second Name	Surname
Options	Title	Middle Initial	Designation
	Nickname		
Business Rules	At least one required	Optional	At least one required
Composite	Customer = Data Element 1 + Data Element 2 + Data Element 3		

Table 5.1 – Data dictionary table

Uncovering this kind of insight before decisions are made about customer data is crucial because you know that the data insights might not be as accurate if the data points aren't better reconciled and managed.

Business analysis professionals facilitate understanding and work to get everyone on the same page. A data dictionary is how you define important terms in multiple formats and use them in the right context at the right time for the right reasons. While *Table 5.1* is simple in concept, think about doing this kind of work daily. A person who gets excited defining the structure, alternatives, business rules, and more relating to a single piece of data should specialize in areas of the organization that focus on data. The energy you get from working with data terms lets you know that having a data analysis specialization might be the best thing for you and will help you enjoy your analysis career.

If you are looking for positions that might be data-centric in their daily activities, some common job titles might be as follows:

- Data analyst
- BI analyst

- Data scientist

- Data engineer

But even if you do not specialize with a core "data" job title, you can get this kind of work experience and enjoyment in positions that might include the following responsibilities:

- **Data collection and cleaning**: Gathering, cleaning, and organizing data from various sources

- **Analysis and interpretation**: Identifying trends and insights through statistical analysis

- **Visualization**: Creating reports and visualizations to present findings to stakeholders

- **Collaboration**: Working closely with business leaders to understand their data needs and provide actionable insights

- **Advanced analytics**: Utilizing statistical methods, machine learning, and predictive modeling to analyze complex datasets

- **Data engineering**: Building systems for collecting, storing, and analyzing large volumes of data

All these positions and responsibilities require analysis work. And this is just one area of specialization your career can take. Let's now look at another very common specialization with technological roles and activities.

IT systems analysis

If you have the same natural curiosity for technology as a data analyst has for data, then focusing on analyzing technology solutions might be the best direction for your career. A fact now and for years to come is that technology is going to play a crucial role in how businesses deliver customer value, even if their products and services have nothing to do with technology. Technology is ingrained in our daily work and lives and is not going away anytime soon.

Specializing in technology could mean two different focuses. You could be a generalist and seek a position such as a technical solutions architect, who designs solutions that consider an organization's entire infrastructure stack. This is a great position because you learn about each area in a tech department and get experience in the specialized areas. Often, senior technical business analysts will transition into these roles quite nicely, taking advantage of both their tech and analysis backgrounds.

On the other hand, if you are just starting your career journey, almost any technical analyst position can be a great way to start specializing and building up your analysis skills. A position such as a technical analyst assigned to any program, system, or component of technology is a great way to define your specialization and analysis processes. Positions such as this could have the following job titles:

- Technical analyst

- Program analyst

- Application analyst

- Systems analyst

- Business systems analyst

If you venture into one of these roles without much experience, this just means you want to first learn as much as possible about the specific technology you've been assigned to. Learn how it is set up and configured in the organization. Learn where and how it is used and how it is connected to other technologies. Then, explore online resources to find out what else the tool or technology can do. Learn from user communities how others are leveraging the tool's capabilities and aim to get training and hands-on experience in test and development sandboxes as much as possible. This is what makes you a subject matter expert, or SME, in the technology. While you are doing all this, practice your analysis skills: ask good questions, interview users, and document system processes and data flows. When you know the technology, you can focus on your analysis skills. Your analysis skills will keep you sharp when you find gaps or opportunities in what is and is not being used in your technology.

When you start with this approach, you become an invaluable resource because there is a constant challenge with technology: its constant and rapid evolution. Technology is changing so quickly that there needs to be people who can dedicate their attention to learning what emerging capabilities could be valuable to the business. Of course, the business needs to be able to articulate its strategic goals and intended direction. But they may not know what they need until they see it. And you can't show them ideas until you know what the technology can do. This kind of *chicken and egg* question is exactly where you sit. In *Figure 5.2*, you can see how you can start on either business opportunities or technology capabilities. You learn technology capabilities and seek business opportunities to leverage those. And you seek understanding on the business processes to define needs that you can then address by seeking out the relevant technology. And so, it may feel like a continuous cycle, as shown in *Figure 5.2*:

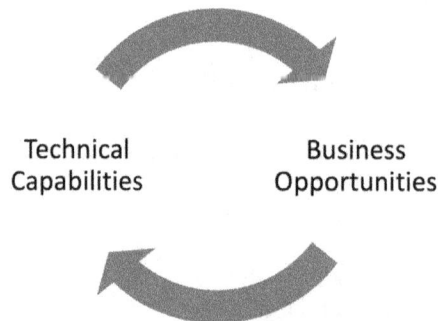

Technical Capabilities   **Business Opportunities**

Figure 5.2 – Relationship between business opportunities and technical capabilities

When looking for positions that help you specialize in technological areas, look for roles that include the following responsibilities:

- Analyze and optimize business processes through technology
- Elicit requirements from stakeholders and translate them into technical specifications
- Facilitate **user acceptance testing** (**UAT**) to validate that systems deliver necessary business value
- Troubleshooting and problem-solving to identify and resolve the root causes of issues
- Evaluate existing systems for optimization and increased value delivery
- Collaborate with technical teams to deliver technical system designs and solutions

When you specialize in a certain technology, you can provide organizations with the insight they need to take advantage of that technology in a way that drives them forward. But only when you take the time to dive into understanding the features, functionalities, and applications of the technology does this value truly emerge. But even in the technology space, there is even greater specialization in areas that are key to the business.

Cybersecurity

Cybersecurity is a critical area in technology that will only continue to grow and be of value as long as customers and organizations continue to use technology. This is not just a technology concern but also a business concern, given the reliance organizations have on technology. Business analysis professionals will find themselves having to learn basic cybersecurity considerations for defining requirements and successful solutions on any technical project (IIBA, 2024). Since failing to properly address cybersecurity requirements in any initiative can make or break an entire organization, prioritization of cybersecurity skills continues to grow in almost every organization in every industry in every part of our digitally connected work. Specializing in cybersecurity is an excellent focus if you enjoy being part of technical solution design teams. Solution architects often have strong cybersecurity backgrounds to combine with their infrastructure knowledge. And when you can layer on your business skills, enabling you to understand the strategic value delivery processes of your organization, you become critical to any project that harnesses technology.

A cybersecurity specialization will have you spending significant time asking about the following:

- Access control – *who has access to what and from where?*
- Authentication methods – *how will we prove that the person is who they say they are?*
- User management – *who needs access to what, and how can we give them only that access during that time?*

- Disaster recovery and backup plans – *how long is the business comfortable with not being able to operate? How much data is the business comfortable with losing or not being able to restore?*

- Audits and testing – *how do we know our systems are secure? Do we know how much they can handle before a breach is possible? What do we need to report on to prove our security stance?*

These questions are excellent areas of cybersecurity concentration for a business analysis professional who centers their career on the business side of analysis. This kind of specialization is often a great place to be pulled into a more technical SME role on any change efforts. Yet the technical security analyst role is truly valued by business sponsors when you show that you can relate your technical knowledge to what the business is trying to achieve. That desire to focus on value can lead you into even more areas of specialization where you focus on a single line of business, a process, or even a single product or program.

Product management

Product management has grown in popularity with the rise of agile methodologies and approaches. The value of this role is not just managing a product from day to day but in acting on behalf of the customer to define the most valuable features and ideas that are viable to the business (Atlassian, 2024). Again, you are combining the subject matter expertise: knowing your customer and your product intimately with their needs, wants, and desires. You then couple this with your knowledge of the organization's capabilities, what the markets are doing, and how competition and the industry as a whole affect your product decisions.

You might first get experience of working in agile teams and defining needs in terms of value to your customer. As you get to know your target customers and audiences better, you may feel a strong desire to represent them directly and influence the business decisions being made. Agile skills of thinking like your customer, prioritizing delivery (and willingness to accept constant re-prioritization), and keeping focused on value implementation are critical in these roles. They are great if you enjoy the agile mindset and have a passion for representing your customer (IIBA, 2017). Concentrating on agile practices can be a natural place to move your analysis career, especially when you are starting out and looking for more hands-on experience.

Agile

Agile is more than a simple methodology; it brings flexibility and adaptability into your change efforts. Agile is a mindset and a skill set that can be a powerful addition to any analyst's toolbox. Many organizations have found success by using agile approaches and often prefer that their teams and product delivery cycles run in an agile manner. The first step to specializing in this area is to get on an agile team. This can be a great first move if you are new in your analysis role.

In an agile environment, a business analysis professional will often still be assigned the requirements elicitation for a project or initiative. The trick with agile teams is they often like requirements to be captured in user story format. A **user story** is a short, concise statement of value in terms of the customer (IIBA, 2017). While many teams will want particular formats, the goal again is to express statements of value. This is a good idea wherever you work with requirements. A user story, though, puts the user directly in focus.

> **An example format of a user story is**
> As a WHO I need WHAT so that WHY.

The *WHO* portion describes the customer with enough detail and specificity so that you can picture the customer of the requirement or desired functionality. The *WHAT* is the desired functionality or capability. The *WHY* becomes the business value. Even if you do not write requirements in this format, simply thinking about every requirement, every piece of work on any initiative in this format – customer, need, and value – is a great way to ensure your work is always valued. This is often the first skill explored and achieved in agile teams.

Agile environments can introduce you to a host of other skill sets and techniques that are valued in agile work and strengthen your business analysis expertise. **Estimation** is done and redone frequently, so you'll develop the ability to provide clear specifications and improve your communication skills to help ensure items are estimated correctly the first time. **Prioritization** is an activity you will have to facilitate over and over again. Agile environments always want to deliver the highest-value activities. What provides the most value for the customer? That is the feature that you prioritize. You handle the changing work around you this way. Agile emphasizes **collaboration** so that there is constant feedback on what is or is not working well to help everyone stay focused on how much value is being delivered. These are all skills you will both explore and expand when working in agile environments.

Getting comfortable with these areas as well as learning different agile techniques, as described in the *Agile Extension to the BABOK Guide* (IIBA, 2017), will help you hone your agile skills. This will be exactly what you need to find better career paths in agile environments – demonstrate your agile mindset through the application of these approaches. Building your experience by working on teams that welcome change and in fact even expect things to change will help hone your mindset so that you have the expertise needed when projects call for adaptability. Not everyone gets this perspective. Having experience and expertise in agile environments is a specialty that is not only desired right now in many organizations but, due to the dynamic nature of the world around us, will be desired for years to come. If you get excited about change, if you like exploring ideas to see what works and enjoy facilitated discussions around user experience and expectations, then working in agile areas may be just the specialization to leverage your interest and your analysis skills.

Financial analysis

Not everything in business is based purely on customer wants. Good attention to detail, particularly numbers, is important for any organization that wants to make informed financial decisions and follow suitable strategies. Analysts who enjoy numbers and exploring the financial aspects of a project might seek specialization in finance. This has a two-way focus, like much of your business analysis work. You could seek analysis positions in the finance department, where your primary duties are financial data analysis, with secondary work focused on driving positive business change based on those insights. Alternatively, you could do business analysis work within organizations whose mission is financial services and products. Both perspectives are quickly becoming popular and in need of more people with technical data and financial skills coupled with the business acumen needed to make informed business decisions.

If you take a financial analyst position, you will be expected to know about financial equations and formulas. You are looking to mine and analyze data to compare solution options and inform decision-making processes. Financial information that supports strategic business decisions includes the ability to analyze the following:

- Metrics and **key performance indicators (KPIs)**
- Initial and ongoing costs
- **Return on investment (ROI)**
- **Net present value (NPV)**
- **Internal rate of return (IRR)**
- Risks and potential impacts
- Payback period
- **Total cost of ownership (TCO)**
- Value realization
- Cost-benefit analysis

These may not be everyday activities for some positions, but you could also find yourself doing even more in-depth financial calculations in certain financial analysis positions. If you get excited about calculating these results and comparing them for financial decisions, then this world of financial data analysis may be perfect for your specialization.

Now consider a second option to specialize in financial analysis. You could do business analysis work as an assigned BA in a financial institution or industry. This kind of position means you will have to at least know what these terms and other financial lingo mean. You may not be doing the calculations, but you will have to spend time facilitating with teams to seek out the data that helps drive the business decisions you are working on or supporting. Understanding the financial processes and the data used and flowing into reports, ledgers, and other outputs will be critical to your success. Just like any other business analysis position, the more you dive into the industry in which your analysis work is taking place, the more valuable you become as a resource to any team. The question becomes how much you want to be hands-on with the financial data and defining insights versus focusing on leveraging the outcomes of the financial analysis work to drive the business decisions.

Risk analysis

Given the volatility of global markets, supply chains, and other factors, the financial sector continues to seek and develop strong financial analysis skills. *Risk analyst* roles are often central to these efforts. These are analysts who assess the risks of certain actions and explore their potential impact on business outcomes. What is really great about these positions is that they are not just found in financial teams but also in marketing and technology teams, and even at the enterprise level in organizations that often take a more risk-adverse approach to their investment strategies. This is a great way to explore a business, coupled with technical skill sets.

Risk analysts have to be very comfortable with probability and estimating impacts. Benchmarking, market analysis, metrics, KPIs, risk analysis, and management are key techniques that they regularly employ (IIBA, 2015). These roles help decision-makers understand the ramifications of their decisions. Most of this work is just estimation; things are not certain. But a lot of work goes into simulating possibilities, and it can be thrilling to present these possibilities and their potential business impact to decision-makers. With the constant changing of the technology, policies, and politics of our environments, risk analysis positions will deliver value for many years to come. But even in these processes there can be room for improvement.

Process improvement

One of the areas that provides the most value, and where business analysis professionals often let their skills shine, is process improvement. Some organizations may have robust Six Sigma and Lean teams that focus on process optimization and reducing waste in operations. In this position, the focus is on understanding and analyzing current business processes to find opportunities for improvement. Defining current processes, measuring output, suggesting and implementing changes, and then remeasuring the processes will keep you focused on the details of the work within an organizational context in this type of work. You get to focus on the specifics while considering the impact on the bigger picture. These roles can often require certifications in methodologies and process improvement approaches that you might need to consider if you are interested in this career path. While it requires additional work, there can be clearer promotion paths as your experience (and certifications) grow. Accepting a position in process improvement will often require you to use techniques like value stream mapping, **suppliers, inputs, process, outputs, customer (SIPOC)**, and root cause analysis, along with metrics and KPIs to help quantify the value of the improvement efforts.

But even if there is not a specific process improvement position at your organization, many analysis positions can focus on process improvement. Take, for example, a *service desk analyst*. While many service desk positions are about answering questions, most of them are about solving problems. Using techniques like **functional decomposition** daily to break down issues into smaller components so that the service is focused on the particular element in question is key to daily work. When you understand the process occurring at a more detailed level, you are in a great position to optimize the process to not only solve the immediate issue but then to help prevent it from occurring again.

Recognize if you are a person who loves to take things apart to simply know how they work and then put them back together again. If this sounds like you, asking your employer or prospective employer about the amount of time your job would focus on process improvement activities is imperative. You will get to build on your process modeling and analysis techniques to get more insights on value delivery and help organizations to maximize their existing investments.

Each of these areas of specialization is simply an option. They are not your only options by any means. Consider how each area of specialization introduces new tasks and techniques to your daily analysis work that you may not use as frequently if you choose to be more generalist in your business analysis career path. Business analysis is not a one-size-fits-all role, but a field with diverse specializations that cater to different aspects of organizational needs. So, next, let's talk about the things to ask yourself to help you decide whether specialization is right for you and, if so, how to choose the right one.

How to choose the right specialization

So, how do you choose the right specialization? Well, in good business analysis fashion, the answer is simple: it depends. First, ask yourself whether you even want to specialize in your analysis work. If you are just starting out, staying general can be a great way to learn about your analysis tasks and techniques. This means taking entry-level business analysis positions to get accustomed with the analysis work.

But the question is then whether you like a particular topic more than others. You are going to use most of your analysis skills and techniques wherever you go. That is the great thing about business analysis. The question to ask yourself is whether there is a subject area, an industry, or even a job market area that interests you more than others. This is not just a question about whether you like it or not but about whether you are passionate for it. Would you be willing to spend time outside your regular work hours attending user groups and professional association events at your own expense to learn more and connect with others doing the same kind of work? Does it excite you to enroll in a class to learn more on the topic, in addition to the daily work at your organization?

You want to always make informed decisions, especially with your career choices. This is what business analysis is all about – making data-driven and data-informed decisions that strategically align with goals. You need to take this same approach with your career. Ask yourself questions regarding what you feel excited about. Identify areas you have a natural curiosity for, and check whether it would be easy to sustain that curiosity for a period of time. If you didn't do your **SWOT** analysis (**strengths, weaknesses, opportunities, and threats**) in the previous chapter, now is a good time to go back and explore not only what you want to do, but also what the industry is doing and how that aligns with your interests. What potential opportunities do you see in your areas of interest? What threats might exist to limit your opportunities and advancement conditions? Each career move should entail all the analysis of a good business case. You are driving your own informed decisions.

While you are deciding what works best for your passion and interest in the business analysis domain, it can be beneficial, especially financially, to analyze market trends and demands for the business analysis profession. Having a career path that is not only exciting but in demand in a way that can pay your desired salary and support your lifestyle is how you get the best of both worlds.

Analyzing market trends and demands

In the world of analysis professionals, you will encounter various market trends and demands. You may see the value in your business analysis work, but the organizations and industries in which you work may have shifts and even radical swings in how and when the demand for business analysis professionals grows or shrinks. Specializing in technology, particularly a form of development or coding, might be extremely profitable as technology capabilities advance and organizations are exploring how best to integrate technology. But consider the no-code or low-code solutions that are coming onto the market, putting advanced programming capabilities into the hands of the general user. Your specialized skills become less valuable because the technology has changed. It was nothing you did or did not do. The environment and context around you has simply changed. So, whether through formal or informal techniques, stay abreast of current trends in business analysis in general and in the different areas of specialization. Positions and titles will come and go. New techniques will emerge. But constantly growing your skills and adding to your toolbox will never go out of style. You simply want to be mindful of all the forces at play when it comes to your analysis career.

Applying force field analysis

Balancing your interests and passions against the effect the economy and industries may have on your career can be a way to constantly adjust and align your career path. Let's use one of your great analysis approaches on your career again. **Force field analysis** is a technique that looks at the forces acting upon a situation or topic (IIBA, 2015). These are the forces that both push you forward and push against your progress towards your goals. In general, the topic is in the middle and then you simply list the items to the left and right that are pushing against the topic, as shown in *Figure 5.3*. The size of the arrows indicates the strength of each force.

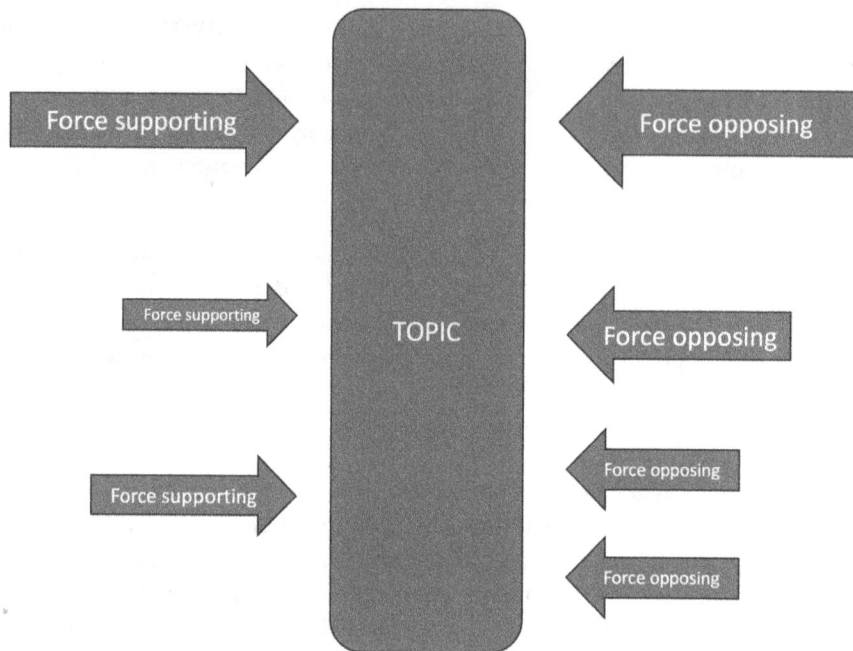

Figure 5.3 – Force field analysis structure

For your career, lay out the forces that are supporting your success. Consider things such as the following:

- Experience
- Certifications
- Subject area knowledge
- Training
- Industry trends
- Current job market

But these factors can also push against your career progress:

- Lack of experience
- Lack of certifications
- Broad knowledge, no depth
- Lack of formal training
- Industry trends shifting demands
- Oversaturated job market

The more you can brainstorm, the better the picture you will have of those forces that are weighing on your decision to specialize or not.

The challenge is to remember to continually analyze your career. Lessons learned are powerful motivators and provide insights into not only what worked well but also what you enjoyed in your analysis work. Remember to review your past work and define actions that can support your SWOT analysis work. As shown in some of our examples, even when you do not change anything, the world in which you perform analysis work is constantly evolving. But just like the agile mindset, you can go into a successful analysis career having changed specializations many times or even having switched between specialization and generalization. There is no right or wrong answer to whether to specialize. The trick is that you want to have made a well-informed decision and with a solid business case that supports a long-term, successful career rather than a job for the next few months. So, to help you in your decision, let's take a look at some of the pros and cons of specialization in your career.

Benefits and challenges of specialization

The reason why there is not a single answer as to what you should or should not do with your career is that it truly does depend. It depends on you and your work experience, the organization you work in, the industry, and the market, as well as your own drive and personal aptitude. Again, we want to make informed, data-driven decisions to get the maximum value from all our investments of time and energy. So, like any good business case, there are advantages and challenges with specializing in your analysis career that you should address when you make career choices.

Advantages of specializing

Specializing is sticking to a single niche area and working your way forward within that niche. The advantage of this approach is being able to see clear career paths or at least professional growth. Tasks get bigger and more complex the longer you stay in a certain specialization. More advanced applications of tools and learning task-specific techniques come into play the longer you stay in a single area of work or business. Your general business acumen for the topic will make it easy to be seen as an SME in that area of the business. It can also narrow your scope and focus when you want to address your career goals.

Certain training programs, certifications, and academic courses are more specific and tied directly to your area of work. Conferences and professional associations have a clearer relationship with the work you are doing because you focus on a specific topic. Consider how many financial associations or professional organizations there are out there. Then consider how many professional business analysis organizations have open membership. In any specialization, business analysis is a valued skill set, much like communication and team building. It is not the only work you do, but it is valuable for getting the work done.

It can also be quite easy to start a new job search. You know the area of business or the general departments of an organization in which you would find your work. Only mature organizations have business analysis teams. Some do not even have "business analyst" as a titled position! Yet most organizations have IT departments and finance and marketing teams that actively recruit good team members who can have a positive impact on delivered value.

Consider that just in your area of specialization, you will often then repeat tasks and techniques. The more you do the same things, the better your skills are in future activities. Specialization allows you to hone a specific set of skills to be an expert on that topic area. In contrast, if you worked in a more general business analysis position, every assignment may be different and require a variety of techniques to complete different tasks. You might get a greater breadth of technical knowledge with these analysis skills, but there may never be the opportunity to repeat the same tasks and so you will lack the depth of work that is more systematized. However, this can also be a hindrance as specialization does introduce some challenges.

Challenges with specialization

There are challenges when you start to specialize in your business analysis career. One of the things you might notice even in your own assignments is that specialization can lead to you assuming that your specialty area is the *only* type of analysis work you do. As you become an SME, stakeholders may not see you as a business analyst. They see you as an SME. So, people will seek out your skills in your area of specialization, not for analysis. When this happens, you don't want your analysis skills to be overlooked, or worse, wasted. Those analysts who become really good at getting agile teams running smoothly might then only be sought after as a Scrum Master or even product owner. Sure, both of these roles get to do analysis work, but this perspective limits the amount and types of work you might be assigned. The same applies to task work. As good as the repetitive nature of certain tasks and techniques can be to increase your confidence and success, only doing a select few tasks or techniques will greatly limit and hamper your analysis skills progression. In fact, you could get so focused on your area of specialization that you lose some of those more holistic business perspectives of a business analysis professional. You can slowly slip into a permanent SME position rather than continuously growing and expanding your analysis knowledge and experience.

You could also face challenges if your area of specialty is in a market saturated with analysis professionals. Job markets can act like a pendulum and go from needing lots of positions filled to there being no demand. This is why the analysis of your career, in particular SWOT analysis and force field analysis, needs to be periodically redone to look at what is happening in your context. Know that even if you get into an area of work that you love, the environment around you is constantly changing and evolving. You want to keep track of this because things could change.

Take, for example, AI. This area is in high demand right now as companies look to upskill and leverage this technology. Not many people have this deep specialization, which makes it highly sought after and well paid. As more and more people get skills in working with and designing AI solutions, the demand will be more easily met, and the job market will become more competitive. What used to be a specialization will almost have become a generalization, an expectation even, that everyone knows how to do. If this is your only specialization, how will you stand out from the rest of the community? What if this technology advances so far that many of the positions no longer exist because of the processing power the technology has evolved? If your only skill set is automated, not just your position but even your value can become obsolete. This is why it is so important to always build and revise the business case for your career decisions. Your own analysis work will always be the key to your next great career move, but it requires active analysis on your part. Reflecting on your experience with the motivation and long-term vision you have for future analysis work, coupled with your insight into your environment, is where you define those elements for making informed career decisions and avoiding challenges with specialization.

Overcoming challenges with being specialized

Like most of your analysis work, there will always be opportunities and threats in what value you deliver and how. You can easily address these challenges using your great analysis skills. First, keep an eye out for industry and market trends. Find out how they relate to your specialty area. What effect or influence might they have on the kind of analysis work you perform? What are they doing to the job market? How is your own organization responding? Look broadly at what your current organization is doing and what the industry is doing. This doesn't only mean seeing what analyst positions they are hiring. Rather, is your organization hiring more and more IT staff after having outsourced most of the department for years? Is the human resources department shrinking while more consultants are being hired for project-based contracts? Just by noticing these trends, you can have an earlier insight to course-correct and pivot your career in a proactive manner rather than having to react to a negative change in the market.

You should be on the offensive in your career. Continuing to always professionally develop your skills will help put you in more demand. Look for topics that are considered fringe topics for your work. These are topics that have a small relation to your work but might not be completely related. A great example is in IT: definitely take some cybersecurity classes to understand the foundational concepts. But if there is a cloud architecture or virtual hosting course or event, attend it to learn more about what technologies are out there and how organizations are using them.

Most of the learning you will do will be an investment in the future. It is okay to learn something interesting that you might need later in the future. The same goes for certifications. First, certifications will give you an advantage whenever you are seeking more benefits in your current position or transitioning to another position. Second, certifications make you dive into concepts and industry knowledge to understand the foundations and core standards for that area of specialization. Again, looking for topics that are related but also expand your current horizon is a great way to continuously build your value. For example, consider ITIL certification if you work at all with IT. This is not a programming certification but rather helps you understand the software development life cycles, even if you only ever get projects that work in one area (Bharadwaj, 2024). Now you are building both your specialization skills AND your analysis skills, which helps insulate you from specific market shifts.

No matter how niche your work or industry may get, do not be afraid to go back to those business analysis foundations. Those core analysis skill sets and competencies are the most transferable skills, no matter how the world changes. Seeking business analysis training, pursuing another BA-related certification, or seeking a new business analysis position can help you root yourself in those foundational skills and explore what started your career. The greatest thing about being a business analysis professional is that you have the power to shift from generalist to specialist and back again. This power comes when you rely on the core skill sets and value delivery models that make business analysis the sought-after competency that it is today. The decision of when, how, and where is up to you, and you should apply that very skill set for informed decision-making of a long and successful analysis career.

Summary

This chapter's goal was to introduce you to some areas of business analysis specialization to help you explore the many faces a business analysis career can take. Each area of specialization will have unique tasks and techniques that are tailored to the specific area of work, yet they will all rely on foundational business analysis skills. Having to learn to be a good business analyst in your own career is a challenge. Using your SWOT analysis, coupled with a broader scope of analysis of markets and trends, you should identify the forces acting upon your career. Then, you should continuously review and revise your career analysis plan so that you are constantly adjusting to avoid any roadblocks that could come from focusing on a particular area of analysis work. One of the greatest strengths in your toolkit to be a relevant and sought-after analysis professional is those powerful certifications. In the next chapter, you will explore certifications in the deeper context of how to focus and approach certifications with a plan for success.

Further reading

- Atlassian. (2024). What is product management? *Retrieved from* `https://www.atlassian.com/agile/product-management`

- Bharadwaj, A. (2024, August 10). *What is ITIL Certification (With Types and Benefits). Indeed. com. Retrieved from* `https://www.indeed.com/career-advice/career-development/what-is-itil-certification`

- Coursera. (2024, March 27). *What is Business Intelligence Analyst? Making Data-Driven Business Decisions. Retrieved from* `https://www.coursera.org/articles/business-intelligence-analysts-what-they-are-and-how-to-become-one`

- International Institute for Business Analysis® (IIBA), (2024). *Business Analysis Specialization. Retrieved from* `https://www.iiba.org/career-resources/business-analysis-specialization/`

- International Institute for Business Analysis® (IIBA), (2015). *The Business Analysis Body of Knowledge® (BABOK®) Guide. International Institute of Business Analysis*, Toronto, Ontario, Canada.

- International Institute for Business Analysis® (IIBA), (2017). *Agile Extension to the BABOK Guide v2. International Institute of Business Analysis*, Toronto, Ontario, Canada.

- Vavra, B. (2015, Jan). Data is the new currency. *Plant Engineering*. Barrington Vol. 70, Iss. 1, p16-17.

Unlock this book's exclusive benefits now

Scan this QR code or go to packtpub.com/unlock, then search for this book by name.

Note: Keep your purchase invoice ready before you start.

6

Business Analysis Certifications and Training

A professional certification can get you the interview you need, the raise you deserve, and the position that sets your career on a path to long-term success. Business analysis is a career path that values and encourages certification, as meeting the entry-level skill requirements and demonstrating the rigorous understanding needed to pass certification exams is valuable both to you and to any organization that hires you. Because of this rigor, only a select few in any country hold the most valuable business analysis certifications today. The process is demanding and intense, but it's also one you can succeed in by applying the same valuable business analysis skills that make you a great candidate in the first place.

This chapter provides an overview of the key certifications and training programs available for business analysis professionals. You will learn how to prepare for certification exams and choose the right training resources.

In this chapter, we're going to cover the following main topics:

- Overview of key certifications
- Training programs and resources
- Preparing for certification exams

Overview of key certifications

As mentioned in prior chapters, certifications can be the key differentiator to demonstrate your business analysis skills when reviewing your experience in a resume or LinkedIn profile. They are based on industry standards and give human resources specialists and others an unbiased way to compare individuals and what they could possibly bring to the table. Having a professional certification lets them know that you not only have the experience and knowledge in a given subject matter area but that you are dedicated and professional in your approach to work to attain these sought-after designations of professional achievements. Regardless of where your analysis career takes you, obtaining a certification concentrated in business analysis topics will ensure you dive into the core skills and competencies that will be valuable no matter what work crosses your desk.

For any certification, you will want to be a good business analyst and know the following before ever starting your pursuit of one of these great options or any others that come on the market:

- Who is the certification for? Who is the target market?
- What are the requirements for the application?
- What is the process to obtain the certification?
- Know the application processes as many have pre-requirements
- Know the examination process and understand both the question structure and examination format
- Know the maintenance process, if any, to avoid losing credit for your hard work due to a missed document.

When you think about who the certification is for, think about their understanding of the certification and its value. A hiring manager requiring a specific, advanced certification for a position that you are applying for is a different audience than going to your current manager and asking for a raise. What your stakeholder thinks of the certification can also sway your decision, so let's start with the one that is most recognized in the field of business analysis.

Certified Business Analysis Professional

The **International Institute of Business Analysis**® (**IIBA**®) is the global association for business analysis professionals. They focus on defining the standards for what quality analysis work means regardless of your industry, specialization, or even experience. As such, they have the premier business analysis certifications, with the key being the **Certified Business Analysis Professional**® (**CBAP**®) certification. At this time, this is *the* senior or elite certification for anyone pursuing business analysis as a career and not just a hobby or side interest. However, being the elite certification means it expects you to be of elite caliber (IIBA, 2024).

Consider the requirements of this certification. IIBA (2024b) defines that the prerequisites to simply apply are as follows:

- You must have completed over 7,500 hours of business analysis work (can go back 10 years)

- Your business analysis experience must cover 4 of the 6 knowledge areas with at least 900 hours

- You must have obtained 35 hours of training (professional development) in business analysis-related topics over the last 4 years

- Gather two references from supervisors of your business analysis work or other CBAP holders

- Agree to their code of conduct

- Agree to the terms and conditions of the certification

- Pass the examination

This can feel like the most daunting part of the whole process. Yes, gathering the necessary documentation can feel like an incredible obstacle. But simply think of it as its own business analysis work. You have to dig through your old records (*document analysis*), ask supervisors and references for points of contact and support (*interviews*), and review your own work to ensure it is worth the effort (*business case*). Being committed enough to analyze yourself is a great sign that you are ready to dive into a certification that can bolster and drive your career forward. Be ready to spend time on this effort. Be ready to also spend money (cost for applications and exams, plus any training or support resources). But if you pass this rigorous certification process, you demonstrate your commitment to the practice and profession of business analysis. And that is exactly what supervisors and hiring managers want to see.

The CBAP is also becoming more recognized by organizations as a leading business analysis certification, and as such, is increasingly becoming a requirement for mid- to senior-level business analysis positions. This makes this certification valuable even if your current position does not require it, as your future position just might. Remember, it gives potential employers an unbiased industry standard to compare you against other candidates. Earning your CBAP validates that you are familiar with the business analysis concepts that drive value and that you know when and how to best apply them to business analysis scenarios in addition to your experience. Even if you do not think you will need the certification for career growth in your organization, business analysis professionals have used the event of obtaining the CBAP to justify a raise in salary. This is quite common, particularly in the consulting world, and makes you a more valuable asset as you have proven you not only understand but can also demonstrate the tasks and techniques of someone who knows the power of business analysis.

Case study

There is so much value in business analysis certification – from the process to getting you to understand industry terminology and really analyze your own experience to the application in the exam's scenario questions. Consider this simple example of how a certification governed by a professional body, composed of individuals who actively practice the art and discipline of business analysis, can offer an unbiased validation of one's business analysis capabilities.

A business analyst sought the CBAP certification while working as a technical business analyst at an organization. They got support from the organization, which agreed to pay for certification exams and applications if you passed them. However, even after receiving their CBAP and being "officially" recognized for their advanced skills, the business analysis professional could not convince their boss they should get a raise.

They then applied to another company for a senior business analyst position. They got the position and even got their desired salary raise. They asked the hiring manager later what it was that helped select them. The manager stated that even though there were other candidates who, quite frankly, appeared to have more experience than this analyst, the hiring manager valued the certification. The hiring manager felt the analyst would know what should be done in certain scenarios based on good business analysis logic and best practices. The work is constantly evolving, and prior experience is not necessarily going to help in new and innovative scenarios. So, having someone who knew the industry standards and core foundations to deliver business value was more important to the hiring manager for future endeavors.

This is like having the IIBA vouch for your skill sets or even give you a recommendation for your analysis experience. And any professional organization is a powerful reference you would want on your resume! But look at certifications as not just end goals but as stepping stones that can build on each other as you grow.

Certification of Capability in Business Analysis

The IIBA (2024a) put out another certification in 2011 that requires less experience than the CBAP does. It can be a great stepping stone if you do not have the experience yet to go for the CBAP. It is the **Certification of Capability in Business Analysis**™ (**CCBA**®). It follows a similar structure to the CBAP, requiring documented experience, professional development hours, references, and agreement to a code of conduct and terms and conditions. It differs from CBAP in the following:

- Less business analysis work experience: 3,750 hours over the last 7 years (compared to 7,500 for CBAP)

- Fewer hours per knowledge area: only 2 knowledge areas need 900 or more hours, or 4 knowledge areas could simply have at least 500 hours (compared to 4 knowledge areas over 900 hours with CBAP)

- Less professional development: 21 hours within the last 4 years (compared to 35 with the CBAP)

Analyzing your work experience can help you determine which certification is right for you. Like the CBAP, the CCBA offers the value of having an unbiased body validate your capabilities against industry standards and definitions. If you've decided that a business analysis certification aligns with your career goals, keep in mind that you might not have all the information you need to choose the right path until you begin documenting your experience.

From an analysis standpoint, the difference between the certifications is small enough that as long as you have been employed for more than five years, then you can really challenge yourself to reflect on your past work – especially the parts that involved business analysis, even if that wasn't your official title. You may not have started your career as a business analyst, but that doesn't mean you haven't done business analysis work. Take someone working in a restaurant, whether fast food or full-service. They've likely engaged in core analysis activities. Did you gather information from customers to meet their needs? That's elicitation. Did you ask about preferences, special occasions, or specific requirements? That's context gathering and interviewing. Great servers constantly assess the current state and respond to change. These are hallmarks of solid analysis work, even if they've never used those terms.

Business analysis is everywhere and will continue to be for many years. The CCBA is not the professional certification standard and is not as well known as the CBAP in some places. However, it is still a valuable certification, and going through the process for your CCBA will only make you that much stronger to easily approach the CBAP process in the future. Just do your due diligence in analyzing your goals and your experience (yes, again, analyze future state and current state analysis, as in the industry guides, on your own career!).

Case study

Diving into certifications is a great way to analyze your work experience. You have to analyze your own analysis work and describe it in terms of industry standards no matter what your employers call it. This can be a great analysis exercise to flex your skills. However, you may feel overwhelmed when first looking at the requirements for the CBAP and so may naturally turn to the CCBA because it requires less work experience. One professional stated this very thing – they would go for the CCBA now and consider the CBAP in the future. As you'll read more than once in this book, sitting down and analyzing your work history in terms of the *Business Analysis Body of Knowledge® (BABOK®) Guide* is a great way to flex your analysis muscles.

In this case, the professional quickly realized they had well beyond the 3,750 hours of analysis experience required for the CCBA, so they questioned whether they should rethink the decision about the CBAP. We did an exercise to keep going back in their work history as many years as the CBAP allowed looking for analysis experience. They shared they had done just entry-level work at a clerical office. That was easy to validate because there was lots of document analysis and they were constantly doing interviews as learned various processes. But they then discounted their work at a small restaurant. We laughed because we talked about all the *requirements* of people's food orders. They fully acknowledged how much work it was sometimes to understand what a person wanted. The act of bringing the desserts to the table to help customers choose (a real-world example of valuable visual prototyping!) was definitely key to success. Before they knew it, they had captured the hours required for CBAP certification. This only came from sitting down and analyzing the details at the same intensity that business analysis professionals attack their analysis work with. But you do not have to wait until you have had years of analysis work to jump right in. Remember that there are great entry-level certifications as well.

Entry Certificate in Business Analysis

For those who are starting their career focusing on business analysis, one of the best ways to dive right in is to earn your **Entry Certificate in Business Analysis**™ (**ECBA**™). This is for those who do not have any experience. You study the core foundational knowledge of business analysis work and the ways you can provide value and then take a 60-minute multiple-choice examination. No references, no training requirements, only business analysis knowledge is required. Simply put, this tests you on the core concepts from the *BABOK Guide* and the Business Analysis Standard without requiring any experience (IIBA, 2024c).

A great characteristic of a business analysis professional is natural curiosity coupled with a desire to constantly be learning. Simply knowing there is a professional association of practicing analysts out there that share knowledge and great ideas should be enough interest to at least check out the online resources at iiba.org. While there, check out the tasks and techniques section, as these can be a valuable resource you can leverage again and again. Then, with just some reading of the materials, a little study time, and an online payment, you can easily take the short examination and have a valuable business analysis certificate in hand.

While it feels like an entry-level checkbox, think of it more as a stepping stone. Certifications are great entry points to larger initiatives and opportunities. They not only make you dive into content that will help you prepare for that next career opportunity but are also the business card that puts your name at the top of the list for the next business analysis assignment, one that can propel your skills, your results, and your career forward.

Case study

College-level students taking a project management course pursued the ECBA certificate because of the minimal requirements and having studied the content as part of their project management class. They had an excellent teacher who used bodies of knowledge like the *BABOK Guide* and the **Project Management Body of Knowledge**® (**PMBOK**® Guide) as course materials. Upon obtaining their certifications, they pursued job opportunities in junior analyst positions. The recruiter reported that every applicant with the ECBA certificate was hired because they demonstrated knowledge of the profession and what the role should be focused on. For an entry-level position, this was like finding gold for the employer. They got wonderful team members who already knew the context and approaches the analysis activities might take. The new members simply had to learn the context of the company and the responsibilities of the position and were able to immediately dive in and start trying those tasks and techniques they had learned about and practiced in class.

These examples are small ways to show that the value of certification can come from non-analyst perspectives of what it means to be a certified business analysis professional. While the certifying board is an unbiased party that aids in credibility, the fact that there are a limited number of certification holders in the world demonstrates the unique value proposition you bring. These certifications are not easy to obtain, yet with the right business analysis mindset, they can easily be put on your career path. Let's now look at those training programs and resources that can facilitate your certification journey.

Training programs and resources

There are ample opportunities and support resources that will help you achieve these valuable certifications. They, like the certifications themselves, deserve to be analyzed for their value for your effort. They each require a significant investment in both your valuable time and money. So you want to be sure that the **return on investment (ROI)**, even of your own career, is the high-quality value you need.

While even my company – Champagne Collaborations (`https://www.champagnecoll aborations.com/`) – offers certification exam prep courses and coaching sessions to personally help you overcome any obstacles on the application, again, the best thing is to be a good business analyst on the training options that work best for you. There are a number of vendors out there who offer services. To help you with this journey, first, there are the personal assessment questions to consider.

Answering these questions as laid out in *Table 6.1*, helps you define the type of certification support you need. The table also has some training and support considerations to guide you.

Question	Training & Support Considerations
Do you know which certification is best for your career position?	If you are unsure, then some coaching or information sessions would be best first. Check certification organizations for free webinars that are helpful for information.
Do you feel confident in documenting the required experience in a way that aligns with the certification requirements?	If unsure of how to define the experience (remember, you must align to the certification's objectives and body of work the test is based on), then consider an exam prep course that includes application support.
Have you ever taken a standardized exam before?	If not, ensure any program includes test-taking tips and strategies so you can focus on the content of the exam.
Are you self-motivated?	If you can prioritize your time and focus your energy, then an on-demand course where you work at your own pace may be best.
Do you learn better in group settings?	If you need the support and accountability of others, finding programs that are live with small numbers of participants can give you the support and responsibility necessary to keep you focused and on track.
How do you prefer to learn?	Many programs offer content in more than one medium. Having the ability to hear, see, and even touch training content helps to ensure concepts are not only memorized but can be recognized and applied.

Question	Training & Support Considerations
Do you like working on the computer?	Look for online programs and even asynchronous ones that allow you to be on your own device in your own location.
How are you when it comes to prioritizing your time?	A structured program that has a set start and stop date will help hold you accountable. Deadlines will drive results and make this an achievable objective rather than an ongoing pressure.

Table 6.1 – Personal considerations and recommendations for certification prep programs

Walk through these questions first to help you narrow the scope of your training focus. You want to make informed decisions. This is what business analysis is all about – making data-driven and data-informed decisions that strategically align with goals. You need to take this same approach with your career. Identifying good questions and then finding the data that helps to answer those questions is great business value wherever you apply it. Again, it helps you recognize how much business analysis work you *do* perform so that certifications should be on your career path if not already!

Application support

While it may seem easy to get some good study questions to practice and be ready for the examination, if you do not get your application approved first, professional certifications such as the CBAP will constantly be out of reach. You first want to ensure you get an approved application. The application is where you document your experience. This is where you get a chance to prove you more than exceed the minimum requirements for being a credential holder.

Any good training program should include support to help you with the application process. Consider the references and professional development hours and even accept the terms and conditions and code of conduct as simple "to do" items on your task list. Do them and get them out of the way. The bulk of your application is in your documentation of your work experience. Any certification prep program should include how to best approach the application in a way that gets approval the first time (there is a fee to resubmit and often a waiting period if you do not pass the application the first time so you have a solid business case to get the application right the first time!).

Look for a coach to advise you on how to translate your experience in terms of the body of knowledge. Your work as a system analyst, for example, may never have been described in terms of "eliciting requirements from stakeholders using interviews and workshops," yet that is exactly what you did. You simply called it "documenting system needs by meeting with the stakeholders." Can you see the difference? You have to translate your experience into the vocabulary of the global Business Analysis Standard. But if you can do this, you are demonstrating your understanding and application of the body of knowledge, which is exactly what the certification aims to do. Until you get comfortable with this context, you could find yourself struggling through an unscripted and chaotic pile of notes. Good examination preparation begins while you are simply filling out the application.

Using the application to dive into your studying

One trick here is to use the study material while working on the application. Doing these two items in tandem is a great way to not only break down the work into manageable segments but to also help validate your understanding and better prepare you to pass the examination. Here's how you set yourself up for success for both the application and the exam.

First, read the body of knowledge. The goal here is to just get introduced to the concepts and vocabulary. Don't worry about taking copious notes or anything just yet. Simply get familiar with the content.

Then, go start your application. This can be just setting up your template on where you are going to capture your work experience. Fill in whatever you can capture without having to look up details.

Now, go back to the body of knowledge and pick one topic or knowledge area. Here's where you zero in on your studies. Do whatever approach helps you understand the topics and remember the vocabulary, tasks, and techniques.

Then, go to your application and capture the work experience where you have done that knowledge area you just studied. The topic should be fresh in your mind so that you are looking for those elements.

Unsure how to translate some work experience into the terms of the body of knowledge? Or not sure if you actually performed the analysis work described in the body of knowledge? Those are both signs to jump back to that topic and the body of knowledge content and study a little deeper.

As you study some more, jump back to the application to record your experience in those terms of the body of knowledge.

Continue this cycle until your application is completed, having dived through the body of knowledge content quite well to set yourself up for just some final studying for the exam! *Figure 6.1* has this process laid out so you can see your steps and how the studying time can help you with your application while your application can help you know what to study.

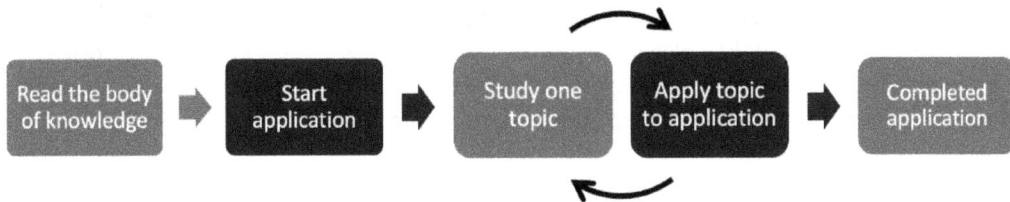

Figure 6.1 – Study cycle for certification requiring application

The right training program and approach will not only get you ready for the certification but often will focus on the examination itself. Regardless of whether you pick a training provider or simply use your personal and professional network, you will want to ensure you spend time specifically preparing for the examination portion. Let us now consider how to best tailor your examination success plan!

Preparing for certification exams

Achieving a professional certification from an international body dedicated to defining the practice and role of business analysis activities means you are accomplishing a major milestone in your career. This means that you do not take the examination lightly. These are standardized tests that seek to be agnostic of industry, technology, background, location, nationality, and more. They are looking to see whether you know business analysis from the terms and perspectives as defined by the governing body. Your application demonstrated the experience you have in doing business analysis work. The examination then looks for you to demonstrate your knowledge of the standards and body of knowledge. Once you accept this fact, then the following advice on how to best prepare for, study, and approach the examination will be your key to success.

Building a study plan

Most successful certification journeys begin with a solid foundation of a laid-out study plan that works for the applicant. Again, you will be analyzing yourself to know how you study best. Are you a person who likes studying with others for motivation and accountability? Or do you like audio or video options that you can do when not in the office? Do you need a quiet space or even prefer physical paper and note cards to write on? First, do your own stakeholder analysis and know your own study patterns and habits. Too many people have failed their exams trying to use others' methodologies that do not fit their own.

With this in mind, a good rule of thumb is to plan your exam date about two weeks after you can commit to the studying time, especially the CBAP and advanced certifications. This gives you enough time to really dive into the exam content without burning yourself out. But for those exams that require applications, also give yourself enough time to put together a solid application. This can take some significant effort if you need to review dates and look up references, so you want to not be rushed. Once it's submitted, you can then plan out two weeks after you receive the application approval for when you may best schedule the exam. *Figure 6.2* gives you a visual of how your study plan should include enough time for the application and the dedicated study sessions.

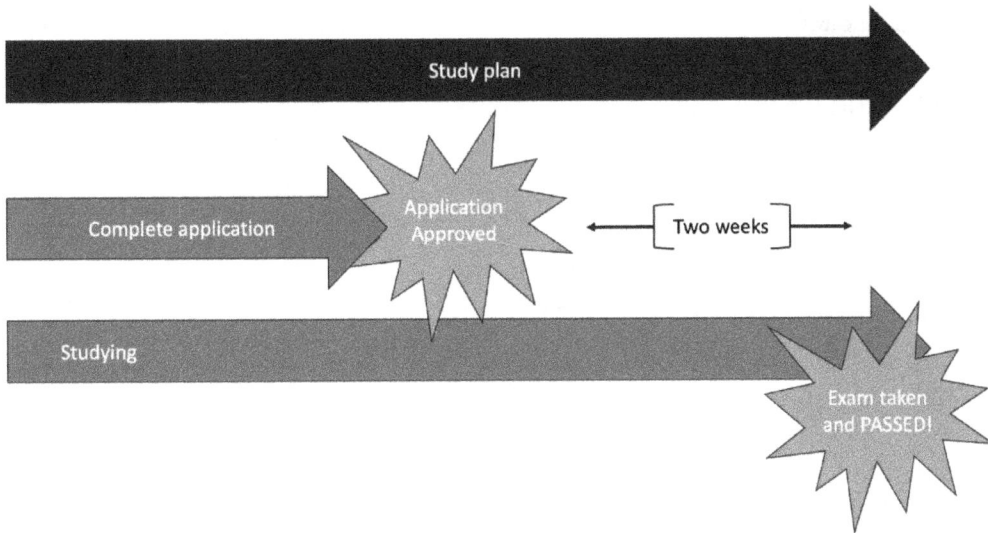

Figure 6.2 – Study plan layout

After that, craft your study sessions. This means what are you actually going to do to "study"? You need to commit to blocking out time for studying without interruptions. Then, create a plan for how to best utilize that important time.

Example study plan

To pass my certification examinations, in the two weeks leading up to the exam, I would carve out the following:

- Every day, get up an hour earlier – spend 60 minutes studying, focusing on a single knowledge area:

  - Do a brain dump (without looking).
  - Review the body of knowledge section to see what was missed.
  - Rewrite the brain dump correctly.
  - As I read the area in the body of knowledge, write down the tasks, techniques, key terms, concepts, and what I need to know. Read each aloud before moving on to the next concept.
  - Do a brain dump.
  - Take some practice questions.
  - Review the answers. For any incorrect answer, write down the question with the correct answer to remember the concept.
  - Do one last brain dump.

- Take flash cards (3x5-inch cards with the term on the front and definition on the back) with me to review between meetings, waiting at appointments, or other break points in the day

- Block one hour every evening to "study," which includes the following:

  - Do a brain dump on the area of interest.

  - Write out 10 techniques and all the information about them.

  - Do a brain dump on the techniques.

  - Practice a few questions.

  - Review the answers. For any incorrect answer, write down the question with the correct answer to remember the concept.

  - Do one last brain dump.

Two weeks of this schedule, which includes dedicated study time and practice with terms and questions, will have you so fully immersed in the terms, concepts, and scenarios that you will hardly be able to get this information out of your head and onto the exam! Regardless of your approach, you want to ensure you utilize a number of elements so that concepts are truly ingrained in your vocabulary. Reading, of course, is a bare minimum. Your studying time should consider the following:

- Restating terminology and key concepts

- Reciting vocabulary definitions without looking

- Writing out concepts (repeatedly!)

- Practice questions

- Timed settings – used for both writing down concepts (read about *brain dumps* in the next section) and answering questions

- Reviewing and identifying images of techniques or task work

- Practicing techniques with examples

Perfecting your brain dump

To help you in your studying, one of the best tools is what we call a *brain dump*. This is exactly as it sounds – you try to write down everything in your brain at that moment. While this can sound almost impossible, there is a method to this madness. You are basically creating a cheat sheet of what you know. Here's how it works:

1. Think about the end of a study session. While still looking at the book for the first time, write down on one piece of paper everything that you need to know from what you just studied. But write it in shorthand with abbreviations, even draw it out. What are the key concepts?

2. Close all books and notes and take out a clean sheet of paper. Set a timer for 5 minutes. Then, write down on that blank sheet of paper anything you can recall. Go fast! This is the brain dump part.

3. At the end of the time, check your notes and materials to see what things you did not write down. What you are doing now is identifying the areas you DO need to study. The things you wrote down are things you already know, so you want to prioritize your time studying the things you still are uncertain about.

4. Rewrite the brain dump list of topics with everything you want to remember. Then, write it again. And again. Then, close your notes and see whether you can do it without looking. You are making a cheat sheet you can use during the exam.

No, you cannot take anything with you to your exam. But you do get a notes section or scratch paper to use. The first thing you will do when starting your exam is another brain dump. If you have practiced this over and over again, it will feel easy. Then, you literally have a list of notes to use and keep you focused as you go through your examination! But this only works well if you practice it during your studying!

Taking the exam

The hardest challenge for many business analysis professionals who have been working for a while is to know that the examination portion is *NOT* about your experience. The application was for your experience. In the exam, you need to answer the questions from the perspective of the body of knowledge. They are looking to see whether you can understand and apply the governing principles of business analysis.

This means you do *NOT* answer the questions as you would do in your job. I know this can sound conflicting, especially if you have been doing certain techniques for years and they work well. The concern is not whether what you do in the real world is right or wrong. The test is looking for you to show you know what the *BEST* thing to do according to the body of knowledge. What the governing bodies put out as the foundational knowledge is what they *MUST* test to ensure the test is standardized; therefore, always think about what the book would want you to answer. A great trick for this is imagining your mother looking over your shoulder as you take the test. What would she want you to answer? What is the "right" thing to select or "should be done" option? It sounds a little funny for a business analysis certification examination, but this is what will keep you focused and eliminate your own bias.

Approach your examinations just like you do any standardized test with the following recipe for success:

1. **Brain dump**: As soon as you sit down, do a brain dump! Get it out fresh! The more you write down, the less you actually have to remember during the exam.

2. **Start answering questions**: Start with answering questions you are confident about. If unsure, skip the question. Go all the way through the exam to the end continuing this method. It is okay if you skip a bunch – this is your warmup time to get comfortable with the format of the exam.

3. **Answer skipped questions**: Go back to the first question you skipped and spend more time now. Answer the question with what you feel is best. "Flag" or "mark" the question if still unsure. Go all the way through the exam to the end until every question is answered. It is okay to still skip questions and simply come back to them, but continue the cycle until every question has an answer.

4. **Review flagged questions**: Go back and review your flagged or marked questions. Pick the best answer and unflag or unmark the question. Go through the exam until all questions are unflagged or unmarked.

5. **Re-read every question before submitting**: With the remaining time, read each question with your selected answer. It should make sense. Go through every question until you have read all questions and answers or time runs out.

Remember to always use the full time allotted. Do not rush. Take your time and read each question carefully, ensuring that you are answering the specific question they are asking. For example, if the question asks for a technique, ensure you did not select a task option. One final note to never forget on these exams is to trust your first instinct and leave the answer as chosen.

> **Do not change your answers!**
>
> Your first choice is normally the correct choice. When you overanalyze a question, you read too deeply into it and can end up selecting an incorrect answer. Go with your first guess and avoid changing any answers, if at all possible. Your read-through of every question with the answer selected will help you validate this.

Maintaining your certification

A final note here as you consider the certifications and their rigorous requirements. Once you have achieved the certification, professional certification standards expect that you will use that certification in your career and be a practicing professional. This means you must demonstrate (submit information via written format and proof of certificates or other validation) that you are actively applying those same skills and techniques that you were challenged on by the examinations. This does not mean you have to keep taking certification exams. What this means is that you need to keep doing this kind of work. Do business analysis tasks throughout your projects. Leverage business analysis techniques in your analysis work. Join webinars on topics related to the profession. Attend conferences and network with fellow professionals. The opportunities are almost endless. The main point is that you still do business analysis work and applications beyond the examination so that you are a practicing professional.

And do not let this stop you at all. Honestly, it probably takes almost as long to document your experience as it did to actually do the work, but that's worth the effort. Just like the certification process, know the requirements and business rules. Any certification will list upfront the maintenance requirements, as they are called. Find these and look for the following:

- Type of work that qualifies
- The minimum amount required to be documented (always a good habit to do a little extra!)
- How each type of work is documented or categorized
- Any rules or limits for how much experience you can submit for a given type or category

Often, these are relatively easy and more about you making the time to update your profile. Also, the experience you need to maintain your certification can be counted for other certifications where the work applies. For example, working on an agile team for a development project is a great way to get experience for both maintaining your CBAP certification as well as your PMP or an Agile certification (the tasks would be different in what you document). But that one project gives you lots of experience to capture. That is the key word – capture. Recording your own experience makes it easy for recertification as well as future applications, and it is one more opportunity for you to practice and see the results of your hard-working analysis skills.

Summary

Certifications are the industry standard recognition you can leverage throughout your analysis career. Just like your analysis work, doing the research and business case for the right certification at the right time is critical to your success. The CBAP certification should be on your career path if you plan to focus at all on any kind of analysis work as it is *THE* certification for business analysis professionals. For both the CBAP and the other certifications, understand that these are rigorous application and examination processes that reward you for your commitment and dedication with valuable credentials. Consider not only the options available but also the resources you have access to and how learning an industry standard and applying it to real-world situations fits into your personality and work styles. Then, develop a plan that will help you execute and achieve these career goals aligned with your strategic direction.

Certifications are one component that is part of a business analysis professional's career path. Next, let's look at the role of technology in your analysis work. Just like maintaining your business analysis certification can continue to propel your career and demonstrate your knowledge, technology can be a valuable tool in how it not only affects what kind of work you analyze but in how and where your analysis work evolves.

Further reading

- International Institute for Business Analysis® (IIBA®), (2015). *The Business Analysis Body of Knowledge*® (BABOK®) Guide. International Institute of Business Analysis, Toronto, Ontario, Canada.

- International Institute for Business Analysis® (IIBA®), (2024a). Certification of Capability in Business Analysis™ (CCBA®). Retrieved from `https://www.iiba.org/business-analysis-certifications/ccba/`

- International Institute for Business Analysis® (IIBA®), (2024b). Certified Business Analysis Professional (CBAP®). Retrieved from `https://www.iiba.org/business-analysis-certifications/cbap/`

- International Institute for Business Analysis® (IIBA®), (2024c). Entry Certificate in Business Analysis™ (ECBA™). Retrieved from `https://www.iiba.org/business-analysis-certifications/ecba/`

- Project Management Institute® (PMI®), (2021). *The Project Management Body of Knowledge* (PMBOK® Guide). Project Management Institute, Inc., Newtown Square, Pennsylvania.

Unlock this book's exclusive benefits now

Scan this QR code or go to `packtpub.com/unlock`, then search for this book by name.

Note: Keep your purchase invoice ready before you start.

Part 3:
Being Successful in
Business Analysis Work

This part starts by having you consider the immense impact of technology on both the work and the context in which business analysis work needs to operate to be successful. That context will also be full of challenges that will test your integrity. The most challenging part of business analysis work is working *WITH* your stakeholders and helping ensure that business value is prioritized, and that it is done in an ethical manner. From this, you will then dive into leadership and mentorship in business analysis work. You will need those leadership skills to be successful throughout your career, and a mentor might be just what you need to keep your career on track for success.

This part has the following chapters:

- *Chapter 7, The Role of Technology in Business Analysis*
- *Chapter 8, Building Effective Stakeholder Relationships and Upholding Ethics*
- *Chapter 9, Leadership and Mentorship in Business Analysis*

7

The Role of Technology in Business Analysis

Regardless of whether your position is in the IT department or a non-technical business area, technology is going to have a significant impact on your analysis work. Technology is evolving at unprecedented rates, and while you do not need to be a technical business analysis professional, you need to be comfortable with your working technologies and stay aware of trends. As both an advisor and an advocate for the business, you should also consider what technology innovations mean for your organization, as these will influence both the solutions you recommend and the approaches to change you support.

This chapter examines the impact of emerging technologies on business analysis work and what you can do to integrate technology into your work and stay updated with technological advancements, regardless of whether you are pursuing a technical business analysis career or not.

In this chapter, we're going to cover the following main topics:

- Emerging technologies and their impact
- Integrating technology into business analysis
- Staying up to date with technological advancements

Emerging technologies and their impact

Technology has seen unprecedented evolutions not just in what you use in the workplace, but in how you use it. Positions are being replaced with technology while new job descriptions are being created to take advantage of the evolving capabilities and innovations. With this massive impact on the profession, there are two key viewpoints to consider as you ponder what technology can mean for your analysis career: the impact on your customers and their solutions and the impact on your analysis work.

Understanding technology innovations in solutions

The technological innovations and revolutions taking place today are going to be directly seen in the solutions your customers and organizations use. Changes to technology are going to both drive as well as enable strategic decision-making. Those decisions are only going to be as good as the information on which they are based. Knowing what is happening with technology helps you be informed to provide those much-needed recommendations and ideas to your stakeholders. You do not need to know about every technology, nor need to be proficient in the usage or programming of the latest tech or applications. Rather, you want to focus on understanding what technological changes can mean for business solutions and the ways in which value is achieved so that you can best enable and support those crucial business decisions.

Understanding cloud computing

We'll start with a simple example, as **cloud computing** may not seem like a "revolutionary" technology like some of the others discussed in this chapter. But the reasons cloud computing became a technology revolution are often true for the other technologies listed here and are worth understanding, as they could apply to future technological evolutions.

> **Knowing *enough* about technologies**
>
> A quick note as we dive right into discussing technology: just like for the other examples in this chapter, do not worry that you are unfamiliar with the exact intricacies of how cloud computing or any other technology works. Rather, have a general understanding of what cloud computing is. This can be as simple as going to your favorite online search tool and asking, *"What is cloud computing?"* This is actually a good habit to get into with all the technologies and even processes you will encounter throughout your analysis work. Know *enough* to have a conversation about not just the *what* of the technology, but more importantly, the *why*. As you will see throughout this chapter, your analysis work will often be less concerned with the *how* of each technology and more about the *why* of the technology and its impact on business value.

First, like many other technologies, the factors driving the popularity, market growth, and shifts in cloud computing did not come from the technology itself. Hosting service providers had been around for years. However, the ability to leverage this capability – shared hosted services – became affordable, scalable, and therefore, able to get into the hands of "average" users. Cloud computing became a convenience due to the ease of access. But then organizations started considering what this capability and access could mean for them. Shifting technology infrastructures, such as moving off of on-premise mainframes to cloud-based servers, were often major undertakings and severe hits to companies' budgets. However, the ability to scale and only purchase the exact services required became an easy ROI for many. So, companies would have to consider their strategic directions to determine whether the cost savings and future reliance on technology would truly be worth the effort. Additional value came from the increased capabilities cloud computing offered, which could lead to better customer service products and influence which projects were prioritized in the organization's backlog.

Company reputations were also bolstered by reduced carbon emissions and smaller environmental footprints. These capabilities, previously unavailable, became a driving factor in how organizations approached change efforts and re-evaluated their current work (Technology.org, 2024).

This simple shift in architecture has redefined solution approaches and even forced organizations to reassess their entire technology strategies because of the capabilities and options cloud computing provides. It made features and functionalities possible for the small business owner while helping large enterprises scale their services. The trick, as shown in *Figure 7.1*, is to understand this pathway, which you can use for any technology that emerges:

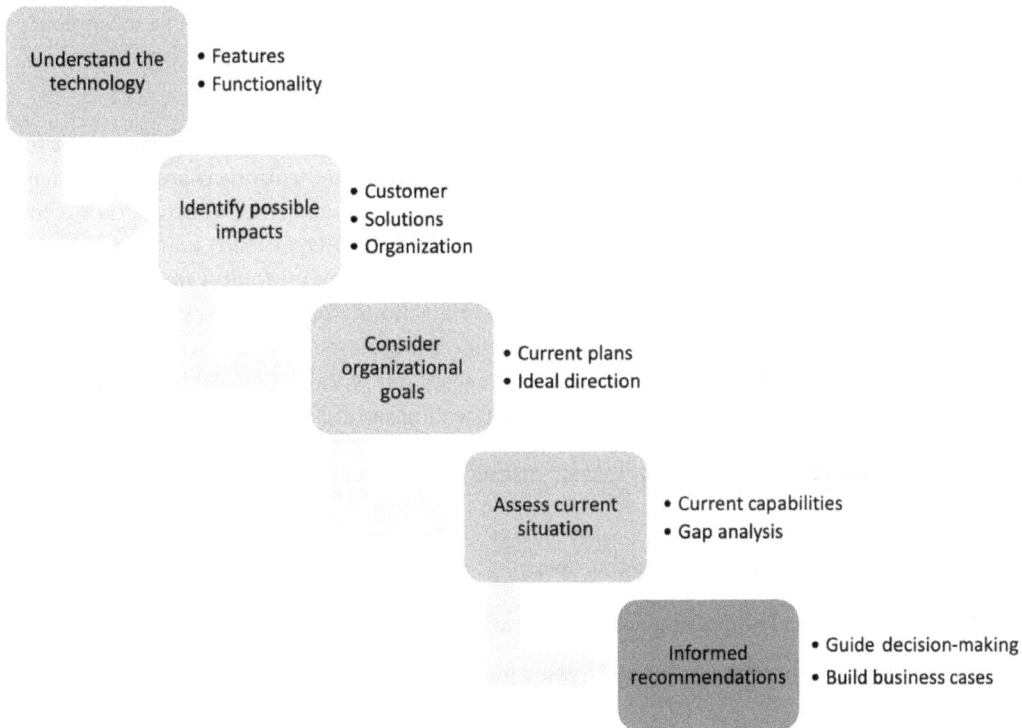

Understand the technology
- Features
- Functionality

Identify possible impacts
- Customer
- Solutions
- Organization

Consider organizational goals
- Current plans
- Ideal direction

Assess current situation
- Current capabilities
- Gap analysis

Informed recommendations
- Guide decision-making
- Build business cases

Figure 7.1 – Process to consider technological impacts

Keep this model in mind for all your analysis work. It will allow you to see whether the organization should take advantage of new capabilities or even rethink the prior work it has done. This is how you balance both the *what* and *why* of technology and keep your facilitative, strategic advisor role no matter what technology appears. Again, highlighting the value of doing business analysis everywhere!

Connecting solutions on the Internet of Things (IoT)

Our world is more connected than ever. This goes well beyond global enterprises, down to the daily interactions of individual stakeholders. Yet the expectations of your end customers are higher than ever: they expect information to be created and stored once but accessible repeatedly, well beyond the original point of capture.

Understanding the technology that results in the **Internet of Things (IoT)** – where a network of devices, appliances, and accessories share data to increase functionality and accessibility – is key to building solutions for your customers and understanding their expectations (Oracle, 2024). Here is another example where you do not need to be an analyst who knows everything about a technology. Instead, these topics and terms are good to be aware of to help you understand their impact on how teams and organizations operate, and especially, your own analysis work.

So, like any of the technologies presented in this chapter, what this means to your analysis work is to consider this interconnected approach in the solutions you support. Your customers are used to their washing machines being able to communicate with their phones, directing their Bluetooth speakers to add items to a grocery list (which are then automatically ordered and delivered), and being able to watch their dog or their front door from their smart watches. These same customers are going to have similar expectations in their business applications and interactions. Your role is to simply ask good questions. Ask good questions that consider how you and your customers interact with technologies daily. Ask good questions that consider how interconnected our world is and just how much data might already be at our fingertips. The following are a few things to consider:

- What applications do we have today that are sharing information and data with other applications or systems?

  - What and why are they sharing this data?

- Where are we already capturing data today that could be used in our next solution?

- Where and how are solutions being accessed today?

- Where are our customers?

- What other solutions are our customers using?

Regardless of your industry or type of project, asking these questions, whether anyone on your team knows about IoT or not, is just helpful in acknowledging your stakeholders' environments and contexts that solutions need to be able to thrive in. IoT, as in this description, is more than simply integrating wireless networks into solutions. IoT is about leveraging the information from existing products to make more valuable and capable solutions tomorrow. The key to successful solutions lies not only in adopting new technologies but also in understanding the broader shifts they bring to activities, approaches, and overall productivity. This deeper comprehension enables organizations to harness these technologies effectively to deliver maximum value.

Considering the impacts of cryptocurrency and blockchain technologies

Cryptocurrency is another technological innovation that is currently having a major impact on solutions for some organizations. Cryptocurrency is digital currency that has a peer-to-peer format that eliminates banks and the fees often associated with the regulated banking industry (Coursera, 2024). First, simply consider the idea that there is another form of currency that your customers may be using to acquire goods and services.

Again, this impacts your solutions as it is not simply a matter of whether your organization wants to take payments via cryptocurrency and the brand reputation that comes with that decision. This will also require a major infrastructure update to accommodate the tracking and recording of such transactions. The ROI of saving money on transaction fees can be outweighed by the change in internal processing structure without even considering your organization's brand reputation.

Second, consider that cryptocurrency was a way of introducing blockchain technology to organizations. **Blockchain** is a way of recording transactions in a secure manner that is not editable (IBM, 2024). But while this functionality is something that did exist previously, blockchain brings speed and ease of access to information, while providing an additional security layer. After just discussing the IoT, consider the massive amount of data that now must be processed and analyzed. Verifying information slows down this process, and duplication and redundant data cause an even bigger impact on performance. With blockchain technology, however, secure and transparent business transactions can occur at higher speeds, with improved data integrity.

Again, you do not need to become an expert on understanding the intricacies of these technologies. What you need to consider is their functions and capabilities, and what impacts they have on your organization and the enterprise area of your solutions. While some brands do thrive on being "first in the market space" to incorporate cutting-edge technologies, it might be valuable to analyze how your industry and even competitors consider these technologies in their solutions. Having a valuable customer-focused use case that drives profitable value is often an easier business case to recommend in your analysis work. You can make better decisions when you understand how including or excluding new technologies affects your solutions and the bottom line. Remember, the technology will continue to evolve regardless of how long your stakeholders wait to make decisions.

Case examples of cryptocurrency impact on solutions

Without even discussing any of the features or logic behind cryptocurrency, an analyst faced a simple business question on a project: *Would we be willing to accept payment in cryptocurrency?* This decision would have a major impact on both the project-based work to deliver the new solution as well as a direct effect on the solution design. As the analyst for this work, you would have to help articulate what those effects would be. Yes, you would need to get some technical stakeholders to help define the requirements for implementing processes to accept, track, and manage cryptocurrency at your organization (and then estimate the cost and efforts). But then you would also have to talk with marketing and do some market research. Is your competition accepting cryptocurrency as well? What is the industry doing as a whole? Is your client base using cryptocurrency for other aspects of their lives? Answers to these great business questions are going to impact the business value of the solution. You can start asking them without knowing all the elements involved in cryptocurrency and how to secure the processes. By not being afraid to facilitate those necessary conversations with the technical stakeholders, you will actually acquire greater knowledge and insight into the technology. That is why asking questions can help you build your experience and comfort level more with each piece of your analysis work, regardless of which technology your scope may touch.

Artificial intelligence and machine learning

At the time of this writing, *the* biggest topic in technology is the explosion of **artificial intelligence (AI)**. For a skilled business analyst, though, its significance is not solely focused on the technological capabilities. AI is another example of a technology that has actually been in use for many years already. What makes its impact so profound is that this technology has evolved to be accessible for the average end user. No advanced training is required to start getting value from it. Applications with free account settings put AI tools for data and information analysis at lightning-fast speeds under the fingertips of every connected Internet user.

Now, as fast and great as this innovation seems to be, it continues to be viewed with skepticism and concern over the security and protection of intellectual property. So, consider these same thoughts in your solutions work. Consider that many AI features are based on fast computing algorithms and the use of predictive models. But the differentiator is the ability to "learn" based on the input received. Computing power is faster than ever in history, enabling systems to take input, feedback, and other responses to shape the next action. As much as end users are getting information, they are giving enormous quantities of data back to your systems. This leaves you needing to ask the following questions:

- What is happening with the data?
- What is the data telling the organization?
- What should the organization do with the insights?
- What predictions can be made with these insights?

Using machine learning technologies that have been pre-trained to mine organizational data for insights can uncover hidden gems of competitive advantage. A great business case is to leverage all that data on your customers that is quickly amassing. Yet this technology comes with a cost. Considering AI and all the other emerging technologies listed so far, using the model in *Figure 7.1*, have you asked what capabilities the organization has? Not just infrastructure, but in terms of talent management? Who is going to not only build these solutions but also support the solutions that integrate these emerging technologies?

Then, with this data and insight, are you building solutions that safeguard this data? How do you prevent the system from making up connections or insights because it followed a "bad" or inaccurate pattern? Productivity can go up exponentially, but so can the risks, not just when the technology is implemented incorrectly but also when it is not used in the right manner and context.

Consider how many **business-related questions** you need to ask to get the maximum business value from AI technologies. Use the following questions not only for AI-related solutions, but also to simply consider whether you should have any AI-enabled technologies as part of your solution work:

- What are our business processes today? Are these documented?
- What tasks are repeatable?
- What information sources do we have?
- How consistent/accurate/up to date are our data sources?
- Where do we store our information?
- Do we have staff knowledgeable and experienced in these technologies and/or processes?
- How is our corporate culture when it comes to change? Are staff willing and welcoming to change how they work?
- What is the talent management strategy or processes at our organization? Is there any work or HR support for tracking capabilities over roles?

These additional questions and concerns are where business analysis professionals can shine. You can couple the knowledge of what capabilities and approaches are now possible when integrating these emerging technologies. You can balance out risks and rewards in solid business cases that think through how you can approach solutions differently. Then, you can build business solutions by considering how the technology, the processes, and even the people and organization have to change to be able to leverage the capabilities in the solutions of tomorrow.

Building the technology business case

To help us consider the business analysis perspective on technology, let's consider a business case. A business case is the justification for a course of action. It lays out not only the pros and cons of a potential decision, but it also includes alternatives and risk analysis. You can use the template in *Chapter 2*. So now, let's consider the business case for AI.

First, you always want to be clear on a goal. What is the goal we want to achieve by leveraging the technology? The key word here is *leveraging*. There is a difference in being a technology company where technology *is* your product and being an organization that utilizes technology to provide your services. An example of the latter would be a financial institution or an insurance organization. Both rely on technology, but financial or insurance products and services are what each, respectively, provides. So first, you want to identify a business need or opportunity that needs to be solved. For our business case example, we could use the goal of increased staff efficiency.

Now talk about the current state. What is or is not happening right now? With technology, this could mean you have old systems that do not talk to each other. Do you have manual processes that use paper to complete transactions? But then flip the viewpoint and identify what your competition and industry are doing. And how has technology changed recently? The expansion and evolution of technologies could actually create the opportunity that the company needs to take advantage of. When it comes to AI, it offers great opportunities for process efficiencies by both streamlining and automating manual, redundant work processes. Also consider that your organization does not want to be left behind or outpaced by your competition because your competition decided to use AI technologies to improve their operational processes. Do not be afraid to consider both internal and external factors, as this gives a much clearer picture of what is (and is not) happening today.

Once the context is clearly articulated, you can tell the story of what the team or organization could be doing if the technology is properly leveraged. For the goal of simple staff efficiency, what could the teams be doing if even 20% of their work could be automated or streamlined? Would that be 20% more time to onboard new clients or build stronger relationships with existing clients? Could available time be research and development cost savings (rather than expenditure) giving your teams the time to explore ideas and custom development work? Don't just talk about the goal, but rather explain what it means to the organization in terms of value.

Now the work comes in analyzing the options. Don't be afraid to get more technical here or bring in an SME to assist you. You want options, including alternatives and substitutes. This is where the pace of technology will force you to optimize your own research analysis processes to quickly learn what is available to organizations today. Even with evolution, it is still back to good questions that you should ask; for instance, in your effort to boost efficiencies with AI technology, you might ask the following questions:

- *What applications are automating business processes using AI today?*

- *What service providers are helping organizations transition to integrating agents and more into their work?*

- *What upgrades are now available to technologies that are integrating AI capabilities?*
- *What factors out there are causing people to either fully adopt AI integrations or remain hesitant about implementing them?*

Using the business case template, each option needs the costs, risks, and impacts. This is where you either want to leverage your technology background or enlist the help of a technical SME because there are additional considerations for emerging and rapidly evolving technologies that impact your business case:

Factor	Consideration	Comments
Features	What value does each tool option offer?	Are there additional features that might not be needed or used initially, but might be great to consider using as staff get more comfortable with the technology?
Data availability	Will the tool need access to data sources?	Where are those data sources? Are they accessible today? Will there need to be migration? Transformation?
Security	How does the application secure the information used?	What security standards does your organization have today? What concerns does the security team have about the technology? And why?
Compliance	What are the compliance requirements?	How will the new technology show compliance with rules or regulations? Are there rules or standards governing what technology can (or cannot) be used today? Are regulations or legal rules changing?
End user costs	Licensing per user?	What are other similar technologies doing with their pricing? (i.e., are they licensing AI features separately or including them in existing subscriptions?)

Factor	Consideration	Comments
Implementation costs	Is additional hardware or software required? What will it take to get this? implemented successfully?	Ask what is needed to make things work – both technology and soft skills (training, communication, change in business processes). Does the new solution even require a different skill set than exists at the organization today to implement, maintain, support, or augment it (i.e., does it require external vendors or consultants?)?
Performance requirements	What are the performance requirements to gain maximum value?	Greater performance means greater infrastructure, which often means greater cost – can you minimize costs and still provide the value of the application?
Evolution risk	Will the technology evolve before you can implement the tool?	Could it be better to wait for the technology to mature and be more common than using it right away?
Current state evaluation	How efficient is the current state?	Do processes need to be reviewed and improved before adding additional technology? Does the data need to be "cleaned up" or organized before other technology will work?
Current technologies	What applications do we have already that can do the same work?	Are current applications being evolved to include AI technology or capabilities? Are there multiple applications that, if reconfigured, might be a better solution than a new application or service?
Change management work	Will the staff *WANT* to adopt the solution?	What is the culture of the organization? Is it risk-averse, so team members are wary of new ideas? Is your company a long-standing organization wanting to "do things how we've always done them" type? Or, will people be excited to learn how their jobs can be made faster and easier? Have you considered training? Communication? Marketing?

Factor	Consideration	Comments
Transition requirements	What is required to transition from the current solution to the new solution?	What things, albeit one-time requirements, need to happen – such as data migration? Old system backups for historical copies?
Staff capabilities	Do you have the staff competencies to not only install, but support the end solution?	Training is not just for end users, but for your support systems – help desk, human resources (talent management), finance (budgeting and operational costs), and technology management.
Defining the value	Is it easy to measure efficiency today?	What baseline metrics do we have? Will you need to get baseline metrics *BEFORE* you even select the tool?

Table 7.1 – Technology options considerations

As you define the factors listed in *Table 7.1*, build out your recommendation and alternative options, including the pros and cons of each selection. You want your approvers and sponsors to not just see different options but understand how their decisions will impact both the business and the intended goals. But to get buy-in for the initial steps and evaluation points you give, consider two important factors:

- How new the technology is for the organization
- How fast the technology is evolving

These factors are important in technological business cases as they greatly affect how and when you can show the value of the efforts. A culture hesitant to adopt technology like AI is going to require a longer time for change management efforts to work to get end-user adoption, so that you can have the desired efficiency improvements in operations. However, investing in a technology today that might evolve in the near future could be a costly business consideration if you could wait to get more features for less money, and more easily address your efficiency business needs.

While technology holds great potential, it needs to be articulated from the point of view of the business. Use the following process to help you in building your business cases.

1. Define the business need or opportunity.

2. Describe the current state – not just of the business but what is happening with technology and your industry's adoption and integration of technology.

3. Articulate the future state – how do you want your employees and customers to view your integration of technology into products and services?

4. Define the options – research what the latest capabilities are in all areas of technology (i.e., hardware and software as well as people skills).

5. Define the potential costs, risks, and impacts for each option.

With this great research into the technological capabilities available to your organization, now is the time for you to think about the applications of these technologies in your own analysis work.

Integrating technology into business analysis

Regardless of the evolution technology may undergo, remember to always start with your business analysis goals *first* and then look for the best way to accomplish those goals. There is no *best* application to use for business analysis work. The *good* tools are the ones that help you accomplish your goals more efficiently and effectively. So, always start with a clear goal. Then look for the tools that provide those capabilities that align with the effort. Let's look at a few areas and examples to see how you can integrate technological innovations into your analysis work.

Enhancing decision-making

Business analysis professionals' roles or responsibilities are to help stakeholders make informed decisions. These decisions are often made based on insights into the organization's data. As a result, business data analytics has evolved as a technical competency where business areas hire professionals to mine their data and build large data warehouses they can pull their insights from.

With the evolution of technology, an expansive amount of data can now be amassed, organized, integrated, and assimilated into descriptive visuals within a matter of minutes, which data professionals can interpret and apply to business decisions. It is important to realize that the actual data analysis is not about the data. It is about the *insights* the data provides. This is then expanded with visuals that help show the data in formats more easily consumed by your stakeholders. Your analysis work delivers the most value when you help stakeholders answer the "So what?" question about the data and these presented insights. Given what the data shows, what should the organization do? The more data analysis technologies and visualization tools you integrate into your analysis work, the more time you can spend on the justification portion, rather than diving through data dumps. Organizations need to make decisions faster than ever and do not have time for manual correlation.

Example of the power of visuals

Consider how these technologies can build even greater predictive models that apply directly to task management. Common backlog management tools like Trello `https://trello.com/` and Jira `https://www.atlassian.com/software/jira` are great ways to track work, including your own business analysis work. If you have not used these in your work, that's okay. Simply know that these are great task management tracking tools for your analysis work.

Now imagine you showed stakeholders the list of requirements you had identified – in this case, user stories you were tracking in these tools. How much more value could you provide if you presented that same information in a table format like *Table 7.2*?

Story ID	Title	Status	Story Points
US-101	Login functionality	Done	5
US-102	Password reset	Done	3
US-103	User dashboard	In Progress	8
US-104	Profile editing	To Do	5
US-105	Upload document	In Progress	8
US-106	Download report	To Do	5
US-107	Search feature	To Do	3
US-108	Notification system	To Do	8
US-109	Admin panel	To Do	8
US-110	System performance improvements	To Do	13

Table 7.2 – Example user stories in table format

Looking at *Table 7.2*, would you know the team is behind schedule? Could you make decisions about what to prioritize moving forward?

Now consider *Figure 7.2*, where there is a visual chart to show the work that is completed (also known as a **burndown chart**). Burndown charts visualize how much work is left to complete and at what rate the team is completing the work. In *Figure 7.2*, the straight line is the planned work while the other line is what the team has actually completed.

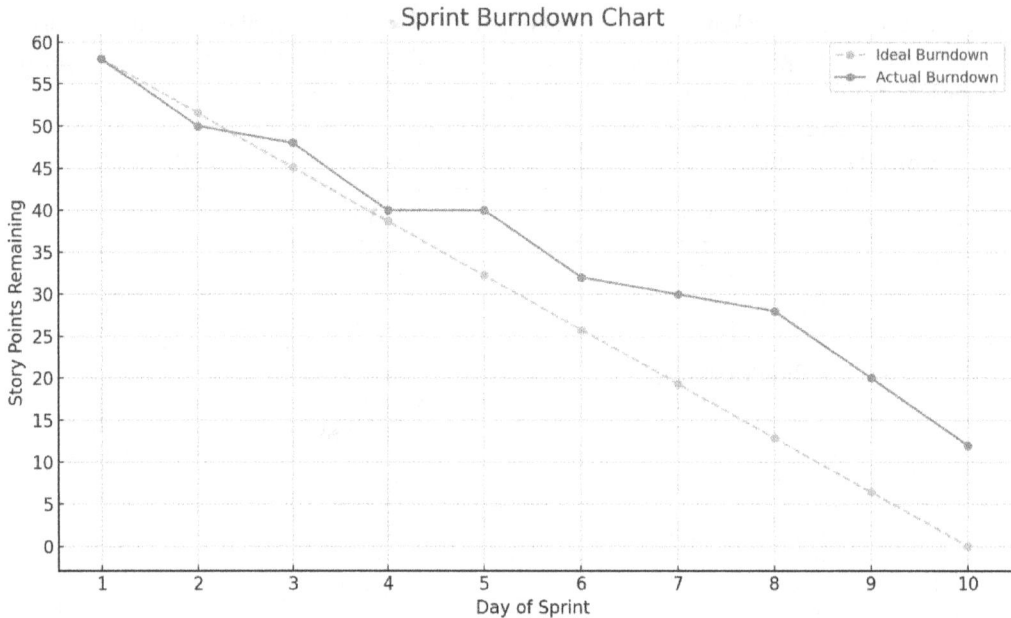

Figure 7.2 – Burndown chart of example user stories

Knowing that a burndown chart's goal is to show a comparison of planned versus actual work, does the visualization in *Figure 7.2* have more impact? Does it show the insights from the data in a way that speeds up informed decision-making?

When you know your cadence of work, you can predict how much work can be accomplished moving forward. You can even analyze the impact of adding more work or justify hiring another analysis professional. Leveraging the same data analysis practices and system connections you use with your stakeholders can help you stay focused on the highest-value delivery activities in your analysis work.

Facilitating collaborative experiences

Beyond simply connecting stakeholders in remote and hybrid meetings, the advancement in collaborative technologies enables you to conduct effective and efficient meetings and workshops now more than ever. Gone are the days when meetings were about agendas and simply going through a checklist. Now you must connect stakeholders from around the world to collaboratively build solutions. Often, in these dispersed and hybrid environments, the business analysis professional will spend more time getting stakeholders to collaborate than they will working on the actual solution. But this is where you shift from being an SME to truly being an advocate for business value. Facilitating collaboration means focusing on getting the stakeholders to collaborate on the solution. You simply enable that wildly productive environment with your incredible facilitation skills!

Current collaborative software includes whiteboarding and annotation features to allow real-time interaction on solutions. Miro `https://miro.com/` and Mural `https://mural.co/` are great examples that include engagement activities in the form of reactions and even real-time video feeds right inside the collaboration space. These powerful tools can help you focus on your facilitation goals and to achieve them.

For example, these collaboration tools have AI features that do summarizing and note-taking and even suggest next steps or action items based on the context provided. Knowing this, you can focus on keeping everyone engaged, helping them participate, and helping them clarify and refine their ideas and inputs. You can even turn on AI notetakers in your meetings (tools like Zoom AI Companion: `https://www.zoom.com/en/ai-assistant/`, Fathom Notetaker: `https://www.fathom.video/`, and Otter.AI: `https://otter.ai/`) to keep track of what is happening and summarize your next steps, so you focus on the outcomes.

These are all different apps that have features to support your facilitation goals. By the time you read this, they may have evolved further, and new, more advanced capabilities may have entered the market. However, these are great examples of how you have to balance learning that these features exist with then modifying your actions to leverage these capabilities and focus on maximum analysis value. Remember, it's not about knowing all these technologies and being an expert on what they can and cannot do. Rather, shift the focus to what you are trying to do in your daily analysis work and seek tools that enable your success. The more you do this in your analysis work, the more you will understand the impact these technologies can have on how organizations operate and help you define key business value.

Improving your analysis productivity

Now, as much as technology impacts your customers and their solutions, make sure to spend time reflecting on your own work. By this, we mean leveraging technologies to improve your work and efficiencies. Based on the office productivity suite that your organization uses, you want to use the respective AI companions daily. This means if you use Google, then integrate Gemini (`https://gemini.google.com/`) into your daily processes. Microsoft users will leverage Copilot (`https://copilot.microsoft.com/`) in their work.

A simple example comes in dealing with your email inbox. AI technologies help summarize emails and then identify tasks, even creating appropriate task trackers in your Trello or Jira backlogs, when configured correctly. Even using AI email features to draft emails, proofread your work before sharing, and find the best available meeting times with colleagues can save you valuable time and energy so that you can focus on the analysis work and not daily task management. This comes from knowing what the different technologies can do. But then the business value is using them to accomplish your business analysis work with more efficiency and effectiveness.

One of the best ways to learn is to try doing it yourself. Understanding the business value of these technological innovations can be easiest when you try to incorporate them into daily activities. Consider the power in using virtual desktops. Basically, your laptop connects to your "computer" at the office. Anywhere you go, you can work productively if you can connect to your computer. You do not care that there is no physical desktop computer taking up space. That is simply added value. You do not notice how quickly a new user can have a computer fully set up, ready to access in just a few minutes. This is where the business value begins to emerge: by minimizing operational costs to support and maintain the solution. Even further monetary value emerges in the reduced number of physical devices needed to leverage this technology. Then, if your organization uses the device location or even your smartphone as an authenticator, you don't even notice how you can skip the additional verification on login when the device recognizes you on company property or a known and trusted network. You simply enjoy the business productivity. But you also leave the business case full of value by integrating these different technologies into your daily activities.

No matter the direct effects of tech on your work, every time you learn about a new technology, don't just ask what it can do, but maximize your value proposition by always asking "what else?" Not just *what* else, but *where* else? *Who* else? It's the business application of the combined features and functionality to achieve a desired business goal where value can emerge. Seeing the value in your daily analysis work can be one of the most motivating factors for you to dive further into the technology for long-lasting, valued solutions. Even though technology is developing at unprecedented speeds, there is a lot you can do to stay informed about the value these tools provide by exploring some of the ideas in the next section.

Staying up to date with technological advancements

It was referenced in earlier chapters that one of the best skills successful business analysis professionals have is the ability to learn about new topics as well as to quickly understand and adapt concepts into their work. This same approach to constantly learn is the approach you also need to take to technology. As your role shifts to an advisory role for your organization and clients, they will also look to you to have knowledge of trends in the industry and what forces should be considered as they strategically move forward. The challenge is not to be distracted by all the "shiny objects" that emerge in different applications and technologies. But rather, focus on the business value and potential business impacts these innovations can have. Just like integrating technology into your own analysis work, you want to not just focus on the *what* but also the *why* of the technology. You have several areas you can turn to in your own approach to building your own knowledge of these technologies.

Start exploring trending topics

When you hear others discussing technologies, or if you like reading online articles and news sites, start exploring trending topics in your preferred learning format. Here are some great ways to jump right in and begin your exploration:

Style	Options	Notes
If you like...		
Reading and research	Use AI companions to pull summaries and articles to explore and read	Make sure to check out sources and see what others are saying on the topic
Visuals	Sign up for a webinar	Connect with and follow authors and organizations on LinkedIn
Learning by doing	Sign up for free trials of online apps and "lite" versions of software to explore their features	Look for templates and examples
Connecting with experts	Follow and connect with experts on LinkedIn	Schedule an online video meeting to ask them what insights they've gained from their learning and exploration
Collaborative discussions	Join professional associations	IIBA® and PMI® offer local chapter events and professional development activities
Communities	Seek out conferences and events	The "latest and greatest" is often covered in the presentations. Also, meet with vendors who share their own evolutions and ideas

Table 7.3 – Ideas for exploring topics based on learning style

Beyond the ideas in *Table 7.3*, consider using the technology itself. A good example is using **Perplexity** (`https://www.perplexity.ai/`) to ask it, "*What should I know about [topic]?*" Then use the prompts to ask more questions and explore the topic further. View the sources that are referenced. Ask Perplexity for industry experts talking about and actively working with the technology to follow and see what they are doing. This technology mines the data and information out there for you, if you just know the right place to start and some great questions to ask!

Leveraging your professional communities

Now, to know what technology is doing specifically in the business analysis space, turn to your business analysis communities to see both what technologies are impacting their work as well as how they are integrating technological advances into solutions and more. Webinars and conference topics are great insights into seeing new and emerging case studies of where and how technology is being applied. This is also the group you want to turn to for how technology can impact your analysis work. For example, if you were curious about AI, seeing the different ways analysts use ChatGPT (`https://chatgpt.com/`) to be more productive at some of the membership webinars can help you be more efficient and inspire you to think about what else those capabilities could be applied to in your analysis solutions. Check out who the presenters are on the different topics and connect with them on LinkedIn. Connect with me to jump right in and see not only the topics I write about, but also those topics and other authors that I share information about: `https://www.linkedin.com/in/jamie-champagne/`.

Now, these were direct applications on your analysis work, but don't be afraid to go further. Seek out communities of interest in technology. Going to not only conferences but also local user groups where they discuss technologies can be insightful to understand more about technology innovations. A good example is checking out cybersecurity groups or data analysis events, as these areas cover many technologies and discuss current issues and challenges that will emerge in your analysis work. And of course, stay abreast of what is happening in your industry. What applications are other organizations finding with emerging technologies? Even read news articles about mistakes other companies have made by not understanding capabilities or ensuring they thought through the entire solution approach.

Those same technologies that you are using to research and explore data and the impacts in your analysis work can be used to improve your own learning. Take, for example, AI. While it can mine and summarize information about your customer solutions or even your own analysis, make sure to have AI go to work for you! Taking time to ask AI about the emerging trends, the applications of newer technologies, and even to simply ask your favorite chatbots what you should know about a technology, can be both efficient and effective ways to quickly dive into new topics and find the best resources to learn more. But again, seeing the application of the capabilities is where the true value is at. The more you can do this in your own work, the easier it will be to explain and leverage in your business solutions work.

One final thought on technology in general: consider your analysis career path and the decision to be a more generalist or specialist in your analysis work. This means deciding whether you want to know about more types of technologies and what is available from a broader spectrum versus learning about specific applications and helping others get the most value out of those specific technologies. For example, would you go to a technology conference or a Microsoft conference? The technology conference would include broader technologies across vendors and industries, while the Microsoft conference would help you learn more about the Microsoft stack. You would learn lots and make valuable connections at both events, yet you have to ask yourself what you will do with those outputs. What do you need most when you go back to your office? The challenge is that there is no singular answer. You simply have to do the analysis work in the strategic direction of your own career goals. Both directions have space for long-term career success when aligned to your larger career vision.

Summary

This chapter highlighted just a sample of technologies available and even more will be on the market before you finish reading this book. The trick is not to be distracted by which app or other shiny object comes to market, but to constantly seek out the value in the application of the capabilities. Technology innovations are making stakeholders rethink their approaches to solutions. This awareness and ultimate success come best when guided by a knowledgeable business analysis professional. Understanding not just what these technologies can do, but how to extend the scope for long-standing operational value is where you turn "upgrade projects" into valuable solutions.

But you have to dive into the technologies yourself and seek out the application in your daily work and how you approach business analysis work. Technology's rapid innovation requires that you stay on top of trends and applications. Not because you have to be a technology analyst to be successful in the future. It is rather that you will be outpaced, outmatched, and even made obsolete by an analyst who can leverage these technologies for faster, more informed decision-making and business solution recommendations.

But the interconnected world of systems and sharing of data for greater insights continues to raise concerns in the community, not just about cybersecurity, but also ethics and businesses' responsibilities to their customers and communities. In the next chapter, you will build on this chapter's focus on collaboration and enhancing decision-making by considering how to build effective stakeholder relationships that allow you to uphold ethics and professionalism in both the solutions you recommend and in your quality analysis work.

Further reading

- Coursera. (2024). *How Does Cryptocurrency Work? A Beginner's Guide. Retrieved from* `https://www.coursera.org/articles/how-does-cryptocurrency-work`.

- IBM. (2024). *What is blockchain? Retrieved from* `https://www.ibm.com/topics/blockchain`.

- International Institute for Business Analysis® (IIBA®), (2015). *The Business Analysis Body of Knowledge® (BABOK®) Guide.* International Institute of Business Analysis, Toronto, Ontario, Canada.

- Oracle. (2024). *The Internet of Things. Retrieved from* `https://www.oracle.com/internet-of-things`.

- Technology.org. (2024, January 25). *The Impact of Cloud Computing on Our World. Retrieved from* `https://www.technology.org/2024/01/25/the-impact-of-cloud-computing-on-our-world/`.

Unlock this book's exclusive benefits now

Scan this QR code or go to `packtpub.com/unlock`, then search for this book by name.

Note: Keep your purchase invoice ready before you start.

8

Building Effective Stakeholder Relationships and Upholding Ethics

Business analysis can be fundamentally simple in its thought process. However, it gets exponentially more complex in execution as it requires you to work *WITH* people. It's this collaboration *WITH* your stakeholders that enables successful solutions to be designed. Without it, your hard work and analysis skills will simply be wasted.

This chapter focuses on the importance of building strong relationships with stakeholders, with a particular emphasis on communication and collaboration skills, managing stakeholder expectations, and ethical considerations. You will also learn how to uphold the highest standards of professionalism, ensuring that your interactions and decisions are ethically sound and respected by all parties involved.

In this chapter, we're going to cover the following main topics:

- Communication and collaboration skills
- Managing stakeholder expectations
- Techniques for successful stakeholder engagement
- Ethics and professionalism in stakeholder relationships
- Upholding integrity in business analysis

Communication and collaboration skills

In general, business analysis work is very easy. The structures are simple, and you work to define value and ways to achieve that value. However, one of the biggest challenges with business analysis work is considering the human element. As mentioned in the introduction, what this means is, to be truly successful in this profession, you have to work *WITH* stakeholders. You do not work for stakeholders. You do not go around stakeholders. But you work to collaborate *WITH* them to define solutions and act on them.

Truly successful business analysis professionals learn how to develop effective communication and collaboration skills for working *WITH* their stakeholders. The more you get to know your stakeholders, the more the solution designs will meet their needs for long-term value, versus a temporary appeal to their wants. You have to elicit those needs clearly enough to design solutions that deliver the necessary value. But stakeholders often only see their role or perspective in the enterprise. Honestly, many stakeholders are not used to working with a business analysis professional and can appear aloof, negative, or even confrontational simply because they do not understand. That is why this human element is so challenging. You have to bring clarity to not just the business challenge but also the business context. Being clear on what is needed over what is wanted can be one of the biggest obstacles any business analysis professional faces.

Let's see now how you can build clear communication into your analysis practice by both defining your role as well as your stakeholders' expectations.

Understanding the importance of clear communication

Clear communication will be both the success measure as well as the challenge of your analysis work. Most analysts will see this in two parts:

- Defining your role in any change effort
- Defining stakeholder expectations

First, consider that many people will not have had the pleasure or delight of working with an overly passionate business analysis professional before! Especially if you are placed on project-based work that has you working with different areas of the organization, many stakeholders may not understand your role. Your first communication challenge is to define the value you bring:

- Be clear up front about what you plan to do, what you consider your responsibilities, as well as what you consider outside your responsibilities
- Do not be afraid to be upfront with others and state that you are *not* the documenter or note-taker

- Be clear about your expectations to meet with different stakeholder groups to document their current challenges and potential future opportunities

- Most importantly, be ready to articulate your role and the value you'll provide throughout the endeavor

The more comfortable you get with articulating where and how you can provide the most value, the better.

But just as you want them to understand you and your role, you need to understand your stakeholders and where they are coming from. Context is going to be key to finding those solutions that last beyond a single iteration. Your analysis work means more than eliciting requirements. In every interaction, you want to focus on eliciting *understanding*. The more you understand where stakeholders are coming from or what the root of their frustration is, the more aligned your solutions will be with their needs. You have to ensure you understand their communication with you. Ask yourself whether you understand what others are describing. Can you picture the same picture as them? A different perspective on outcome means you will end up with solutions that do not align with stakeholder expectations, let alone business needs.

Exploring an example in understanding

Consider an example of a marketing department wanting to update their organization's website. The initial mockups did not get much feedback from the project team, but when presented with the test site, some of the marketing members had a lot of questions and ideas about the visuals. One of the biggest comments the technical team got was to make the website "prettier" or even "more on brand." The technical team struggled because they had used the brand assets and color patterns provided, but what they thought "prettier" meant apparently did not match what marketing was looking for.

What would you define as the requirements for "prettier"? Do you understand what the expectation is for the final product? Are you visualizing what the stakeholders are describing? Do you know how to understand what your stakeholders are envisioning?

This is your challenge as a business analysis professional. With that, let's look at some ways to facilitate effective communication throughout your analysis work.

Communicating effectively with business analysis techniques

Your business analysis skills help you define the "what" by focusing on the "why." Your techniques are the "how" to reach that intended value. In your business analysis planning work, when you are first assigned an initiative or topic to research, make sure your first steps include identifying your stakeholders and analyzing their needs. Consider everyone involved, not just in delivering the product or service, but also in making the changes and supporting the solution after it's in use. Spending time analyzing your stakeholders will actually save you valuable time in the long run. This can be as simple as *Table 8.1*, where you lay out the stakeholders and define their preferences.

Role	Communication Preferences	
	Receiving	**Sending**
Sponsor	Summary email with report in PowerPoint attached	Verbal updates to project manager
Project Manager	Task list updated in SharePoint	MS Teams project channel team chat
Network Administrator	Visual diagrams and models sent via email	Manually marked up artifacts sent via email (scanned and attached)
Help Desk Manager	Pre-arranged in-person meetings	Pre-arranged in-person meetings

Table 8.1 – Example stakeholder communication table

As we can see in *Table 8.1*, different stakeholders are going to prefer different forms of communication. This is why knowing multiple techniques to help engage and communicate with your stakeholders is essential to your analysis work. Every group of stakeholders is going to be different, and so the more ways you know to work with them, the more options you have to create a communication approach that works well for both you and your stakeholders. But then also use this as a starting point that you constantly revisit as you work with your stakeholders. Needs and preferences may evolve, so be welcoming to not only evolving your communication but also the format, frequency, and even style to help keep stakeholders engaged.

In the next sections, let's walk through some of the most common stakeholder communication techniques you will want to have in your toolbox throughout your analysis career.

Focus groups

Focus groups are great when you have a specific question or topic in mind and want to get various stakeholders' feedback on it. Typically, you are the moderator with an interactive group where you seek feedback and understanding of the group's perspective on the question or topic at hand (IIBA, 2015). Your prep work for facilitating this engaging, and often lively, discussion begins with you not only narrowing down the focus of the group (hence the term "focus group") but also what specific questions you want answered or need feedback on. Determining ahead of time if you want feedback on how things exist today is part of your prep work, so you can clearly define questions you need input on ahead of time. These could be questions such as *"What are your opinions on today's product X?"* or, if you are looking for new ideas and fresh insights, *"What would you like to see in this product?"* or *"What would you require to make this more valuable or something you would use more often?"*

With this in mind, you can carefully determine the right audience mix. This could be a range of specific people (i.e., current customers, current product users, or people with different backgrounds and identities). Or this could be a targeted segment that is focused on a unique niche or perspective, such as individuals who live within 10 miles of the organization and are over 70 years old. Then your work rests on your facilitation skills, encouraging conversation about the questions or the topic as well as different opinions and viewpoints with the group, and seeking additional insight and ideas based on the participants' contributions.

Focus groups are great for seeking information, but you are limited to the audience you select. This could inadvertently introduce bias into the elicitation results, for better or worse. Focus groups provide the input. They are a technique to elicit information. You will still need to review and analyze the collected information within your larger change effort before moving forward. That valuable information is also heavily dependent on the facilitator. Yes, you can drive the output – not in a demanding way but rather in how well you are prepared for the focus group. As will be continuously emphasized throughout this book, your facilitation skills and the ability to help others provide quality information are often key to success. Use the same prep work you would need for any meeting but spend a little more time on getting to know your participants so you can really engage them, appealing to their strengths while keeping focus on the tasks at hand. Focus groups are a great way to build relationships with your stakeholders and get them engaged and excited about the work you are doing. However, focus groups are just one elicitation technique. Moving on to the workshop technique can be more powerful, where you actually work on the solution during the session.

Workshops

Workshops are going to be one of the most common tools in your toolbox for bringing stakeholders together, and as your facilitation skills grow, you will quickly find workshops being a "go-to" technique that you find yourself using often.

What differentiates workshops from focus groups is that you have an intended work product that your stakeholders will work on during the session. At the end of the session, you want to be leaving with something in hand or completed, or at least something that helps move your effort forward. Common workshop goals for analysis work often include the following:

- The initial elicitation of requirements

- Requirements reviews

- Test plan walk-throughs

- Lessons learned or retrospectives (IIBA, 2015)

Workshops can vary in how you execute them, as they depend not only on the stakeholders but also on the goal of the session, the environmental context of the effort, and even your own facilitation skills. This is why it is key when you first start doing workshops (and honestly, even as you progress in your analysis career) to follow some core structure and setup. This includes:

Objectives	Considerations
Defining the goal of the session clearly	What do you intend to produce?
Defining the necessary stakeholders	Invite those who can help produce the end result, and ONLY those people whose contribution is necessary
Defining the structure	How will you get the stakeholders to the desired end product?
Defining the environment	Is this in person? Virtual? Hybrid?
Identifying what information you need to facilitate	Do you have background information such as stakeholder attitudes and influence, supplies and interactive element components, and anything else required to facilitate?

Table 8.2 – Structure to prepare for workshops

With this simple structure, you can be successful as you simply help the stakeholders to deliver the end goal. The biggest challenge comes in your facilitation work. You want to do as little of the work as possible. Your goal is to get the stakeholders to collaborate to achieve the result or produce the necessary product(s). With this attitude, it becomes easier as you simply guide the conversations to help everyone stay on track while setting up interactive elements to help engage the participants in the session outcomes. To help with this, technology can be one of your biggest enablers here. Let's see how.

Collaboration games

Collaboration games can feel similar to a workshop (and most times they are!), but the idea behind collaborative games is that you are encouraging the collaboration among your stakeholders by having them focus on an activity. With remote and hybrid teams, the use of technology can make collaboration games feel like a foundational element of most of the workshops you run.

While it may not feel like a "game" per se, simply connecting online with other team members via online collaboration tools such as Zoom (https://www.zoom.com/) or Microsoft Teams (https://www.microsoft.com/en-us/microsoft-teams/) offers your stakeholders several ways to engage in the session. From responding to chat messages, sharing visuals, or annotation on the screen together, these tools can keep people engaged in content while you facilitate achieving a specific session objective. Even asynchronous tools like persistent chat channels (such as those on Zoom and MS Teams, but also others such as Slack (https://slack.com/) and WhatsApp (https://www.whatsapp.com/)) offer ways for stakeholders to engage with each other to collaborate towards a common goal. When you turn brainstorming into a challenge, voting into a game, and even encourage some charades or drawing contests as ways to get to your products defined, your stakeholders are having fun, which is why these techniques are like games.

But while these technologies help you enable collaboration, do not limit your focus to technology. All collaboration games begin with a goal. Always define clearly what you need your stakeholders to deliver from the session. Just like workshops, you want specific stakeholders invited and *only* those people who will help achieve the goal. The trick is to then consider the structure and how you will get people to engage.

Perhaps try an ice breaker for a new team in order to open everyone up to sharing, which might be needed during some brainstorming work. Or perhaps collectively build a process map of how the team thinks work is carried out today and then show them a pre-recording of the process and what actually happens.

Technology has become a great enabler of collaboration games. You can use simple tools such as *Wheel of Names* (`https://wheelofnames.com/`) to pick who goes first, sharing through the online meeting platform. You can get more interaction through apps that have surveys and responses like Sli.do (`https://www.slido.com/`), Mentimeter (`https://www.mentimeter.com/`), and Poll Everywhere (`https://www.polleverywhere.com/`).You can get more complex and create huge layouts in *Miro* (`https://miro.com/`) or *Mural* (`https://mural.co/`) that walk participants through multiple activities, ending with them creating mockups and potential layouts for your solution, all while recording the process within the technology.

Collaboration games are often the enabler of your workshops or other elicitation sessions. They are both the tool and the technique. So, while it can seem like things are all "fun and games," there is a serious purpose and structure to them. The true secret to running great facilitated, collaborative games comes not just in your setup of the collaboration space, but in your prep work to facilitate those outcomes. What information do you need prepared to help turn your invitees into immediate participants? What questions do you need to ask for everyone to be focused and moving in the right direction, such that the participants are answering the questions themselves and moving forward?

Consider the following checklist whenever you incorporate collaborative games into your analysis work and toolbox:

- What's the goal?

  - *What needs to be delivered via the collaborative game?*

- Who needs to participate?

  - *Do you have all the right players?*

- What is needed for the "game" to happen?

  - *Include seating or area layouts, materials and supplies, workspaces or whiteboards, and easels*

  - *For virtual settings, consider setup, accounts, access, and screen-sharing tools*

- Define how you will capture results

  - *Where does the output go?*

  - *Is what is created, discussed, or utilized recorded and documented anywhere?*

- What are the action items or follow-up actions?

  - *What is going to happen next?*

  - *Where or how is the output used?*

Regardless of the communication technique you choose, aligning your approach with your stakeholders can be the best method for helping to ensure your analysis communications are effective. And just like preparing for a focus group, workshop, or collaborative game, spending some time preparing for how to engage with your stakeholders can be your key to success.

Communicating remotely

As mentioned regarding collaboration games, integrating technology into your techniques can enable greater collaboration and insights than simply a face-to-face meeting. It also enables you to work with teams remotely or in virtual and hybrid environments, where not everyone is in the same room. When you do, though, this means your communication has to be even more focused. You will still need to use your analysis techniques but consider that people may not see or feel your body language and emphasis. Or conversations may be much more structured as you have to wait for the other person to be completely done with their statement before the next person speaks to avoid talking over another person. The trick to successful remote and virtual communication often boils down to two things:

- Overcommunicate
- Consider what makes it easier for your stakeholders to participate

Overcommunicating does not mean talking more. Overcommunicating examples for, say, a requirements elicitation session, might be as follows:

1. Send an email to give all stakeholders background on the change effort and the role they will play, along with information on the first session and why you are approaching it the way you are planning.

2. Send a confirmation email invite for the requirements elicitation session, clearly articulating the goals and outputs of the session, along with a brief agenda. Also include an explanation of why you invited each of the individuals – articulate their role in the effort.

3. Send a reminder for the event prior to it, re-emphasizing the importance of their role.

4. Conduct the elicitation session.

5. Send an immediate recap (or as soon after the end of the meeting as possible) of what was achieved and the next step 6.

6. Follow up one week later on the next steps and what the stakeholders' work on the effort means.

It might feel like a lot of work to send reminders and re-emphasize roles, but the easier you make it for your stakeholders, the more they will participate. That is why whenever you have people participating in multiple formats, you work to make it as easy as possible for them to participate and not be a bystander.

All the same rules apply to virtual environments – roles, meeting purposes, constantly communicating – but you might have to adjust your processes so that it is easy for stakeholders. That is, if someone has trouble with their microphone during a virtual meeting, can they use the meeting's chat feature? Can they send you information ahead of time that you can present and share with the group? Hybrid formats require you to treat everyone equally, regardless of their participation format, so that people feel like they are on an inclusive team. I have some courses on LinkedIn Learning to help you figure out logistics and engage with both virtual and hybrid environments (`https://www.linkedin.com/learning/search?keywords=jamie%20champagne`). But the trick is to really focus on overcommunicating to make the work feel as inclusive as it does when working in person.

Additionally, accents and cultural norms can challenge your communication when you introduce remote and virtual formats. The lack of body language or expressions can make it hard to interpret meaning, so don't be afraid to restate comments to ensure you have both heard *and* understood what is being said. Avoid jargon, slang, and colloquial phrases as much as possible to, again, make it easy for your stakeholders to understand you as well. Even technology such as translation tools is going to be required in your work as you scale to more global operations. Don't fear these features and elements of your communication but simply acknowledge them as facts in an expanding analysis space. Stay focused on your communication goals and then simply ask, "What is the easiest way for my stakeholders to confirm understanding?" Success will follow this approach much more easily than frustration over having to constantly restate or reexplain your work.

Now let's look at how to manage stakeholder expectations beyond a single meeting and what you can do to effectively communicate throughout an entire initiative.

Managing stakeholder expectations

Figuring out another person's expectations can be very difficult, especially if you don't have much experience eliciting understanding. You will also find it even harder if you limit your interactions with the stakeholders and wait until the final solution has been completed to see if you have met your mark.

This means that to be successful in your analysis work, you must constantly work *WITH* your stakeholders. You want to think about how you will engage everyone before, during, and after implementing any solution. Your analysis work will generally be focused on defining requirements in enough detail so that the resulting solution meets the stakeholders' expectations while addressing a business need. So, you are going to want to think about how to engage the stakeholders for their input, feedback, and ultimate approval during all phases of your analysis work. Your communication approach, techniques, and artifacts that are produced will enable collaborative relationships to happen and be successful.

Openly communicating your planning and estimation work

Many times, your analysis work will be performed as part of your duties when assigned to a defined project. There are goals and objectives that must be met while working within constraints. While there are a number of stakeholders on projects, the primary stakeholder that you need to get comfortable working with when assigned to a project is the project manager.

Think of the project manager as the one responsible for ensuring the project is completed successfully. They often have a project plan tracking what must be done and by when to ensure the objectives are met. So, when working on a project with a project manager, ask yourself whether you have a business analysis plan. Do you know what you are going to do in your analysis work to ensure the successful solution is delivered, implemented, and utilized to return the desired business value? This does not have to be overly complicated, but defining what you are going to do, with whom, when, and how can not only help keep you on track but can also be a great communication tool with all your stakeholders.

Your BA plan is focused on your analysis deliverables and actions to get those accomplished. You want to include in your BA plan both what you are doing and how you are doing it, including the following:

- *List your business analysis deliverables*: Write down all the artifacts you think you will need to produce during the change effort.

- *Identify the stakeholders*: Define who you will possibly need to work with to deliver those artifacts.

- *Estimate the duration of your work*: How long do you need to complete each deliverable? This means that if you were not interrupted, how long would it take to define the work? Be realistic. Acknowledge that both you and your stakeholders often have other assignments that could extend the time it takes to deliver on assignments. The duration may be something that changes as you get into performing the actual analysis work, as you work with your stakeholders, or even as you learn about their availability.

- *Identify dependencies*: Listing out dependencies, conditions, or constraints can help with your estimates. Think of what needs to be done/has to happen (or not happen) so that your estimated duration can be met. Even articulate some of the potential risks with your approach. Identifying this and laying it out creates clearer assumptions and realistic expectations.

- *Define the techniques*: Given what you need to produce, with whom, and by when, *now* you identify the best technique for the goal. List out initial ideas when making the plan. But again, be open to the idea that as you learn more about your stakeholders, the techniques might need to be changed or altered to accommodate your goal and your stakeholders.

Like your requirements tracking, a simple, relatable list or spreadsheet can work. An example is shown in *Table 8.3* with the analysis deliverables for a project to replace an old office machine project.

BA Deliverable	Stakeholders	Estimated Duration	Dependencies or Constraints	Techniques
BA Stakeholder List	Project Manager	1 hour	Will be updated as project progresses	Item tracking
Requirements Traceability Matrix (RTM)	Project team SMEs and other analysts	4 weeks	Multiple elicitation sessions with different stakeholders as well as reviews	Workshops Reviews Interviews Document analysis
Current State Process Model	Project team SMEs and other analysts	2 hours	Initial session, then a verification review	Workshops Process modeling and analysis
Future State Process Model	Project team SMEs and other analysts	2 hours	Initial session, then a verification review	Workshops Process modeling and analysis
Prototype feedback	Project team End users	2 hours	May need asynchronous option if all stakeholders are not available	Workshop Surveys
Test Plan	SMEs and technical analysts	16 hours	Dependent on RTM Needs multiple reviews with SMEs and analysts	Item tracking Reviews
Post Launch Survey	End users	4 hours	May need asynchronous option if all stakeholders are not available	Workshop Collaborative games Surveys

Table 8.3 – Example BA plan

Now the trick is to *use* the plan you create. This will make this planning work more valuable. When creating a plan, especially for projects, building this out with the project manager can help you both get on the same page. The project manager can build out their plan of tracking the project work, and you can align your deliverables based on what helps achieve the project and product goals. Then you can use this plan when introducing yourself to stakeholders and articulating what the analyst role does. A visual model with time frames can really help things be clear for the stakeholders. For instance, in *Table 8.3*, listing out that you will be gathering the prototype feedback as input into the solution before it goes live helps stakeholders know that they will get a chance to share their thoughts and ideas before things are final.

Like most of your other work, the initial planning is just the starting point. You may find that the plan itself will evolve, including having to create additional artifacts that help the team as you go. An example BA deliverable may be to create a business case to help with vendor decisions or design options. It may not be needed when you start, but as there are multiple considerations once the project is better understood, you realize it is then needed. By adding the business case deliverable directly into your plan, you bolster your successful communication while also addressing expectations. Even the example of changing the technique to better align with stakeholder styles, preferences, and even working environments, can help demonstrate to your stakeholders that you truly are there to help them achieve their business goals. But they need to see a plan or something tangible communicated so that they align themselves with your goals as well.

Integrating the power of feedback

The power of "showing" – not just "telling" – your stakeholders your analysis work will become a critical part of your analysis approach, helping ensure engagement and communicated expectations. This means you need to shift your mindset to constantly seek and be open to feedback. Now, this does not mean you have to do or accept every piece of feedback; consider it all as input to be analyzed as to how, where, and when it might fit in your work to deliver value. It is more of a habit to get accustomed to seeking feedback throughout your work. The two techniques to help you build these communication practices are continuous reviews and retrospectives.

Continuous reviews

Referring back to *Table 8.3* (under columns 4 and 5), notice that there is mention of reviews or verification activities in the BA plan. This is a great approach to your work if you have time. There is the work needed to first draft your deliverable, but then consider it as a *draft* only. Whatever you generate, seek out feedback on what can be done to make it better. This is not to say your work is not good. It is simply about seeking input on what could be added for even greater results. This habit of continuously seeking feedback helps improve your deliverables and helps you understand expectations better, which leads to better solutions.

Especially as you are starting your career, getting a peer business analysis professional to look over your plans, approaches, templates, and more can be really helpful to have the insight of someone who has done similar work before. Seasoned analysis professionals still do this today for anything that is high risk or high visibility to help ensure they are not overlooking any aspect.

In your work, you want to build in feedback loops throughout any initiative. It can be as simple as stating that any business analysis artifact will be reviewed by the project team before moving forward. You can keep it simple by using various forms of **surveys**. Surveys are simply a way of eliciting feedback through questions. They can be as informal as a simple email or more robust, like an online form with conditional questions that depend on the previous answer(s). These are great to get in the habit of sending out when you may not meet with those stakeholders again. Just don't be afraid to add a question or two about your own success as a business analysis professional. Even a question such as, "What value did the analysis role play in helping this effort?," can give you some great insights.

But then, in larger artifacts, such as lengthy requirements documentation, **reviews** are actually part of the plan, as it may take multiple iterations for all the unknowns to be defined and addressed, or ideas to be explored. Many times, stakeholders need time and space to think through concepts and what could be viable for the long term. When you hold multiple sessions over a few weeks, you create the space for more insights and ideas. Reviews help not only gather additional ideas and input but also validate that the information you are working with is still accurate and correct.

The power in conducting review sessions is that you help the stakeholders engage with the analysis artifacts. They get more familiar with what you produce. And yes, while I will even admit that a project manager once told me that my requirements review session was about "as lively as watching paint dry"; they also commended the session on being a great validation of the requirements and actually facilitated the test plan being created almost *during* the session because the stakeholders were really thinking through each element and asking questions to help articulate their expectations of the end solution.

As you get more comfortable, consider doing more interactive and facilitated review sessions over just emailing out the documentation. You can start to bring the stakeholders into the content, and you will validate your assumptions if what you are picturing is the same thing as your stakeholders.

Retrospectives

Beyond reviews, though, you want to ensure in every effort you embark on that you incorporate time for retrospectives. **Retrospectives** and **lessons learned** are great techniques to identify what is working well, what could be improved, where there were failures and mistakes, and (most importantly) the corrective actions needed to ensure future successes. Projects will often do this to identify ways to do future projects more successfully, but these sessions are also powerful in improving your analysis skills with feedback as to what went well and what to improve next time. Plus, retrospectives are a great way to build deeper relationships with people whom you will often work with again in the future.

Retrospectives can be as simple as discussing your work with a colleague over a cup of coffee or tea. Or they can be more complex as a facilitated workshop where feedback is collected, tracked, and assigned. Regardless, feedback is a gift that you want to seek out and collect throughout the effort.

Here are some areas where retrospectives can not only help your current effort but will be investments in your career:

- *While reviewing your BA plan*: At this point, you can ask your project manager and stakeholders about what to include in your BA plan that is helpful to their understanding, or simply what information you included that was never used by anyone else.

- *After a workshop or session you facilitated*: You could provide a short survey post session to gain feedback on your facilitation style, setup, and engagement activities to help you plan the next one. *Any* stakeholder feedback as to the style and approach for eliciting the necessary information can be very helpful (i.e., do they even like workshops?).

- *After the completion of a project or initiative*: You could interview the project manager (PM) on what worked well and could be improved, when there is a project with both an assigned PM and BA. You could also review BA artifacts with other BAs to create templates and examples to help all analysts in the organization. You could post surveys or hold small focus groups with stakeholders as to the power the business analysis role added to the effort, and their feedback for future efforts.

Regardless of the technique or approach you use, the power is in simply eliciting the feedback. When you show you can take feedback and adjust your work to best support the stakeholders' goals, you will often find much more support from your stakeholders for your own analysis work. Ultimately, you are building feedback loops that help everyone get the most out of the effort while providing open access, and these together will help address any unstated expectations earlier on, when you have more options to accommodate changes.

Next, let's look at some of the techniques you want to ensure are part of your analysis toolbox so that each engagement with your stakeholders is successful.

Techniques for successful stakeholder engagement

In your analysis work, it is important to think about how you are collaborating and engaging *WITH* your stakeholders. You are not their order taker, nor are you to simply demand information from them and walk away. The focus of your analysis work is the delivery of long-lasting value. You do this by building relationships.

For now, let's look at the foundational actions you can take regardless of the stakeholder, environment, or change effort you are working on to find long-lasting success. Analysis professionals who have solid relationships with their stakeholders will find it easier to ask questions, inquire about alternatives, and especially present information that may not be in alignment with what stakeholders are asking for. These are all scenarios that we will talk more about later in this chapter. But again, for now, let's focus on two key business analysis knowledge areas.

Business analysis planning and monitoring

Business analysis planning and monitoring is often the knowledge area people tend to skip or spend the least time on; however, it can be one of the most foundational aspects of your analysis work. This area includes techniques you need to both prepare yourself for successful analysis work as well as to ensure you continue to do quality work. In general, the tasks include the following:

- Planning your business analysis approach

- Planning your stakeholder engagement

- Identifying and defining your business analysis governance plan

- Identifying and defining your information management plan

- Identifying areas of performance improvement with your business analysis work (IIBA, 2015)

The more time you can put into planning your analysis work, the easier your analysis work becomes. That is especially true with your stakeholder engagement activities. To add to what has already been discussed in this chapter, really consider doing some analysis work on your stakeholders. Once you think about or all the possible stakeholders you might need to deliver your analysis work to, you want to do further analysis with a technique such as impact and interest mapping.

Figure 8.1 shows how you would plan your engagement based on your analysis of each stakeholder.

	Low Interest	High Interest
High Impact	*Keep satisfied*	*Keep engaged*
Low Impact	*Minimal effort*	*Keep informed*

Figure 8.1 – Interest versus impact mapping

On the surface, some stakeholders are not as engaged as others are, which means you might have to plan to do extra activities to keep them not only informed but also more participative in the actions of the change work. *Figure 8.1* will have you ensuring your highly interested and high-impact stakeholders attend every meeting, or even have you work your schedule around theirs to accommodate their attendance. While also looking at this analysis, you may realize that a weekly summary email to your highly interested but low-impact stakeholders might be enough to satisfy their curiosity.

Ultimately, though, you have to do the analysis in the first place to help plan your analysis activities. Then, you have to continuously reassess your stakeholders throughout your effort so that those who need to stay engaged are properly connected to the activities being done.

Elicitation planning and managing stakeholder communication

Stakeholder analysis work should help you determine the best communication methods and preferred technology for your stakeholders. You then want to plan the elicitation sessions to maximize the stakeholders' time and input while delivering on the desired outcomes.

Using the stakeholder analysis work you have already done, now think about what your stakeholders need to be successful in the elicitation session. If you are doing a workshop to elicit requirements, do they need background information or understanding of current processes, the issues, or other concepts before you start? If you want to run a focus group on the use of a current app, for example, should you do any interviews first to get a sense of each stakeholder's usage before they join for a group session? Really think through what you will need to show, say, and walk through in your elicitation work, such that your stakeholders can easily contribute the necessary information.

Here is where the task of planning your business analysis information management is so important. You not only need to keep track of all the information you are going to need to communicate, but you also need to know where you will put all the information, data, and artifacts generated during your engagements with the stakeholders. While your stakeholder analysis might show that most of the team is just fine with an email, when you send out a document via email, where is the authoritative source saved? Do you have a Microsoft SharePoint project site or a team Google Drive to save it to for reference later? Or perhaps your requirements list is stored in a location that stakeholders can easily reference as you define requirements and their attributes? Actually, here, it's about thinking about what makes it easy for your stakeholders to access the information. The last thing you want is more confusion if you are putting Microsoft documents in Google Drive and it changes the formatting and creates frustration. Simply go back to what makes it easy for others and you can make it easy on yourself! Creating a clear organization method will be key to helping you and your stakeholders stay informed of the change work and leverage the reusability of the team's hard work.

Also, try to consistently communicate information and respond to requests in the same manner to help build stronger working relationships with your stakeholders, whether it is treating all stakeholders equally in the sharing of information or simply being consistent with your own methods. An example, back to the SharePoint project sites, is to consistently always link the documents, each of which has version control. Even if a senior team member asks for a copy of the report, still send the SharePoint link. This helps standardize your communications as stakeholders know what to expect. It can also help drive home the behaviors you need for them to become contributing collaborators and actually use the documents you create.

Finally, don't be afraid to use those same techniques used for deliverable feedback for feedback on how the communication is going. Mid-project, set up a small focus group to get feedback as to what is working well with the communication and what could be improved. Actively seek input and ideas to make it easier for people to contribute and participate, versus spending valuable time searching through emails and folders for information. A communication plan shared with your project manager and stakeholder team can even be a great thing to create, so everyone knows from the beginning what to expect. When you not only do what you say you will do, but you are consistent in your actions, you will start to build the reputation you need to have valuable, long-lasting professional relationships. This integrity is what you need, as ethics and professionalism are key qualities of successful analysis professionals.

Ethics and professionalism in stakeholder relationships

Ethics and professional conduct are leadership qualities of every successful analysis professional. Like many other valuable traits and characteristics, these are not unique to the business analysis profession; however, those business analysis professionals who embody these characteristics are the ones who find greater success. Regardless of how you might feel about a certain project or effort, acting professionally and upholding a strong ethical practice and approach will be key to experiencing successful stakeholder interactions.

Let's walk through some examples in the following sections so you can more tangibly picture what ethical considerations there are in your analysis work that will apply to any field, background, and technology.

Ethical principles in business analysis

So, what does *ethics* mean in the business analysis space? Essentially, this can be broken down into doing the right thing at the right time, even if no one is watching. Do you act and perform in a way that *should* be done? Not in a way preferred or that could be done, but rather, are you always focused on what is the *best* way for the organization?

Let's consider a simple lunch conversation with a colleague. You mention that you will need to change the design of your product after speaking with the technology team, even though the plans have been submitted. As your colleague just happens to be the financial approver for the project, they easily say, "Sure, no problem." Now, when you get back to the office, what might be the first thing you do? Do you tell your sponsor you got the financial approval already for the change? Or, instead, do you document the proposed change and submit it in writing to your colleague, the financial approver, and the reason for the requested change?

The correct answer is to follow the official, pre-determined processes and get changes confirmed and communicated (documented) even if you know the approver or received verbal approval. Being ethical is about you doing the right thing regardless of who is watching, or in this case, regardless of who verbally approved the request. The organization's process is to submit a written request, and so you follow through on this process. You might not think this is a big deal, but it is still an ethical process and practice that should be followed. Simply looking at your actions and decisions that need to be made and always making the "right" decision is how you uphold ethical principles in your analysis work.

If you need help, imagine your mother standing over your shoulder, watching you work. What would she want you to do? That is how you can help focus on staying ethical and building solid trust with your stakeholders. As mentioned earlier, the more you do what you say you plan to do, the more trust stakeholders will put into you and your skill set. Trustworthiness is a trait that is noticeable in all successful business analysis professionals.

Ethics in action

Ethics in analysis work does not necessarily mean that people don't want you to do the right thing. Ethics for analysis professionals means that hard decisions are going to enter your day-to-day activities. Like our example, you will face some hard decisions for your own analysis processes. Your decision-makers may follow processes when convenient for them. The challenge is that sometimes they will then try to go around approvers or include others when it becomes inconvenient. This is why your business analysis plan can be so valuable. It sets out expectations. When expectations are not being met or other ideas come into play, simply ask the decision makers what makes the most sense. That's generally the best practice. But then, what if you're not sure they are making a decision that is best for the team or the organization? That is when your analysis comes into play.

You will face different scenarios with your stakeholders when it comes to ethics. Here is another example where a small IT request came in to replace the server for one of the teams. The analyst got the estimate of all the work required, hard and soft costs, and presented the business case so that the executive could submit it for funding approval and get the project moving forward. The executive saw the cost sheet submitted for their approval, for which they'd have to pull from their budget. While the analyst included labor costs in the "soft costs," as they are part of employee salaries, they were nonetheless listed as costs. The executive was livid and called the CIO, saying that the IT team was full of incompetent and lazy staff and that they (the executive) were just going to go buy the server from an online vendor and plug it in themselves for 1/20th of the cost. *What would you do?*

This is going to happen more often than you want in your work because you are doing analysis work as part of a larger picture. You did just as you were told and followed your process, as instructed, for the analysis team. Never feel like a "bad business analyst" because someone disagreed with your analysis work. But do just that – focus on the analysis work. Stay objective and see this great example as follows: while the analysis work was the deliverable, or product of your effort, your solution to this "small request" also needed to include stakeholder analysis and what information they needed to not only support the analysis but understand where the analysis was coming from. Our irate executive was not familiar with the funding and approval process. They were not aware of the IT processes to safely and securely implement technical solutions that access private and sensitive information, let alone the testing, integration, and management of all technology assets.

The CIO in this case was very supportive of the analysts on their team and defended the work, and they offered the analyst an opportunity here. The analyst jumped right in with a quick process model that was needed to articulate the IT procurement process at the organization, which no one had done before. The analyst also realized the IT request process at the organization was more of an "order-taker" process that just tried to implement what was asked for, rather than analyzing a business need. What this means is that the analyst had only analyzed one solution option. They had not given alternatives that would help the requesting executive see the advantages of the recommended approach. The original work was not thrown out but expanded on, and the analyst worked to build a better relationship with the executive to know more about the work they do and how they operate in their area of the business. In this case, it was lucky that there was support for the analysis process and the opportunity to explain, as not every organization stands up to loud voices of dissent. It might have been much easier to just cave in and let the executive have their way. But then, later, there would be much more burden on the organization when there are issues with integration, support, warranties, and future upgrades. This is why objectively looking at your analysis work and aiming to ensure all aspects of *solutions* (not just products!) are considered (which includes understanding your stakeholders and spending time to get them involved in the analysis work) is so important. It can feel easier in the moment to "just do something," but that does not deliver longer-term lasting results.

Now, consider this scenario: your analysis skills are needed as part of a reorganization at your company. Part of the reorganization is the elimination of a few positions. One of those people is your friend who started at the company the same year you did. You inquire as to what will happen to the people in those positions, and the team says that they'll simply be let go. The effort has a communication plan that includes instructions for the HR team to communicate to everyone affected by the changes, but you see in the project plan that they don't plan to start the communication out to affected individuals until about two weeks prior to eliminations, as that is what is required by local laws. Stop and pause, and ask yourself: *what do you do?*

There are several considerations that are going to challenge you. On the business side, especially since you have empathy for affected individuals, you will need to consider whether you want to bring up options for the team on their communication and change management plans. Technically, the organization is following the law, so it is legally compliant; however, could you do more for the affected individuals? There are additional options such as starting communications earlier, working with HR on helping reposition staff, and others. Yet each will require careful analysis, including the positive and negative potential risks, costs, and impacts of each alternative. Then you have to be comfortable enough to present these alternative options in an unbiased manner to ensure the team has considered whether it is taking the best approach to the business need of strategically aligning resources.

This might feel easy if you have the perspective of trying to do everything you can to save your friend's job; however, that is not your role. Your role is to maximize the value delivered to the organization. Business cases are easy ways to present unbiased options and ensure the decision-makers have the best information. But you will then be personally challenged because you will know what is happening and never give your friend a heads-up to give them more time to plan. You need to remain unbiased and committed to the task. It does not mean you do not care. This is a great example to ask yourself whether you are not just delivering the best analysis of options for every effort you are assigned, but that you are also considering all your stakeholders and their perspectives when doing your analysis work. At the end of the day, you personally decide whether you support the decision-making processes of the organization or not. So, let's consider some more ways you can stay business-focused and objective while delivering quality analysis work.

Balancing stakeholder interests with ethical obligations

Normally, decisions are based on data and information. These decisions should be very logical. But know that you will also face pressure from the stakeholders you work with and the positions and influence they exert on the change efforts. Following the agreed-upon processes and clearly articulating unbiased information is how you can best address stakeholder interests that may feel like they are causing uneasiness in your work.

Take, for example, defining the requirements for a new product. The product owner wants a few more features as they know it will help it sell, and they think the additional requirements won't take a lot of extra work. They ask you to add these few feature requirements to the next release. While you know the product owner is always keenly aware of what the customer would like, you are concerned about skipping the technical review, scoping, and prioritization activities that you have followed for the whole project thus far. The product owner says not to worry and tells you again to just add in the requirements. *What would you do?*

The right thing to do, the ethical consideration, would be to still seek out the technical review so that there is the necessary information about the requirements. This information would be valuable to the prioritization activities to help balance the importance of these requirements against the other already prioritized work.

But then, also consider your communication with the product owner. The justification for the review is simple: you want to have all the information possible so that any decision-making is done with the most accurate and up-to-date information, such that the decisions are data-driven. This will help the team know they are making the right decision, regardless of whether it is to include these features or even reprioritize the work.

That is why you often follow the process – to support data-driven decision-making based on the full understanding of the entire context and potential risks and impacts of any change.

Now, there are often a lot of trade-offs and a need for shared understanding when working with a cross-functional group. This means you might have people from different areas of the business – such as marketing, HR, IT, facilities, and others – all having to collaborate for a positive, impactful change. While each of the stakeholders may have a bias toward their respective areas, your focus should remain on the good of the overall business. The question *"What is best for the organization?"* should guide your decision-making.

However, imagine this – say you report to a manager in the IT department. After a critical design review meeting, the HR department really wants to prioritize the capabilities tracking aspect of the new system, while IT is pushing for better infrastructure before even talking about system features. Your analysis has you agreeing with the IT team members that the infrastructure should be designed first. Then the team can talk more about adding extra features. The HR manager accuses you of being biased since you work for IT (even though everyone works for the same company). *What would you do?*

The best thing to do here is to still lay out the information and the business cases that justify any recommended course of action. Regardless of who you work for, the data should help support the decision. As you walk stakeholders through the data and how you came to your conclusion, the stakeholders might buy into the decision more and more in seeing that the decision was not about who your boss is, but rather what is best for the business.

Throughout your career, you will want to leverage your objectivity as an advantage to the team. Being impartial and focused on what is best for the overall organization is what sets you apart from your SMEs. By not "owning" any of the processes or products in the scope of the work, you can then focus on unbiased and fair decision-making processes to achieve results that have the maximum positive impact. But it can feel challenging as you build rapport with your stakeholders and aim to please and satisfy your team.

One of the best things you can do is to work with your decision-makers to confirm the decision-making processes *prior* to starting some of the work. Most of your work will be to facilitate teams – people with different viewpoints, experiences, and opinions – to come to a consensus on a decision. If, for example, you know that requirements will need to be prioritized to ensure the scope of the effort stays on track, then facilitating a session where the stakeholders confirm the process and criteria that will be used for prioritization can be extremely valuable so that no personal opinions creep into the discussion when it is time to prioritize.

Other common items are to agree on the change process. How formal will requirements or design or process changes be? It can be good to have your sponsor sign off ultimately on any change work, but this can also be a big bottleneck if the sponsor is not intimately involved with the features and functionality.

Ultimately, the first challenge is to gain agreement on how actions with the business analysis deliverables will be handled. Once you have this, you will build trust and become respected when you follow and uphold these processes. That is the integrity needed to see success in your business analysis work, as we will see in the next section.

Upholding integrity in business analysis

The pressure of ethical concerns is not just in the planning but in the execution of business analysis work. What this means is that once you reach agreement on how things *should* be done, you need to follow those processes and uphold those agreements.

The work you put into planning your stakeholder engagement and collaboration includes where and how you document the information shared, consumed, and produced. Your collaboration spaces, where all team members have access, are one of the greatest tools you can use to help drive visibility and transparency in analysis work. Think of not just sharing information in the collaboration space so that it is easy to access but also to use it to show the process and be as open as possible in what is happening.

Let's take a simple 4x4 matrix that is a great technique to help you categorize and compare options. The setup is quite simple:

1. You define the criteria upon which to rank the topic.
2. For each option, rank it on where it stands on each criterion listed.
3. Compare the results of the ranking.

Figure 8.2 shows how you can display the options, communicate, and keep an unbiased opinion while using data-driven insights to help facilitate decision-making with the team:

	Price	Customer Satisfaction	Ease of Implementation	Ease of Maintenance
Feature 1	Low (3)	High (3)	Mid (2)	Low (3)
Feature 2	High (1)	Low (1)	High (3)	High (1)
Feature 3	Mid (2)	Mid (2)	Low (1)	Mid (2)
Feature 4	High (1)	Mid (2)	Mid (2)	High (1)

Figure 8.2 – Example decision matrix

Figure 8.2 shows the criteria used to rank the features. The criteria ranking then helps with the decision-making. The table gives a clear, specific process for the decision based on objective measurements. Then, when you couple this with your communication and engagement plans, you can walk stakeholders through these so that they begin to own their decision. Your analysis work enables successful collaboration and effective and efficient execution. And again, when you are consistent with both your methods and your communications, you will build the trust needed to be successful, even as you encounter obstacles in your analysis work.

Exploring ethical examples for analysis integrity

Now, no matter how clear you make the decision-making or specify the details in your communication, in your analysis career, you might be faced with scenarios that challenge both the integrity of your analysis work and even your own personal character. Agreements at the beginning of your efforts that define what information is confidential and what information can be shared can be a great foundation when you are pressured to share information beyond the scope of the team. Part of your information management plan is ensuring confidentiality and data security in stakeholder interactions. When you uphold these processes, you uphold both your and the analysis work's integrity.

In your facilitation work, especially when conflict arises, understand that fair does not mean equal. Decisions, prioritization, and approvals may not be aligned, nor disseminated equally among different areas of the organization; however, as long as you stay focused on how to bring the entire organization the maximum value, you will build the justification your stakeholders need to see. That visibility, the transparency in the process, and the commitment to analyze to the best of your ability and resources are how you collaborate *WITH* your stakeholders and together define great value for your organization.

Summary

Clearly and effectively communicating with your stakeholders is the key to building relationships with those you will work with during your analysis work. Engaged stakeholders are required to help you define, discuss, and work through their expectations so that you build business solutions that deliver the greatest value. Part of that clear communication comes from openly sharing and being transparent, leveraging collaborative tools and technology, and then planning for engagement.

But engagement is not a one-time workshop or session. You want to build working relationships so that you can continuously seek feedback and input from your stakeholders. Building in space for retrospectives and lessons learned, both during and after your analysis work, is key to managing the engagement. The more you demonstrate your commitment to upholding stakeholder expectations and showing your integrity by doing what you say you are going to do, the greater that feedback and trust loop gets. To help you with any difficult or even unethical situation that you may face, having someone who can mentor you can be a critical resource to help give you ideas and focus on that value delivery.

The next chapter will build on these stakeholder engagement and communication skills by exploring additional leadership skills and how mentorship can be a critical component to long-term success.

Further reading

- International Institute for Business Analysis® (IIBA®), (2015). *The Business Analysis Body of Knowledge® (BABOK®) Guide.* International Institute of Business Analysis, Toronto, Ontario, Canada.

Unlock this book's exclusive benefits now

Scan this QR code or go to `packtpub.com/unlock`, then search for this book by name.

Note: Keep your purchase invoice ready before you start.

9

Leadership and Mentorship in Business Analysis

Leadership is a role that is filled when people see that the right thing needs to be done at the right time for the right reasons. Don't confuse this with managing. Managers ensure work is getting done according to plans, structures, or processes. Leaders are people who step up to the challenge and help teams be successful. That is exactly what business analysis professionals do. Daily, you have opportunities to enable others to be successful and build your leadership skills. Knowing what these are and ways you can build them throughout your career will be key to your success. But just like your ability to support others, you will need to identify sources of support for yourself. One of the best relationships you can build is with a mentor. Yet, finding and cultivating a beneficial relationship can be just as time-consuming as your analysis work.

This chapter explores the role of leadership and mentorship in the career of a business analysis professional. You will walk through activities that will help you both identify and boost your leadership skills. To support you in this work, defining what mentorship means and looks like to your career will help you in building effective mentoring relationships for long-term career success.

In this chapter, we're going to cover the following main topics:

- Developing leadership skills
- The importance of mentorship
- Building an effective mentoring relationship

Developing leadership skills

Leadership skills in business analysis work often center around communication, collaboration, and facilitation work, especially in helping others with informed decision-making and strategy. While many techniques can be learned in formal training courses with practical exercises, most of your leadership skills are going to grow as you apply them in your analysis work. Seeking these opportunities will help you see greater success in your career, but we need to define these skills first. Then, like any good change effort, you will couple it with some measurements. You can use the assessment described in this chapter to help you see not only where you are at right now but perhaps realize how many leadership activities or qualities you have actually been working into your analysis work. When you know where you are and where you want to go, then a growth plan is easy to set.

Understanding analysis leadership qualities

Business analysis work is focused on enabling others to be successful in delivering extraordinary business value. This means that besides doing the analysis work, you will then need to not only communicate that work, but must work to influence decisions, motivate stakeholders, and encourage proactive change attitudes. For this to happen, this is where you need your leadership skills.

While only a sampling, here is a list of leadership topics applicable to your analysis work:

- Emotional intelligence (EQ)
- Active listening
- Conflict resolution
- Difficult conversations
- Public speaking
- Business acumen
- Facilitation
- Written communication
- Confidence
- Trustworthiness
- Respectfulness and humility
- Servant leadership
- Strategic thinking
- Optimism
- Open-mindedness
- Influence
- Vision
- Motivation
- Proactive
- Opportunistic
- Commitment
- Flexibility
- Determination
- Accountability
- Negotiation
- Strategic planning

- Problem solving
- Decision-making
- Innovation
- Cultivating curiosity
- Teambuilding
- Building diversity
- Consultive approach

- Goal setting
- Mentoring
- Delegation
- Giving constructive feedback
- Difficult conversations
- Managing change
- Stress reduction

If these competencies interest you, you can read more about how they apply to business analysis work in the *Business Analysis Body of Knowledge® (BABOK® Guide)* (IIBA®, 2015). As you review this list of skills, you will notice that most are not limited to business analysis work. However, like many of the characteristics of successful analysis professionals, having these as part of your value proposition will make you an even more successful analysis professional.

Measuring your leadership qualities

Change work is about going from a current state to some future state. The same analysis work can be done on your own leadership skills. Thinking about where you are and where you want to be is a valuable activity to put in your career growth plan. Use the worksheet in *Figure 9.1* to seriously think about how comfortable you are with applying each of these items in your daily analysis work. Yes, daily. Leadership is not a tool that is only used for certain scenarios; rather, it is a mindset that is demonstrated and ingrained in all you do. For now, just rate yourself in the **Where you are now** and **Where you want to be** columns and don't worry about the last column. We'll come to it shortly. Take a moment and read through the items in *Figure 9.1*.

Personal Competency Assessment

Rate yourself for each of the topics below using the five point proficiency ranking below. Take a close look at where you're at and where you want to be. Use your results to craft your development plans.

Competency Ranking
1. Not familiar with this topic
2. Basic knowledge of this topic
3. Can follow instructions to perform this topic
4. Can generally do on my own, perhaps with a little help or advice
5. Am comfortable performing this skill well or even demonstrating to others

Leadership Skills	Where you are now	Where you want to be	Actions and opportunities to build these skills
Emotional intelligence (EQ)			
Active listening			
Conflict resolution			
Difficult conversations			
Public speaking			
Business acumen			
Facilitation			
Written communication			
Confidence			
Trustworthiness			
Respectful and humble			
Optimistic			
Open mindedness			
Influence			
Vision			
Motivation			
Proactive			
Opportunistic			
Commitment			
Flexibility			
Determination			
Accountability			
Servant Leadership			
Strategic thinking			
Problem solving			
Decision-making			
Innovation			
Cultivating curiosity			
Teambuilding			
Building diversity			
Consultive approach			
Negotiation			
Strategic planning			
Goal setting			
Mentoring			
Delegation			
Giving constructive feedback			
Difficult conversations			
Managing change			
Stress reduction			

Figure 9.1 – Personal competency leadership assessment

Look at all the items listed in *Figure 9.1*. Then consider your own skill set. For each of the items listed, think about what you do or do not do in your analysis work. Give yourself a score using the competency ranking provided. Just go with your first thought – don't overanalyze! No analysis paralysis here! Then think about where you want to be. Think about the type of analysis work and kinds of initiatives you prefer to get assigned; what skills will help you be the most successful in those areas of work? Measuring those skills and improving them to be at a higher level is how you strategically use them to be more successful in the kinds of analysis work you desire. Simply ask yourself: If your career were very successful, what scores would you want to have? Put those answers in the **Where you want to be** column. Now, as a good analyst, you can actively measure where there are gaps in your own leadership activities. But as you read each of these competencies, what areas excite you or get you to think that you would really enjoy more of that kind of work? Those are the ones you want to pay attention to. Those are the ones that you want to start thinking about how you shift the measurement from where you are today to what level of competence you want to have tomorrow. That is what the final column is for: defining concrete and specific actions that will move that measure of success toward your intended goal. We'll come back to fill in further details later. For now, just like your analysis work, having simply a measure of the current state and future state can be enough of an insight to motivate you to make changes or seek out new ideas. To help you think about how to know whether your skills are being effective, consider the following:

- How resistant to making changes are your stakeholders?

  Effective leadership results in stakeholders who are committed to the change work and eager to take action to make it happen.

- Do your teams have a clear vision of the future state (that was collaboratively defined)?

  Effective leaders help teams set actionable visions that drive focused and proactive work that results in accomplished goals.

- How well do different stakeholders collaborate and work collectively on deliverables?

  Effective leadership facilitates active collaboration where the stakeholders are doing the work, and the facilitator is simply the guide.

- How constructive is the conflict that emerges in your analysis work?

  Effective leadership encourages different views and ideas that are then worked on through creative problem-solving.

Use these questions to help you assess your leadership skills and measure how effective you are today in applying these skills to accomplish your analysis work (IIBA, 2015). But like any good leader, the value in your analysis work is only felt when there is action taken. Now that you know where you are and are thinking where you would like to take your skills, it is time to define the actions that will help you grow your leadership skills.

Growing your analysis leadership qualities

The most important part of any analysis work is answering the "So what?" or "Now what?" question. The same applies to your personal analysis. Change happens when you define specific actions and assign them clear due dates.

So, now that last column on your assessment sheet (*see Figure 9.1*) is for defining specific actions you can take to practice, build, and grow your specific leadership skills. You want to think about specific verbs and actions in your items. Consider them as tasks. Assign a due date. And write it down to hold yourself accountable. The actions column is how you move yourself from where you are to where you want to be. But discussing your goals and acting on them have two entirely different outcomes.

Defining the actions

As much as this book encourages you to use your good analysis skills in your work, it is even more crucial to analyze your capabilities and competencies. Analyzing where you are and where you want to be is critical to your success, especially in the leadership roles and opportunities you will be exposed to in your analysis career. Being able to define your starting and end points (the **Where you are now** and **Where you want to be** columns of *Figure 9.1*) makes it much easier to identify the steps to get you there. In business analysis work, you define current and future states. This is often the project scope definition as the team then works to achieve the future state by making some sort of changes (the work of the project). This is what you get to do with your career. Each one of those skill sets listed is like a mini project. You have business goals or outcomes to be achieved. So, now you need to define, scope, and build out the project to achieve those objectives.

Let's look at the example of public speaking. Perhaps public speaking was *NOT* your favorite course in college; however, it is a skill that is often required of successful analysts to present recommendations, conclusions, and other analysis work to decision-makers. In *Table 9.1*, you might list that, currently, you feel uncomfortable speaking to executives. This is a great scenario where public speaking is a key skill set today, and why this skill can really help your professional career. Then you realize that, for career success, getting comfortable presenting regularly to the executive team would be a solid foundation in this skill area. So, the actions can then come simply from brainstorming ideas.

In *Table 9.1*, under the **Actions to get you there** column, there are some small things, such as presenting to your own team, that you could do to reach this goal of speaking publicly – not quite the pressure of the executive team, but a great venue to practice. And that leads to the idea to present to your manager with the expectation that they can give you immediate constructive feedback. Going even further, presenting topics to the department for practice is a true business analysis idea as, again, it allows you to practice, and sharing your knowledge with others is a true value addition! Again, the first step is to just brainstorm ideas. Go ahead and even think about what actions you might add for your own career if public speaking were an area you wanted to work on!

Where you are now	Where you want to be	Actions to get you there
Uncomfortable speaking to executives	Seen as a trusted advisor, presenting regularly to executives	Present recommendations to the team at weekly status meetings
		Practice presentation with manager for feedback prior to executive presentation
		Present a monthly "lunch and learn" presentation to the department

Table 9.1 – Structure for defining the actions to move from the current to the future state

Now, the actions are powerful when they become true tasks. This means, for each item you listed in the **Actions…** column, you want to be clear on what you need to do to complete that action and give a date by which it needs to be completed. For the first idea, to present at weekly status meetings, the actions might be as follows:

- Identify topics of interest to the team
- Schedule weekly time to present
- Perform first presentation
- Confirm subsequent weekly presentations

You have just broken down a goal into smaller, more manageable pieces (the **decomposition technique** at its finest!). Now, each of these tasks can be assigned a due date by which you want to complete it. This makes the actions much more attainable. Having a due date can help you be accountable to your own plan.

Notice that there has been nothing stated about where you need to be to be a senior or a mid-level analyst. These skills are meant to be applied and grown no matter where you are in your analysis career. Even senior analysis professionals, including myself, are still working on improving different ones daily. The first part, though, is to simply recognize where you are and where you want to be. Then follow through on that growth by identifying the actions you can take to make an impactful change. Just looking at the list, here are some action items I think about as I think about what actionable impact I could make:

- Asking stakeholders why they feel a certain way
- Using an AI notetaker so I don't take notes and can pay more attention
- Asking questions to simply try to understand a conflict (not solve it right away)

- Asking a financial team member to explain a profit and loss statement to me

- Asking to help support another analysis professional's workshop to watch how they facilitate

- Using a chat prompt to review my writing for feedback on professional verbiage

- Ensuring I do what I say I'm going to do – and email or call the stakeholder before I'm late delivering on an action time

- Committing to obtaining another certification

- Helping another team member get their certification

These are just some simple ideas that could apply to a number of those skills. Again, do not worry about right or wrong answers. Normally, any action is forward progress! Go ahead and lay this out for all the areas of your skills, knowledge, and expertise that you wish to grow. Again, it is totally okay if many of these are skills you haven't thought about in your career yet or even need to do some research to understand their place in your analysis work. This means that you can only improve them!

Every item you think you could stretch to greater value, add it to the list with a current state and desired future state assessment. Then, simply brainstorm the activities. Before you even break down the action items into discrete tasks, though, you might find yourself making a very long list of things to do that feels like additional work over your already assigned analysis duties. First, know this is a good thing! Most analysis professionals value their professional development because of its automatic positive ROI. The greater their skills, the greater the value the business analysis professional can provide. And the greater the value, the more they are a truly appreciated asset to the organization. However, it would be overwhelming to try to address every single idea right away. So, this is the point where we introduce the analysis of priorities and strategic planning by building out a leadership roadmap that allows you to strategically align when and how you incorporate these valuable growth actions into your analysis career.

Creating your leadership roadmap

Brainstorming ideas is great to get actions written down and captured. But being a leader means you often have to have a strategic focus to your work and where your energy is spent, regardless of whether you are in a junior or senior position. Creating a career roadmap that is more centered around your skillsets is a great way to focus on your skill development while building agility into whatever positions you find yourself in throughout your career.

Start first with simply labeling four columns of work as **Now**, **Next**, **Later**, and **Not Now**, as seen in *Table 9.2*.

Now	Next	Later	Not Now

Table 9.2 – Structure for building your career roadmap

Then you want to start putting in the roadmap activities you plan to do to move your skill sets from entry level to applied successful practitioner. These can be in more than one area of your analysis work and can be done over different time periods. Let's consider an example of a business analysis professional who finds themselves working in remote and hybrid environments. They work for a major corporation, so IT is governed by the organizational IT department, which has to authorize certain applications and programs. The business analysis professional finds out that the collaboration tool of choice for the organization is MS Teams. They were used to Zoom, so they now have to quickly get comfortable with MS Teams features and nuances. They have also been taking some business analysis techniques courses. One technique, the business case, they find particularly useful and are trying to think of ways to integrate its usage into daily analysis activities. With this background, and some great analysis ideas around their skill sets and technical competencies, they started listing out some ideas, as shown in *Table 9.3*.

Now	Next	Later	Not Now
Run virtual team meetings using MS Teams	Run hybrid team meetings using MS Teams		
Articulate the value of business case formats/ templates as a tool for faster and smarter value delivery	Present business cases for approved changes to the project sponsor	Present business cases for approved changes to the executive team	
			Project manager training
		Run a UAT	

Table 9.3 – Example leadership skills roadmap

In this example, one of the first items was to get comfortable with not only remote teams but in running meetings in the remote environment. Okay, to start with, the analyst has decided to focus on just virtual teams right now using MS Teams. As we see on the roadmap, they will next work up to running hybrid teams. This is an easy example to break down a complex objective into discrete tasks that are more easily accomplished. So, the analyst can continue with the example on the business case formats. They consider where the business case format might be of the most value. In their organization, there are often last-minute demands to jump into projects forced upon the team with little background and clarifying information. This seems like a prime opportunity to introduce the business case structure.

However, first, they want to work to communicate *why*. Using a business case template is going to be helpful for not just the analyst or the project team; business cases are valuable techniques for communicating and overall project scoping. They introduce clarity and specifics that might be skipped in ad hoc and varied approaches.

The more the analyst can communicate the template's value, the easier it is for them to get buy-in on the projects that utilize business case structures. And the more they use the business case structure, the more they see that the right projects are getting the resource required with an increase in communication and understanding.

Once they start garnering greater support for solid business cases, they put on the roadmap opportunities for more strategic analysis or complex discussions, giving them a chance to present well-founded business cases. More strategic discussions or meetings will give them opportunities to use this structure to clearly communicate business value to decision-makers and gain experience in getting their recommendations noticed. And so, they add on to the **Next** and **Later** columns to work on these presentations.

But just like the clarity of project scope needed for successful project work, they scope out what they will *NOT* do in the **Not Now** column. They always wanted to do project management training or earn project management certifications, but right now, the focus of their career is on the business analysis aspects. They know project management skills are important to work with project teams, even if you are not titled as a project manager; however, it is simply not a priority right now. Getting the teams working together on MS Teams is an immediate need and takes precedence now. But again, this is not to say that project management upskilling won't happen. They are simply saying "not now." With a product roadmap, not having those specific dates but relative timeframes for each column, they give themselves permission to always readjust. Things can be later, but when that later is depends on other priorities and changes in the environment and operational context. The world will keep changing, and so committing time to review the priorities and re-prioritize them as things change is critical to using this as a successful career directional tool.

That includes adding, in the **Later** column, things you want to try. For example, the analysis position in this example may not necessarily run user acceptance testing (UAT) today; however, the analyst saw in the last project how much back and forth there was between the requirements and testing work as the users engaged with the solution. They would like the opportunity to run their own UAT for a big project, but not just yet. Or, perhaps when a better project comes along that would give them the autonomy, depth, and bandwidth to properly explore UAT in more detail. So, the opportunity to be responsible for UAT is simply saved for later. Putting these items on the roadmap gets you thinking about the opportunities while allowing space to focus on your priorities now.

Use this same model for yourself now. Think about the actions that will enable you to upskill in the various aspects of your career. Then, lay out very clear and actionable tasks on your roadmap using relative timeframes for **Now**, **Next**, **Later**, and even **Not Now**. Go ahead and create a view in MS Teams Planner, get out a Kanban board, or create one in Trello (`www.trello.com`). This is a great exercise in and of itself to help you prioritize. What can add immediate value now? What might depend on other factors or need more information? Those can come later. But with all this effort, the trick then is to constantly use, review, and update this roadmap. Always add new ideas where you see fit. Growing your leadership skills is much more attainable when you have plenty of ideas and options to apply to each initiative.

As both your work and positions evolve, come back to your roadmap and reprioritize what is next in your journey. Think of the roadmap as a backlog itself. As you accomplish those items in the **Now** column, you want to refill them with the next most valuable items. Just like an agile roadmap, what was not a priority last week could be a top priority next week. Do not worry if some items simply stay in the **Later** column while new items keep landing in the **Now** and **Next** columns. You work in a dynamic environment. So, your plans for continued growth should be just as flexible as the environments in which you want them to succeed. The next chapter will give you more ideas on how to work on a career roadmap as a living artifact to help you with your strategic career decisions.

The real challenge is to focus on your own professional development. Do not include in your roadmap just your assigned project work. Sure, a roadmap can help you organize your work on those projects and communicate with stakeholders. But here, we want you to capture those skill sets and competencies that will bolster your analysis skills no matter what project, initiative, or work area you are assigned.

To help you on this journey, let's look at a small example.

Examples of growing and leading on a project

Leadership can emerge in multiple ways throughout your analysis work. A junior analyst started their business analysis position right after obtaining their **Entry Certificate in Business Analysis™ (ECBA™)** certification. They knew what a business analyst role involved in terms of tasks and techniques, but had yet to get experience, and they were very excited for their first project. So, they began with the basics of using item tracking and document analysis to help capture the requirements for the small project they were on. Being new to the activities of an organizational project, they wanted to seek additional understanding of the effort and the impact the solution would have. They asked the project manager if it would be okay to sit with some of the stakeholders to help understand their context. Of course, the project manager loved this idea and helped to coordinate some on-site visits to a few of the key stakeholders' areas.

Now, the business analyst had lined up a few questions to be ready to inquire of each stakeholder. But then they included the request to observe the stakeholders performing the different processes. Each of the stakeholders was very welcoming to have someone take an interest in their work and genuinely curious as to how things functioned. The business analyst was all too excited to learn as much as they could from each stakeholder and found that it helped them picture the organization across the different departments and functions. While it was great context for this project, the analyst realized in later projects how valuable this perspective became. They were able to provide insights and ideas that had greater value by understanding much more intimately the environments and structures the different teams focused on.

But now, to both help with their skills and enforce their learnings, and contribute to the team, the analyst asked their manager if they could share with their business analysis department team what they learned. Instead, of just talking about their observations and referencing their notes, the analyst wanted to practice building some process models as a senior analyst had shown them some examples on other projects.

The junior analyst worked through some ideas and then asked the senior analyst to help review and revise the approach. Having an actual example to talk through with a senior professional gave greater insight and depth to understand not just how to develop a process model but what it was good for. At the time of the weekly team meeting, the junior analyst then used the process models to walk through their learning experiences in the observation activities they got to perform on their project. The team appreciated the insight, as some mentioned that they had never gotten to experience or explore some of those areas of business. The manager was impressed by the initiative and asked if the junior analyst would help create some templates that teams could use on future projects, based on their learning and experience. Of course, the junior analyst was all too happy to contribute and be a value-adding team member. Years later, they were championing the business analysis center of excellence, which still includes some of those templates and job shadowing guides for anyone doing analysis work at the organization.

So, you can see that you do not have to be a manager or in a management position to start building your leadership qualities. Most leaders are proactive in seeking opportunities in whatever activities are laid out before them. This is your challenge – do you see the opportunity to grow your skills, capabilities, and leadership qualities that you can then use throughout your entire career? Leadership is a role you step up to, not a position you fill. One of the best tools to help you on this journey can be an experienced professional to mentor you through the opportunities and challenges. So, as you think about how many leadership opportunities are presented in your own day-to-day work, let's now explore how having a mentor and building an effective relationship with them can help grow your career exponentially and steer you in the right direction.

The importance of mentorship

Knowing where and when, and especially how, to grow your skills can be challenging if you are trying to do it on your own, especially when talking about leadership and your actions and mindset around others. Leadership skills are not like a subject matter area where you can seek out a particular SME to help answer a quick question. Leadership skills take time to identify, try, reflect on, and adjust. One of the greatest tools in your toolbox can be **mentorship**. You could almost think of mentorship as an analysis technique that enables your leadership skills to be more successful. Mentorship is about getting support in an area of your work and/or life from someone who has more experience and ideas on what is possible. These are often more informal reporting structures. The best mentors are often not your supervisors or anyone you directly report to. These mentors can offer an unbiased perspective that can truly give you insight into any situation or opportunity. They are an outsider who, with the right person selected, only has your best interest in mind.

Mentorship is extremely important, particularly for those pursuing any sort of business analysis career. This is due to two key concepts. First, consider that business analysis work is not always going to be an assigned BA role or even called an analyst position. If you follow your passions based on the type of work you do rather than a position title, you could see your career take many turns in different directions.

Having someone you can talk through scenarios with and ask the *"What if?"* questions becomes extremely valuable because they can often provide an outsider or unbiased perspective, especially when you have mentors who have various experiences in those industries, project types, work environments, and more. You get insight into what might be possible with the different positions and can analyze how much analysis work would be required. These are key data points to help make informed decisions. And mentors are great sources of this needed information!

The second part of how valuable mentorship can be to your career is when you advance into more senior positions in your organization. These positions often involve more strategic perspectives and broader enterprise views. Here, leadership qualities begin to emerge with a much bigger consideration for your success than your original analysis positions, which might have been simple, clear-cut analysis assignments. Your data-driven decisions are going to evolve to dealing with personalities, balancing different departments' goals, managing conflict, and more. The situations are no longer textbook-based scenarios that have right or wrong answers. Every day will give you situations where *"It depends"* is the answer to everything. Having a resource available to you in a mentor, someone you can simply turn to and ask about a scenario, will help you stay focused on your goals of adding value and get you over the hurdles you will face as you expand your skills and impact on the organization.

Using analysis techniques to explore leadership

While you work so hard to apply analysis skills in your daily work to benefit your organization, remember that those same skills are incredibly helpful for your own career moves. When you find a mentor who can talk to you about your analysis career and what is possible, walk into that relationship with the same purpose and focus you would use for any project or new initiative. For instance, when you meet someone you enjoy talking to who has the potential to be a great reference, start your analysis work. Use document analysis to learn more about their career and focus areas. If you can review any of their work or at least accolades, it will help to see where they might be coming from if you seek them out for guidance. Then, do not hesitate to create some evaluation criteria to use as you both research and meet further with the potential mentor.

Things can start like any other basic business relationship where you have similar interests or your work has you crossing paths frequently. But then consider what acceptance criteria you would need to trust someone to the breadth and depth you need in the analysis career space to make them a good mentor. A *good mentor* is simply someone who can give you insight and support from having *been there, done that*. They do not have to be a senior leader in the organization. Think about starting a new job. Is there someone who recently went through that process and still remembers everything required to get access, get set up to work online, and start performing? Their advice and lessons learned represent one of the simplest forms of mentorship. When you go back to them to ask questions or ideas on whom to talk to or seek more information, that's mentorship! The relationship, the insights, and the commitment to each other in a mentorship relationship can be big or small; it just depends! Know, though, that the more work you put into preparing and building a solid foundation for any relationship, the stronger the relationship will be to add tangible value as you seek advice on your career choices.

Leveraging storyboarding for your own career

If someone passes your acceptance criteria, a great activity to do with your mentor is to storyboard scenarios and even ideas on your career work. Not all of us may use these to define requirements or users' expectations, but regardless, these can be a great tool to walk through situations you might face and get insights and those precious lessons they learned before you ever have to learn the hard way! A **storyboard** is like a comic strip. It has different steps and actions. Each step or portion of the sequence is visually shown or drawn out and described. Then, the sequence of events can be laid out for easy analysis. *Figure 9.2* shows an example storyboard, keeping the steps simple, but giving the mentor a better description of what the analyst is expecting or seeking in their outcomes.

- Introduces self as BA
- Explains the goal of the session
- Everyone understands and is ready

- During the session facilitating engagement
- Everyone is eager and participating and contributing

- Everyone is happy and satisfied with the results
- The team thanks the BA for their hard work to help them all be successful

Figure 9.2 – Example storyboard of an analyst's goals for a workshop

🔍 **Quick tip**: Need to see a high-resolution version of this image? Open this book in the next-gen Packt Reader or view it in the PDF/ePub copy.

🔓 **The next-gen Packt Reader** is included for free with the purchase of this book. Scan the QR code OR go to `packtpub.com/unlock`, then use the search bar to find this book by name. Double-check the edition shown to make sure you get the right one.

Now, the point of this technique is not to just visualize your expectations. Its value is that you have a great conversation artifact that you can use *WITH* your mentor. Use the storyboard to walk through the realities you might face in your analysis work. But then, it can also be a great starting point to explore options and what might be possible given your approach or background. These storyboards are valuable when you actively work them and discuss the possibilities and impacts of your actions.

Don't be afraid to storyboard different scenarios of both what you have done and ideas you are thinking about doing, as these can also be a great way to define your business analysis plans. What do you plan to achieve? How are you going to achieve it? But then, again, sit with your mentor after you execute your plans. How closely did things happen according to your vision? Mapping out your planned work and then comparing it with what actually happened is a great way to course-correct and prepare for future endeavors. Just like your analysis work, having more data, such as the planned versus actual results, makes having an informed conversation with your mentor easier. Don't be afraid to sneak some analysis work into the discussion! In our example in *Figure 9.2*, simply add a row underneath your storyboard for "actual outcomes" and fill in what actually happened at your last facilitated session.

This is a tangible metric to reflect on planned versus actual outcomes. Storyboards can make it so easy to do your retrospectives with your mentor by reflecting on not just what the actual outcomes were and what you wanted, but also what you will do next, given what you experienced.

This is why mentorship can be so powerful, especially if they are not in your direct chain of command for your work. Doing retrospectives with a mentor is not about having someone point out your flaws. These retrospectives differ from your own analysis retrospectives in that it is about you. It is a valuable use of even a relatively short amount of time to analyze your work and think about what else you can do to grow your skills. Finding someone you can talk through both the pros and cons with is a great example of a mentor, as they can push you to think about what else you could have done. You have someone to drive you to think about bigger and better next steps. You can make your own informed decisions about what to do next when you have someone asking *you* good questions!

Use those same techniques you apply in your stakeholder sessions with your mentors. Reach out on chat to see if they are available when you have a question or concern. Then set up an online meeting with your favorite collaboration tool so that you can show them your question or idea. Give them more to work with in their thoughts and ideas with you. Walk them through your process ideas – even create a process model to help show them. The example in *Figure 9.3* is simple but can easily communicate a challenge. In this case, the analyst was getting stuck on selecting which elicitation technique would be best for their project.

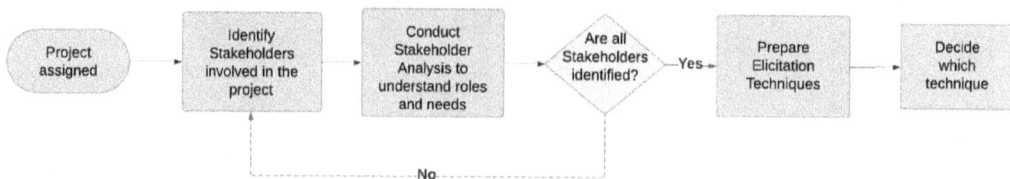

Figure 9.3 – Example analyst's process for preparing for elicitation activities

The model in *Figure 9.3* is great because it shows the mentor the activities the analyst is already doing leading up to the question. Now the conversation is much more focused on the particular part of the analyst's process. But the visual is not the end result. The visual is simply a great facilitating tool to help with the question. The ideas and outcome *WITH* the mentor are the end results. By doing even a simple process model like in *Figure 9.3*, you are actively applying your analysis skills while working on your leadership skills simply by having a great work conversation – how great is that!?

Leadership skills take a lifetime to develop. The work is never done; you simply aim to do better. While this can seem like a daunting reality, know that part of that growing is not just growing your skills, but helping others grow too. It becomes a two-way value-proposition for the relationship, such that each individual finds value. So, consider what you could do to make any of your current professional relationships work well right now. Now let's carry over those thoughts as you explore what is required in an effective mentoring relationship.

Building effective mentoring relationships

Mentorship succeeds when the relationship is not just supported, but fully respected, prioritized, and set up for both growth and long-term success. Like teachers, mentors deepen their knowledge and even identify their own areas of improvement when they share what they know with others. They get the opportunity to turn their past experiences into true lessons learned by helping you apply those lessons in your work. They get an outlet to share their own brilliance with others so that more good can be done. Just like your analysis work with your stakeholders, the collaborative value of your analysis work is often exponentially more beneficial than when done solo. So, where do you start?

Finding a mentor – the hardest challenge

Finding a great mentor can be almost more challenging than your analysis work ever is. This is because of the foundation riding on a strong relationship. Rarely do you find a good mentor by putting a wanted ad out for "mentor for analysis career." More often, you meet great people in your career journey and start to have good conversations with them. You will begin to connect at multiple events and perhaps share the same professional circles. As discussed in earlier chapters, the power of networking at professional events is not just to learn about technologies or new techniques. These events are where you can meet people who are more seasoned in their analysis careers and have a variety of experiences in different areas of businesses or even industries that just might be the perspective you are looking for in your own work. Add to your networking questions some great analysis questions to help you research and do great stakeholder analysis (yes – you *can* do business analysis work while networking at professional social events!). Ask things such as the following:

- What interests them?
- What is their background?
- What are they wanting to do with their career?
- How do they plan to grow in the coming year?
- What have been their biggest challenges? How did they overcome them?

Great questions are *always* valued, no matter where your analysis work takes you. So, then ask some more great questions. But do *not* dive right in and ask, "Will you be my mentor?"! This is too broad an ask with unknown scope and no acceptance criteria or definition of done. Instead, first ask about some of their work and what they are interested in doing. And then feel free to answer those same questions and share with them. Then, if the other person is interested and even excited about talking about those elements, ask if they would be interested in connecting to talk about each other's work some more, beyond the current conversation. Mentorship relationships can be very agile in their development as they can start with small meetings. Perhaps they are informal over coffee or a quick Zoom or MS Teams call. Don't be afraid to share more personal concepts of your work and just learn from each other at first. You do not need to specifically ask them to be your mentor. You can work with someone and be guided and helped by them throughout your career and never call them a mentor. You can take the responsibility to ensure both parties get value out of the relationship without ever labeling the relationship.

But, once you start to build a rapport with the other person, ask for more specific, tangible outcomes. A healthy habit at the end of every call or conversation with your mentor is to set up the time and format to meet next. Putting something on the calendar helps you both invest in the relationship. This investment is needed to then grow the relationship into a value-building asset in your analysis career.

Building the relationship

As you get a great support system set up and configured, then it's on you to invest and nurture this wonderful source of wisdom. A mentorship relationship will give you as good as you give it. What this means is that you will need to do some analysis work to understand your mentor. What are their challenges? What are they facing in their position and context? Being naturally curious about them just as much as they ask you questions is actually a great way to build value in the relationship. You get great analysis practice at asking good questions, and they get space to share and articulate what work they are doing. If you have ever had to conduct training or help show someone how to do something, you will realize really quickly what you do and do not know. What do you not know about their work? What could you find out to understand their perspective better so that you can really get some tailored help from their unique perspective?

Then plan in your actual discussions with the same vigor you plan your facilitation sessions or requirements workshops. Consider the following items as a great checklist that will maximize both the investment in the relationship and nurture a longer-lasting relationship:

1. What is the goal of the meeting?

2. What do you want to accomplish?

3. What questions do you want answered?

    Example: What feedback do they have on your approach for working with certain stakeholders?

4. What have you accomplished lately (or since last meeting)?

5. Be accountable to the mentor for any prior discussions.

    Example: Utilized a new technique using mind maps at the facilitation session last week and found it engaged the stakeholders more on the project than they had been the prior week.

6. Where do you see your challenges? Or, where do you have unknowns?

7. Where can the mentor provide the most insight?

    Example: Wanting to know if smaller focus groups might be better for the next stakeholder sessions, or is there a better technique you should be using that you have not thought of?

8. What are your measures of success?

9. What will make you feel accomplished? Feel good?

10. What validation of your effort do you think you might be able to obtain before the next meeting?

    Example: Able to get consensus in the single stakeholder workshop versus having 2 or 3 more meetings to confirm stakeholders' decisions.

11. What are you going to *DO* before the next time you meet with your mentor?

12. Be clear on what actions *YOU* are taking for yourself.

    Example: Create a template to guide participants in the session and send for feedback prior to running the event.

NOTE

Do *NOT* try to tell the mentor what to do – let them offer up anything they are willing to do!

---

13. Set up the next meeting time. Schedule it before you end your call or meeting to build in the accountability.

Now, here is also where you can practice building those leadership skills. Even if you have an informal relationship, treat it with all the formality of meeting with your CEO. This means simply respecting the mentor's time – show up early to each meeting and make time in case the conversation lingers after the scheduled time. Show your analysis skills and maybe even remember their favorite tea or the way they take their coffee so it is ready when you meet. Prepare for each meeting. Do not fly in at the last minute but let them know you planned around their valuable time to be focused and not distracted. Taking the discussion seriously also encourages your mentor to take the time just as seriously. You are modeling out the behavior you expect of others, and that is exactly what leaders do! If you want quality time with a senior or experienced person, be just as committed, if not more, to their time. Keep this as a healthy habit, as walking the walk of the talk you talk is critical, not just for your current stakeholders but all stakeholders you interact with along the way.

So, what makes a *good mentor*? This is one of those hard questions when looking for a mentor, but easy in hindsight. What this means is that you know you have a good mentor when it works. Mentorship is a collaborative process. That means asking whether you are giving as much as you are getting and seeing that both parties benefit. As you build relationships with others and seek to make quality time for great discussions, use some of these metrics to help you analyze the value of the time spent with others:

- Do you each come prepared to meet?

- Do you each ask inquisitive questions of the other person?

- Are you truly interested in what the other party has to say?

- Are conversations exploratory in nature (seeking understanding versus being judging or critical)?

- Is there motivation and excitement to "do" something after the discussion?

- Do you leave discussions with a list of action items?

- Are you accountable to each other the next time you meet on those action items?

- Do you stay accountable and schedule your next touchpoints (and keep them!)?

As you can tell, these questions can be answered only after you've been meeting your mentor and letting your relationship develop organically. This relationship building is more important than the position or title of your mentor. Again, this is all regardless of positional titles. My best mentors never had the title of business analyst nor even knew what it was, in some cases! Consider a few examples of different positions and how they looked at mentorship opportunities from the lens of a business analysis professional. These are all real-world scenarios I found in my own analysis work. While you may not be the BA in these positions, notice how each of the working relationships with these types of stakeholders not only sought but often created opportunities to incorporate mentorship and guidance into their daily analysis work:

- **The PMO manager**: She was excited to build up business analysis capabilities in the organization, in and outside the PMO office. She sought out ways she could both support as well as learn of opportunities for business analysis work. She would join me (as the BA) and the project manager, both in-person as well as virtually, on project discussions to learn what we were doing in our approaches. But then she often would share some great ideas and encourage new techniques while providing much-needed guidance on tough scenarios. Just being present in the conversation also showed her support of us while allowing her to expand her own ideas.

- **The seasoned business coach**: She had years of work experience and provided advice on lessons learned (*many learned the hard way!*). Conversations were fluid and always about whatever topic I wanted to address, though she would ask what I had accomplished since the last time we spoke. She also pushed me to define goals and objectives through bi-weekly virtual meetings, which were great accountability check-ins.

- **The junior analyst**: Imagine a team lucky enough to get a number of brand-new business analysis professionals right out of college. New to the positions and even corporate work, they kept asking great questions and wanted to know more about the work we were collaborating on. Their insightful questions on project-based work made me challenge myself to think about what optimal approaches might be, as well as best ways to explain our value-adding work. Then during the informal coffees and lunch appointments with the junior staff, we explored the ideas they were excited about, which pushed me to consider my own development path as we discussed what they were looking forward to in this new position.

- **The manager who was also a leader**: We had one-on-one walking meetings where they inquired about what I wanted to do in the position, not just the assigned work. We worked to explore opportunities and seek alignment of the work we were doing with personal goals through informal conversations with concrete follow-up action items on my part. While informal, it gave me a safe space to share ideas while getting constructive feedback, so if I tried a new approach or structure, these conversations with my manager gave me insight and advice so I could be successful when I tried to execute the new ideas.

- **The conference colleague**: A fellow conference attendee at a professional organizational event had similar goals and passions as mine, discovered during breaks and networking time. Monthly calls were then scheduled to meet and simply talk about whatever was going on, yet it energized and excited each of us, even though we were on different paths and goals. It was a safe space to share ideas, get feedback, and see what others were thinking.

These are just a sampling of the types of relationships you can have. While in-person events can feel very conducive to building relationships, others can simply be found online. Sure, you can simply set up a meeting online with your mentor and show up fully present. But then also consider those you follow on LinkedIn (`https://www.linkedin.com/`), for example. Newsletters and posts are great sources of mentorship, especially if you can reach out and ask questions. Mentors have a positive influence on your work. Who are you following online that gives you inspiration and motivates you to take action (that's the important part!)? Or, what about those professional online communities where you can both share questions and provide feedback on ideas? These are great places to seek out information. While these may not feel as personal as a one-to-one, in-person relationship, they can be great sources to help you find a mentor when you have complementary interests and motivations. That collaborative space where everyone is working to lift each other up is the exact definition of a healthy mentorship environment. Just realize you can give just as much value to others as you receive when you are fully committed to professional growth!

Supporting the next generation

Now, the final element in considering how mentorship can best support your career is when you ensure the exponential value of the relationships you have by creating relationships with the next generation of analysis professionals. Just like your own journey, start informally and find opportunities to connect with junior professionals or those just starting out in analysis work. Go to events they go to or, even better, start inviting them to professional events you go to. It is so much easier to meet people at events or know how to navigate conferences if you have someone there guiding you. You could even ask to join their meetings or workshops. Having a second hand to support you is great when you are a junior analyst. Even getting a colleague to go with you to an event can be a great way to unpack and reflect on both the content and the process you both experienced. Feedback is a gift that continuously boosts your career, so seek it out, as well as giving it out as often as possible. Think how great it is when someone joins your work meetings and then tells you how effective your approach or certain activities were, as they could see your stakeholders get excited and really enjoy the work they were doing! Just like that, you will start becoming a mentor yourself.

Refer back and think about that same power and inspiration you got from your mentor. You now get to share learning opportunities with someone who does not have to learn the hard way. You get asked questions from unique and novel perspectives that you might not have ever thought of yourself. You get to practice your own value proposition for business analysis and have a successful analysis career when you explain it to others. You start demonstrating what a mentor looks like without even being asked. The value of your time spent with others will be value added in those future generations that your own mentee might mentor themselves.

Summary

Leadership and mentorship often go hand in hand. Leaders are great mentors to others. Most mentors have great leadership qualities ingrained into their daily work. You will need both throughout your career. Mentors can give you great ideas when challenged by stakeholders or trying to incorporate technology or methodologies in your work. They are a perfect sounding board to ask scenario and "what if" questions to get real-world feedback.

Mentors are not about finding the right person, per se. In fact, you will have a number of mentors who come in and out of your life as you work through your career. Rather, reflect on how much your leadership skills will grow and mentorship relationships will blossom by analyzing your own skills and where you want to take your work. A great action right now is to ask yourself truly where you are and where you want to be in all aspects of your work. Having a realistic, analyzed perspective of where you are, even if you're just starting your analysis career, is what will help you target finding contexts that support your goals.

Mentors are a great unbiased source to give you thoughts on your career choices. It is so much easier to have someone by your side as you navigate your professional journey. What comes out of this leadership discussion is that you need to continually learn and develop professionally to be successful throughout your career. The next chapter will dive into these concepts further so that you can plan out your professional growth and where to find these valuable resources so that you don't just focus on growing your leadership skills but challenge yourself to grow in all areas of your analysis work.

Further reading

- International Institute for Business Analysis® (IIBA®), (2015). *The Business Analysis Body of Knowledge® (BABOK®) Guide*. International Institute of Business Analysis, Toronto, Ontario, Canada.

Unlock this book's exclusive benefits now

Scan this QR code or go to `packtpub.com/unlock`, then search for this book by name.

Note: Keep your purchase invoice ready before you start.

Part 4:
The Future of Your Business Analysis Work

In the last part, you look at what the future can hold for you and your business analysis work. You will begin by exploring how to create a professional development plan that ensures you continue growing and expanding your skills wherever your career may take you. You will also examine the emerging trends – what, where, how, and why analysis work is evolving and is still more relevant than ever before as an in-demand skill set. With guidance on how to assess, measure, and plan your career decisions, the final part of this book leaves you with key action items to immediately consider how great your analysis career can be, whatever direction you choose.

This part has the following chapters:

- *Chapter 10, Continuous Learning and Professional Development*
- *Chapter 11, Emerging Trends and the Future of Business Analysis*
- *Chapter 12, Assessments and Techniques for Career Success*
- *Chapter 13, Final Thoughts and Next Steps*

10
Continuous Learning and Professional Development

One of the most powerful skills of successful business analysis professionals is the ability to quickly learn and adapt to almost any environment or context. Regardless of whether you change position, departments, industry, or entire career paths, you will want to pick up your new context as quickly as possible. This will help you focus on the solution space versus spending time understanding the vocabulary or terminology of the analysis area. Now, you want to apply that same approach of quickly learning and understanding your solution space to your career. As a practicing professional, your skills, insights, and successes should also grow as both you and your work evolve. The best way to ensure your skills never stagnate is to be continuously learning. Regardless of the domain, technique, or skill, finding areas of growth is essential to a long and prosperous analysis career. Then, building a plan that you measure against, supported with valuable career resources, is how you ensure the success of your career planning.

In this chapter, we're going to cover the following main topics:

- Identifying the importance of lifelong learning
- Creating a professional development plan
- Utilizing professional resources

Advancing your analysis career through lifelong learning

As you work in an environment that is focused on bringing change to deliver value, recognize that the one constant throughout your work is going to be change. Even if you do not change, the world around you is constantly changing. That means if you fail to evolve, you may no longer be adding the value you once did. Technology is changing, organizations are changing, and even industries are changing. Are you keeping up? The more knowledgeable you are about these changes and solution spaces, the more valuable your contributions will be, and therefore, the more valuable your solutions will be. But that means you have to continue to improve your knowledge at a rate that lets you compete with the world around you.

Learning for your business analysis career

When it comes to learning business analysis to make you a competitive analyst qualified for senior positions, there are two considerations: the growth of your business analysis skills and the growth in your context area. Growth in your business analysis skills means focusing on learning as much as you can about business analysis work. Primarily, learning what the most commonly performed tasks are and how to execute them can be critical to the success of your business analysis work. But even more critical is learning the techniques business analysis professionals frequently rely on to be successful in their change work and assigned initiatives. Now, *learning* in the context of your career success means that you don't just identify these tasks and techniques but are able to execute and apply them correctly. The body of knowledge out there, like the *Business Analysis Body of Knowledge (BABOK®) Guide* (IIBA®, 2015), can tell you what these tasks and techniques are and describe them in greater detail. Professional development courses, especially live ones with a facilitating instructor, are great ways to be introduced, guided through, and then given the opportunity to practice these activities. And then, of course, career opportunities are the best way to apply the concepts with support from leadership and mentors to help you analyze your outcomes via lessons learned and retrospectives. This enables continuous improvement and learning.

Now you can also focus your professional development on the solution space in which you perform your analysis work. For example, working as a technical business analyst in the IT department, learning more about the infrastructure the organization uses, the security postures and configurations in place, the backup and recovery procedures and facilities, and other technical elements specific to your organization can help you align and deliver solutions faster and more accurately. Even learning about the capabilities of the organization can be incredibly valuable in keeping you more informed in your analysis work. Doing this might require spending time with the different groups in the IT department, talking with leadership, attending status update meetings, and reviewing quarterly update materials and presentations. You are learning more about your work context. As you do, though, you will learn about different IT topics, such as virtualization, hosting solutions, and even perhaps machine learning and AI. Now, for these, your learning may require you to do some additional training or perhaps take some online courses to understand what these concepts are and how people apply them to the IT work in organizations.

Being in an advisory role, doing research on current trends, and frequently reading the latest articles and trade publications can help you feel knowledgeable and apply data-driven decision-making. The more you aim to learn throughout your career journey, in general, the more tools you will have in your toolbox to reference and support your work. Not to mention, constantly staying passionate about design and solution ideas will help you positively stand out from others as a truly valuable business asset to any organization! So, let's now explore a few ideas to help you better think about what business case makes the most sense for your career choices.

An example of learning and applying what you have learned in business analysis work

An organization has a department of business analysts. They have a business analysis manager and a team of five business analysts. The work that they do is all project-related and they are assigned to the top-priority projects of the organization. Their manager walks through the project portfolio with other senior managers, and the highest-priority projects get a business analyst assigned to help ensure project success. The expected job duties, in general, are the same for every project: define the requirements, trace them through design, and facilitate UAT into production, assisting in any troubleshooting, as required. Now, the projects themselves constantly change in context, scope, and products or services. Any business analyst on the team is expected to use their skills to best support achieving the business outcome, regardless of where they are assigned.

One business analyst sees the pressure of the requirements and the testing phases. They see that the better the requirements are defined, the easier the UAT processes become. Because of this, they tell their manager that they want to focus on increasing their requirements capabilities for the year. They propose that they could measure the increase in capabilities by the number of requirement changes, the number of original test cases created, and the number of test cases actually used. The analyst takes online courses that explain how to elicit, define, verify, and validate requirements with stakeholders. They immediately start to apply the techniques and approaches they learn in the online courses in their elicitation and validation sessions in their current projects. The analyst starts tracking metrics back to those goals to see whether they can improve these metrics as they progress with each project. After a year of working on these projects, the metrics show that the analyst has a lower number of change requests on their project than a comparable project. They also received stakeholder feedback that the UAT period ran successfully, as the team had a few prior projects where stakeholders were frustrated with inefficient UAT processes.

In a follow-up with the manager, the analyst discusses what they did that helped make the project successful and why it felt smooth in execution. Along with these details, the manager inquires how the analyst can take these learnings and extrapolate them to the team. The analyst prepares a presentation to demonstrate some of their techniques, as well as sharing some of their learnings from the online courses with the business analyst team at their monthly *lunch and learn*. The analyst, with their presentation and follow-up with their manager, then defines the next areas they want to work on in their elicitation skills and follows the same approach so that they are continuously learning and growing and modeling a culture of continuous improvement that leads to successful analysis teams.

Diversifying your skills

Business analysis is luckily one of those skill sets that is useful wherever your career takes you. The hardest part of your work is deciding what you want to *DO* with your career. You might want to go back to the discussions we had earlier about specialization and designing a roadmap and ask: *what do I need to learn to be successful in those endeavors?*

Often, you will find opportunities and tools you can add to your toolbox that are not limited to business analysis. Working within a team requires leadership, negotiation, and great communication skills, not to mention a lot of patience! Learning team dynamics and personality styles to better understand your stakeholders and how to engage with them for successful outcomes can be great facets to add to your toolbox.

Even exploring deeper into project management and technology development methodologies, financial business acumen, and strategic planning skills can be valuable areas to build your competencies, helping you grow from a good analyst to a great one. Again, none of these are tied directly to business analysis work or business analysis positions, so they can help your career in whichever direction you choose to take it. But it pays to be strategic and aligning your time and financial investments with the career steps that will help you reach your goals. So, let's now look at how you can craft a professional development plan that will help you develop what is best for your chosen career path.

Creating a professional development plan

Creating a professional development plan is a great way to build learning into your work so that it is a planned and, therefore, well-executed part of your analysis work and not an afterthought that often gets skipped for higher-priority work. Using the product roadmap from *Chapter 9*, it can be easy to start with a simple structure of **Now**, **Next**, **Later**, and **Not Now**, as laid out in *Table 10.1*. In the **Now** column, think about what you need to know to be successful in your current work. For example, if you were just assigned a new project in a business area you have never worked in before, such as the marketing department, then in the **Now** column, you could note "learn about marketing". In the **Next** column, you note that you want to improve your requirements analysis skills as you are getting good at the elicitation portion in your previous work. For **Later**, you could note learning more about facilitation with teams, adding it to your roadmap as you recognize how much you like working in project teams. Now, just like your career roadmap, having space to recognize good ideas that might be helpful – even if you're unsure how they fit your career path – will help prevent you from getting distracted. This is what the **Not Now** column is for. This way, you don't forget about the topic but will wait until you have a more direct application to expend resources on the learning effort. In our example in *Table 10.1*, we added project management methodologies to the **Not Now** column as this is not our focus right now in our analysis work, nor in our career paths, but it might be helpful sometime later.

Now	Next	Later	Not Now
Learn about marketing	Improve requirements analysis skills	Grow facilitation knowledge and skills	Project management methodologies

Table 10.1 – Professional development plan roadmap example

Use the roadmap to help you lay out your concepts. Don't be afraid to fill it with all kinds of ideas. You can always add more to the **Later** and **Not Now** columns whenever an idea strikes you, but ensure you keep **Now**, and even the items in the **Next** column, strategically aligned to your current career goals. Again, we want to ensure we do not waste any time, although generally, any learning is good learning. Remember, you are a business analysis professional! Therefore, you want to maximize the value out of everything you do, and alignment is part of your success story.

But as we have described, there are a number of ways you can integrate learning as part of your professional development. Once you have mapped out many of the things you want to do, take a look at what ended up in your **Now** column. Think about *HOW* you are going to execute them. Going back to our example in *Table 10.1*, consider the desire to learn more about marketing. You have marketing projects coming up; even though you are the analyst responsible for requirements, you would like to know about how the marketing team operates, what their threats and opportunities are, how their processes operate, and more. So now think about how you could learn about marketing. Using some good old brainstorming, here is a list of some of the approaches (in this case, techniques!) you might consider:

- Interviews (formal or informal) with marketing staff
- Observation (job shadowing) of current marketing staff
- Document analysis (reviewing existing materials) from the marketing department
- Lessons learned sessions, with other business analysts and subject matter experts (SMEs) who worked on marketing projects before
- Formal training (live or pre-recorded courses, online materials, or programs) on marketing related content
- Informal training (mentorship and peer reviews) on common marketing activities
- Certifications (studying and applying as part of certification process) that may be directly or indirectly related to marketing activities
- Conferences (business analysis, trade, and leadership) to connect with both marketing professionals and other analysts attending the same events

These are just a sampling of techniques you can consider. Even though these are focused on marketing, in our example in *Table 10.1*, these techniques could apply to any topic area you are interested in learning more about. There are many more ways to think about how you can best learn and build your knowledge of your solution spaces. But to be a good analyst, start with a list of ideas on how you can deliver on your professional development goals. Once you have this great starting point, you will want to think through the value proposition story for each approach to help you consider what works best given your context, opportunities, and more. What this means is to essentially storyboard each target on your roadmap (introduced in *Chapter 9*). Walk through not just what you will do but *HOW* you will both prepare and measure your success. Take, for instance, the desire to take a business analysis training class. As a growing professional, you would not simply "take a class." Your storyboard might look more like *Figure 10.1*:

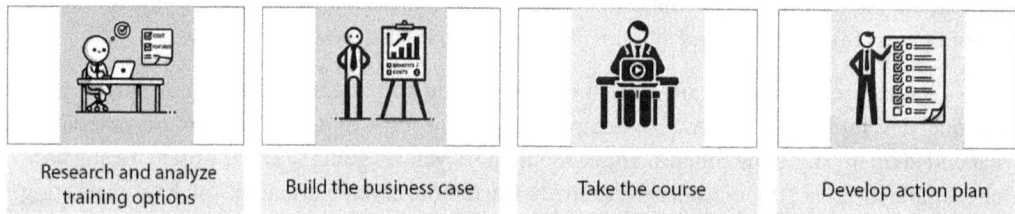

| Research and analyze training options | Build the business case | Take the course | Develop action plan |

Figure 10.1 – Storyboard example of professional development activity

First, you would research and analyze the training options, in terms of both features and costs. Then, you would build your business case for taking the course (and getting your employer to cover the expenses!). Upon approval, you would, of course, take the course. Then, upon completion, you would develop your action plan. You would want your action plan to have measurements in there so that you can compare actuals with this plan. This might include presenting concepts and ideas to your team once a month so that they can get some value out of your learning as well. Let's see what this would look like with the following example.

Example business case approach to professional development

Consider the goal that you want to start using AI more in your business analysis work. You are unsure of how best to incorporate it, so you are seeking training to help. You start by researching available training options for incorporating AI into business analysis. This includes the following:

- Comparing self-paced courses (like LinkedIn Learning and Pluralsight), instructor-led options (like IIBA webinars, live bootcamps, and training such as with Champagne Collaborations), and academic certifications (like Coursera/edX programs).

- Reviewing cost, duration, content, and alignment to your current tools and goals (e.g., ChatGPT for requirements elicitation, prompt engineering, etc.).

- Evaluating value: Which programs offer tangible takeaways? Do they come with templates, case studies, or community support?

For ease of comparison, you create a matrix to lay out the options clearly, as in *Table 10.2*. This requires not only outlining the types of training but also identifying the pros and cons and the costs in terms of both money and time and then considering what each option offers and how it relates to your work.

Type of Training	Pros	Cons	Cost (USD)	Duration	Content	Alignment to BA Work
Self-paced online course	Flexible schedule, often lower cost, on-demand access to materials	Limited interaction, motivation needed to complete, no feedback loop	$50–300	2–10 hours	• Intro to AI concepts • Prompt engineering basics • Using AI in requirements gathering	High for practical tasks, especially quick wins with tools like ChatGPT
Instructor-led workshop	Real-time interaction, ability to ask questions, hands-on practice	Time-bound, may require time off work, limited ongoing access	$300–1,000	1–3 days	• Live demos of AI tools • Group exercises for AI-driven analysis • Case studies and Q&A	Very high if tailored to BA roles, great for immediate team implementation
Academic certification program	Comprehensive curriculum, credible certification, structured learning	Expensive, time-intensive, may include non-relevant content	$1,000+	4–12 weeks	• Technical foundations of AI • Applied AI in business contexts • Projects and assessments	High-level strategy and theory, useful for career growth but less task-specific

Table 10.2 – Training comparison table

Now, with the options more clearly defined, it makes it easy to pitch your business case. Your email to your manager might look like the following business case:

Recommendation:

After evaluating multiple types of training options for incorporating AI into business analysis work, I recommend enrolling in a live, instructor-led workshop focused specifically on the use of AI tools (such as ChatGPT, Gemini, and other generative AI technologies) for common BA activities like requirements elicitation, stakeholder communication, and backlog refinement.

Rationale:

While self-paced courses offer affordability and flexibility, and academic certifications provide in-depth, strategic understanding, a live workshop offers the best alignment with our immediate business goals:

It delivers hands-on, real-time guidance for applying AI in our daily analysis work.

It provides immediate feedback and interaction, helping ensure real comprehension and team alignment.

It allows us to bring back and apply tangible examples, templates, and shared best practices quickly and efficiently.

Current Challenge:

Our team is exploring ways to increase productivity and innovation through AI, but we lack a clear and confident approach to using AI effectively in our BA workflows.

Opportunity:

Participating in this workshop provides immediate skills to:

Streamline requirements gathering and documentation

Facilitate more dynamic and responsive stakeholder engagement

Experiment with AI-generated user stories, personas, and models to save time and enhance creativity

Anticipated Benefits:

Benefit	Description
Increased efficiency	Reduce time spent drafting documentation by 20–30% using AI-assisted generation
Knowledge sharing	Enable team learning through monthly knowledge transfers post-training
Strategic positioning	Prepare our BA team to proactively lead digital transformation efforts

Cost Justification:

Estimated cost for the workshop: $750.

Expected return in efficiency gains over one quarter: ~$2,000+ in saved BA hours.

Intangible benefits include team capability uplift, innovation culture reinforcement, and competitive edge in project delivery.

Conclusion:

This investment in training is not only low-risk and cost-effective but also directly aligns with our team's operational goals. It positions us to be proactive in using modern tools to deliver even more value through our business analysis work.

With this great proposal, you get the approval, so now you would enroll in the course and actively do things such as the following:

- Block calendar time to complete learning modules
- Take notes, save examples, and ask course instructors or peers about real business analysis application scenarios
- If using a course provider like LinkedIn Learning, download the exercise files and apply them to your current project work

With this complete, now comes the most important part – your action plan! *Table 10.3* shows a proposed action plan to implement learnings from the AI training, with baseline measurements and space to track post-training results that you could review with your manager in multiple touchpoints to both measure and demonstrate the value the training is bringing not only to you but also to your company:

Action	Timeline	Measurement Criteria	Baseline (Before Training)	Actual Results (Post-Training)
Share a summary presentation of course learnings	Within two weeks of course completion	Presentation completed and shared with BA team	No AI-related presentations delivered	
Apply at least one AI technique in a live project	Within one month of course completion	Documented AI usage in project artifacts (e.g., requirements, user stories)	No AI techniques documented in any live projects	
Create a team prompt library for ChatGPT	Within six weeks of course completion	Number of prompts added to team library	No centralized prompt library in place	

Action	Timeline	Measurement Criteria	Baseline (Before Training)	Actual Results (Post-Training)
Deliver a monthly "AI Quick Tip" for three months	Monthly for three months	Number of tips shared, and feedback collected from team	No recurring knowledge-sharing initiatives	

Table 10.3 – Example action plan to quantify the ROI of training investments

This kind of detail might seem extraneous, but it serves two purposes that are critical to your business analysis career. First, doing this kind of exercise planning allows you to extract the value out of any decision or action – the same approach you'll use in actual business analysis. So, basically, you get to practice the principles of your work by applying them to your career. Second, the business analysis professionals aim to get the most value out of every effort they make. Planning how you will deliver results from your investment in professional development is another way to demonstrate the value you bring. The more you can do this, the more you will build your value-delivery mindset, which is critical to successful business analysis professionals! But don't stop at planning. Continue to use your plans throughout your analysis work and career adventures!

Using your professional development plan

Once you have a great professional development plan thought out and detailed, the trick is to use it. It is like buying a great tool. If you just leave it in the toolbox and never take it out, you are not getting your value. As a business analysis professional, you want maximum value in everything you do, so time to work out the plan!

First, you want to know what is on your plan and what you are trying to work toward. That means making time to review and revisit your plan often. It can be as simple as blocking time on your calendar once a month to review your plan. This is why lists, or product roadmaps, are helpful because you want some way to track your goals and ideas. But then, more importantly, you want to track the activities in working toward them. Now, how you track them can vary; you want to approach your plan the same way that you do your analysis work: follow the approach that works for you. Everyone's plans can be different, and that's okay. The way you ensure that your plan and the actual outcomes add value is to make your development plan an action-focused resource. The key to being successful with this action-focused approach is to define specific, measurable targets to compare the planned values to the actuals. This is most easily done with dates for your key deliverables.

The first part is the planning and estimation of the work. Deadlines drive results. Period. You need to commit to dates. In your analysis work, you will have to do lots of estimation activities. These estimates need to be confident enough that others can base their decisions on them. This means every chance you get to practice estimating your analysis work will help improve your ability to estimate project- and operations-related work. So, you plan the work and assign it to yourself as actionable tasks with imposed due dates.

Now, those estimations have a purpose as they allow you to measure your success against a clear metric, which is the second part of an action-focused development plan. **Planned versus actuals** are key measurements to use for any process improvement effort and lead to successful retrospective sessions, which we will talk through shortly. These measurements simply mean that you measure the work in the same manner as you estimated. That is, if a task was planned to be completed in two weeks, then measure the actual time taken. If a task was thought to include four focus groups completed by the end of the fourth quarter, then record the number of focus groups you completed by the end of the fourth quarter. It's really simple – no overthinking this! The biggest trick is just to remember to measure the same thing as what you defined in the estimate so that you can accurately compare the actuals to what was planned.

So, you need to work to identify the key things that will be completed for all your planned efforts. Make these as quantifiable as possible. For instance, "research business analysis training options" is good, but what is the deliverable? This is doing work, but what is the return? It is better to define the planned actions in terms of what can be completed. A better option might be to "identify" the business analysis training you wish to take, or even "get approval" for the identified training program you are interested in. Examples like these can be found in the first two columns of *Table 10.4* to give you some ideas. Notice the use of a monthly cadence in the example. This is just one way to structure your time. Use any approach that has a clearly defined date, though, as this will not only hold you accountable but also be crucial for what we look at next.

True value is derived from the professional development plan when you not only use it to guide your actions but also measure your success against it. The plan gives you direction. If you are a good analyst and course correct based on how your actual work turned out compared to what you planned, then the plan is the record of your development. In *Table 10.4*, you can see some examples of deliverables or milestones for a calendar year. Some are simple – there's no need to over-analyze! Simply look at the planned completions and what was actually completed.

But again, the power lies in not only comparing what you actually accomplished versus what your goals were but also defining specific actions you can take. This is true lessons learned. Even though you compared your planned actions to your actual outcomes, you now need to ask yourself, "So what?" Do not assume it is obvious. You may measure and see that there is improvement, but you always need to ask what this improvement means. So, what improved your skills? What are you now going to *DO* with those improved skills? What did you identify in business analysis training, as in our example in *Table 10.2*? It might seem overly detailed and too explicit to write out all the specifics of both the measurements and the action plan, but this is exactly what is needed for change efforts. You are practicing being good at measuring the business value delivered to an organization so far and then asking the strategic questions of what the next best action would be to leverage the opportunity or mitigate and handle the threat of underperformance. Lots of people can talk the talk, but only the best walk the walk. Compare your actuals to your plan. Then, you can course-correct based on experience to either ensure those good outcomes are sustained or to adjust so that you do eventually achieve the desired outcomes.

Month	Planned Completion	Actual Completions	Actions
January	Identify business analysis training	Identified business analysis training	- Update professional development plan - Define date to present to business analysis team
February	Join IIBA	Joined in January for discounted training	- Update annual budget to include membership for entire team
March			
April	Attend at least one business analysis conference		
May			
June	Complete business analysis training program		
July			
August			
September	Provide two presentations to the business analysis and project management teams		
October			
November	Build next year's professional development plan		
December	Review and confirm updated development plan with manager		

Table 10.4 – Professional development action plan example

Following the example presented in *Table 10.4*, you would then set a review time for the beginning of each month to reflect on the prior month's activities. Committing to that review means a commitment to the value of not just planning but your professional development. Even if your organization only does performance reviews on an annual basis, asking your manager or supervisor to sit down monthly and walk through this kind of structure would further leverage the business value of this approach. Your manager or supervisor would get a better sense of what you have been doing, which is excellent for helping you to get promoted and showcase where you have been adding value. But also, they might have broader insights into opportunities that might be on the horizon to adjust your plan based on the successes you have had so far. Look at your professional development plan and see it as an active, living thing that is accessed often to keep you on track. It is not a "one and done" or "to be filed away" report. It is a guide, a roadmap, and an interactive reporting structure that you can actively use to ensure you not only stay focused in your professional development but also are verifying and validating your professional growth. It really is a great way to practice more business analysis activities by applying them to your own career. Consider, though, that you do not have to execute your development plan in a vacuum. There are lots of resources to support your endeavors that let you look at not only what is available to support your learning but also how to leverage these resources as you work through your development plan.

Utilizing professional resources

Your professional development roadmap helps you plan out what you want to do. Professional resources are then the essential tools that enable you to achieve those goals. When you are junior in your career, you might look to your boss or immediate supervisor for ideas on how to best develop. Senior leaders can be great sources of information if you want to grow in your organization. They can give you insight into the skill sets needed to execute the strategic work at the organization while advising on opportunities to grow your leadership qualities by knowing what work is in on the horizon.

But then, also reach out to your mentors. Share your development plans with them for their insights. Having someone outside your organization give you input is a great way to keep your entire career in mind, not just your current employment, as they will have outside perspectives on the market, industry, and even simply what is going on in your regional area. Mentors who are in the business analysis profession but in different industries can provide insights on how to grow your analysis skills from a different perspective. With business analysis being such a transferable skill, you can get insights on techniques and approaches that can be applied no matter what type of project work or even industry you are engaged in. These are all great conversations that equip you with strategic elements for your development plan.

Now, from a tactical perspective, training or taking courses is a very common activity to place on your professional development plan. Formal learning can introduce you to concepts that are new to you and give you the structure to apply them to your own work. Formal learning is easy because it often comes with indicators of success. But learning happens in multiple areas. Look beyond basic schooling through universities or even training providers. Consider what experiences you can get. Are there opportunities to explore not just tasks and techniques but different methodologies, approaches, or industries, and even leadership and facilitation events you can participate in? Even something as simple as helping take notes or managing virtual breakout rooms for another analyst could be an activity. It provides the opportunity to experience perhaps a senior analyst's approach to a requirements workshop or for you to learn about another area of the business while practicing your process modeling skills. There are multiple learning opportunities that can be a great addition to your professional development plan. The trick is to articulate the value and measurable outcomes of your efforts. You have to answer not only how each of these would give value but also how you would prove it (the measurement). Just don't forget that some of the most valuable learning can be found within other organizations you put on your roadmap, including professional associations. But these opportunities are only valuable if you put time and effort into pursuing the growth that they present.

Leveraging the value of your professional organizations

Belonging to a professional organization involves more than just owning a membership card. They are incredible sources of professional development opportunities. Because they are all about the profession, you will get a tailored focus on training opportunities. Professional organizations focus on the trends and innovations in that line of business. For instance, the International Institute of Business Analysis® (IIBA®; www.iiba.org) highlights training on the skills and techniques that are crucial to business analysis professionals today. But these are not just classroom trainings with workbooks and scenarios. Often, professional organizations will have hands-on workshops, guest speakers, panels, and more, which are great ways to learn and explore techniques and approaches you can include in your analysis work. Those same speakers and facilitators are experts you can then tap into for thoughts and advice based on their experience in the industry and profession.

But you have to be proactive with any association you join. You get out of it what you put into it. That means being active. Volunteering is one of the greatest activities you can do to build not only business analysis strengths but also leadership skills, grow your ability to manage projects and coordinate teams, and even learn marketing or technology, depending on what role you support. It is one thing to lead a team at your company, especially as you get into management positions and other reporting structures. However, it is an entirely different challenge when you lead volunteers who you have to inspire and motivate to contribute toward a bigger, collective goal. These are great places to improve your leadership skills when you cannot simply demand others do the work!

Also, ensure you align which professional associations you invest your time in back to your roadmap. Most memberships have great value propositions to them. You want the ones that deliver the most value for what you need to attain in both your current and future work. This is why the roadmap is so valuable. You have a great foundation to go back to. Those milestones you hope to achieve should be supported and enabled by where you spend your valuable time, energy, and money. When worked strategically, it can be the best return on any investment you make.

Learning through certifications

Now, as you explore those professional associations, one of the most valuable benefits is the certifications they offer. Certifications have been discussed in prior chapters as valuable additions to help fuel your analysis career in the direction you want. While many professional certifications can be intimidating due to the requirements for experience, consider certifications as another way to inject some serious analysis learning into your work. This is because to pass any of the standardized examinations, you have to know the content intimately. This work to understand the concepts from multiple sources and bodies of knowledge is learning in its most basic form. But again, this is why your professional roadmap is so important. You will not only want to put certifications on your roadmap but also identify the activities you need to carry out to achieve the certification that is best aligned with your goals. The 7,500 hours required for the Certified Business Analysis Professional® (CBAP®) qualification are not very daunting when you lay out the work over the coming year. Even working on the application in small pieces makes the task of tracking your experience much more manageable. Those small milestones and the ability to course correct as you go make success much more attainable and even something to look forward to.

You will need to consider which directions you want to take your career in. As previously discussed, there are various specialization options and even industries you could potentially do business analysis work in, and there are different certification topics that help push your career into different fields and areas. Consider the topics of concentration of certifications offered by IIBA®. Currently, they offer certifications in agile analysis, product ownership analysis, business data analytics, and cybersecurity. While each of these is still an analysis angle, they each take a different approach with their concentrated subject matter view. Say, for example, you wanted to learn more about cybersecurity. Prepping for and passing the **Business Analysis Certificate in Cybersecurity**™ (**IIBA-CCA**™) is a great way to walk through the concepts and explore elements of cybersecurity and what you can do in your analysis approach to address these requirements.

Do not be afraid to go beyond the business analysis space. PMI® certifications such as **Project Management Professional**' (**PMP**'; https://www.pmi.org/certifications/project-management-pmp) and agile certifications from the Scrum Alliance such as **Certified ScrumMaster**' (**CSM**'; https://www.scrumalliance.org/get-certified/scrum-master-track/certified-scrummaster), as well as others, can give you the skills to be wildly successful no matter what you decide to do with your business analysis career while giving you options. Additional certifications related to the analysis field, such as **Certified Change Management Professional**™ (**CCMP**™; https://www.acmpglobal.org/page/ccmp) from the **Association of Change Management Professionals**' (**ACMP**'), can give you some great perspectives as you work on project-based work and change initiatives. You can even consider exploring DAMA® certifications (such as the **Certified Data Management Professional**' (**CDMP**'); https://cdmp.info/) if you really enjoyed the last data project you worked on and want to get more experience in this area.

Regardless of which certification you choose, each has its value when strategically aligned to the goals you have for your career. Pursuing certifications opens doors for you by validating your knowledge. The additional benefit is that you learn the standard or accepted approach of how other practitioners perform the tasks and activities. Having this foundational knowledge is a great base to use throughout your career, wherever you choose your analysis work to take you!

Summary

One of the greatest skill sets successful analysis professionals possess is the ability to quickly learn and absorb information. Whether it is learning how to perform business analysis tasks and techniques or learning more about your organization or industry, the more you are not only able to understand but can also apply to your challenges and opportunities, the more valuable you will be to any team or organization. But like any good business case, you want a strategic vision and purpose to align the decisions you are making.

Your career roadmap shows the actions you take, but a professional development roadmap shows how you enable those actions to succeed. Spending time thinking through not just what you want but also how you will achieve those professional growth goals and measure and prove your own development is well worth the time invested in yourself. Couple this with the valuable resources your professional memberships can offer, and you have quite the powerhouse. But again, even those memberships should be aligned with your career vision. And, of course, constantly reviewing and re-analyzing your successes and what you have achieved is critical as the profession continues to evolve.

Business analysis work has its own trends and evolving landscape to consider, and course correct back to your own career map. With a clear focus on what you want to do and which direction your professional growth might take, we will take a look at what trends, tools, methodologies, and even technology evolutions are emerging in the analysis space in the next chapter so that you can continually deliver value in rapidly changing landscapes.

Further reading

- International Institute for Business Analysis® (IIBA®), (2015). *The Business Analysis Body of Knowledge® (BABOK®) Guide. International Institute of Business Analysis*, Toronto, Ontario, Canada.

Unlock this book's exclusive benefits now

Scan this QR code or go to `packtpub.com/unlock`, then search for this book by name.

Note: Keep your purchase invoice ready before you start.

Emerging Trends and the Future of Business Analysis

The business analysis community is not immune to the evolution and revolutions of technology. Technology is not only shaping solutions; it is also changing entire industries and the positions that enable them. The concern goes beyond which tools business analysis professionals use – technology changes how work is done in the analysis space and demands a shift in mindset. Analysis professionals must constantly adapt and proactively re-approach their tasks and techniques to keep up with the changes. Technology is an enabling tool. How you integrate it into your work is the key differentiator of thriving analysis professionals and ensures the long-term success of your career.

In this chapter, we're going to cover the following main topics:

- The impact of technology on business analysis
- Adapting to new business environments and models
- The integration of business analysis with agile, DevOps, AI, and beyond
- The future of business analysis: predictions and trends

The impact of technology on business analysis

Consider the impact of technology on the solutions you help teams deliver. Solutions are now more complex, more innovative, and changing faster than ever. Technology is affecting not just what businesses and professionals do, but in *HOW* they approach their work. The evolution of certain technologies, such as **Artificial Intelligence** (**AI**), **Machine Learning** (**ML**), and data analytics, has both driven and enabled organizations to achieve more than they ever thought possible. The amazing thing is that business analysis professionals and those who seek the most business value out of any investment are at the forefront of all these evolutions. They are the ones who help organizations maximize their investments no matter what changes happen in the technical space!

Understanding the role of emerging technologies

The evolutions of AI, ML, data analytics, and even cryptocurrency have changed the way we approach solutions. They bring new capabilities that can make organizations rethink how they deliver value. These technological evolutions have also forced business analysis professionals to shift their thinking. The question is not so much what these technologies do, but rather what vacancy they create for the business analysis professional to fill.

Emerging technologies have two effects for business analysis professionals to consider. First, these technologies are increasingly capable of doing tasks that were previously done by individuals. Simple activities are being automated daily. Seeing these applications in practice causes organizations to think about all the business scenarios, processes, and activities that could leverage the same technology to automate work, decreasing costs and improving efficiency. Take, for example, AI tools that help take notes. An online meeting becomes much more efficient if there are no additional team members attending simply to take notes. The same capability is also useful for in-person meetings, where notes and a listing of action items are needed.

Here's your challenge: when it comes to emerging technologies, ask: where else could we use this functionality? How about in a presentation by executives to a large department? Could the key points and messages of the presentation be captured and shared easily with staff? How about a press release? Then consider, is there clear written documentation that is consistent with the verbal message? You may not experience each of these scenarios, but it is the *extension* of the application of this particular technology that you should focus on. When you can use one capability for multiple business scenarios, you are extending the value of the investment.

Seeking technology opportunities in solutions

To help you think about any new technology and how to maximize the value for your organization's solutions and beyond, use the following checklist as you work with teams. You'll see the structure of solid research reflected in the business case format. But as you go through it, pay attention, in particular, to the added details in step *2*, where you can learn how to integrate emerging technologies by asking good questions instead of worrying about learning every detail of how each technology works:

1. **Understand the business problem:**

    - What is the core business problem or opportunity we're addressing?

    - Who are the stakeholders most affected by the current pain points?

    - What are the measurable outcomes we want to improve?

2. **Ask, "Where could technology help?"**

Efficiency and speed:

- Are there repetitive tasks we could automate with **Robotic Process Automation (RPA)**?

- Could we reduce delays by using workflow automation tools (e.g., Zapier, Power Automate)?

- Could AI agents or bots help triage requests, route tickets, or provide self-service options?

- Are there approvals or handoffs that could be streamlined with smart contracts or digital signatures?

Smarter decision-making:

- Are decisions being made without solid data? Could predictive analytics help?

- Could AI/ML models suggest next-best actions based on patterns we've missed?

- Could a dashboard or real-time KPI tracker support faster, better decisions?

- Could we simulate scenarios using digital twins or modeling tools?

Innovation and creativity:

- Could generative AI spark initial drafts, ideas, or prototypes for new services or products?

- Could image, audio, or video AI tools enhance storytelling or customer engagement?

- Could AR/VR be used for immersive training, walk-throughs, or customer experiences?

- Could we tap crowdsourced innovation platforms to gather ideas from employees or customers?

Enhanced collaboration:

- Could we reduce siloed work by using collaborative digital whiteboards (e.g., Miro, Mural)?

- Could AI-based summarization tools capture meeting notes and decisions instantly?

- Could we create a living, interactive knowledge base using tools like Notion or Confluence?

- Could language translation tools support more inclusive, global collaboration?

Trust, security, and transparency:

- Could blockchain or distributed ledgers help ensure data integrity or traceability?

- Is AI bias or algorithm transparency an issue we need to evaluate?

- Could we use biometrics or multi-factor authentication to improve security?

Customer experience:

- Could chatbots or voice assistants support 24/7 service or onboarding?

- Could sentiment analysis help us better respond to customer needs?

- Could personalization engines improve how we recommend products/services?

- Are there customer journeys that could be streamlined with mobile-first solutions?

Sustainability and resilience:

- Could IoT sensors improve real-time monitoring (e.g., in supply chain or facilities)?

- Could carbon tracking tools or AI for energy efficiency improve sustainability goals?

- Could scenario modeling help us anticipate future disruptions?

3. **Evaluate technology fit:**

- What technologies is the organization already using that could be repurposed or expanded for this solution?

- Are there low-cost tools or pilots we could try without major risk?

- Have other departments or peer organizations used a similar solution?

4. **Build the business case:**

- What is the potential **return on investment (ROI)** (cost savings, speed, satisfaction)?

- What are the risks or barriers to adoption?

- Who would be the champion or sponsor to help explore this further?

5. **Recommend and act:**

- Document the opportunity as an optional or enhancement requirement

- Propose a small pilot or proof of concept

- Align your recommendation with organizational goals and strategic themes

So, rather than focusing on what each new technology can do, your challenge is to consider what other business applications these innovative capabilities could be leveraged for. To help you start, just analyze the analysis activities you perform daily. For each process or technique you perform, consider what technologies are now available to you. Then, consider how those technologies could be applied in your work. To help you get started, *Table 11.1* gives you some examples of exactly this process. Look at what you are doing and consider where those emerging technologies your company is investing in might be applied to your analysis work:

Business Analysis Task/Technique	Emerging Technology	Considerations
Document analysis	AI and ML	Where do you need to research? Where do you need summarization? Where do you need to analyze documentation?
Decision-making	Data analytics	Where are decisions being made based on discrete data? Are there areas of the business that need consistent, reliable decisions to be successful?
Prioritization	Data analytics	Are there areas of work where prioritization processes need to be standardized and streamlined?
Defining design options and risk analysis	Cryptocurrency	Are there areas of work requiring the protection of private or confidential information transfers? Is there a need for data transparency in the work that is still secured?

Table 11.1 – Example BA techniques and the considerations of emerging technologies

Now, the considerations of *Table 11.1* are only the starting point of what these technologies could mean to your analysis work. You then need to consider the second major impact of emerging technologies: what room do they make for advancing analysis activities? To understand this impact, let's consider our example of an AI note-taker tool. You no longer have to spend effort and energy taking notes and ensuring action items and follow-up items are captured. This gives you space to focus on facilitating collaborative work.

Getting teams to brainstorm ideas, think through problem-solving scenarios, and prioritize and plan a collaborative solution is where you add business analysis value. This skill set is far more valuable than simple note-taking and, honestly, requires higher levels of competencies.

But when you are distracted by simple processes and manual activities, it takes time and energy away from focusing on the analysis work. And *THAT* is the value-focus. You need to concentrate on where your most value-adding work is. Then, analyze what other activities are taking your time and energy away from that value-adding work. If you can apply the emerging technologies to those manual activities, you can then maximize the value of both the technology investment and the organization's investment in your analysis skills. So, after identifying the scenarios where you could integrate these advancing evolutions, let's walk through how you can immediately start integrating them into your analysis work.

Integrating emerging technologies into your analysis work

The best way to integrate emergent technologies into your business analysis work is to use the same approach you take with your business solutions. Consider the following as an outline to always use to stay focused on improving your capabilities without getting lost in the technical details:

1. **Current-state analysis**: First, identify your current business analysis capabilities.

2. **Requirements analysis**: Identify the tasks and activities for which you need to develop abilities for your analysis work.

3. **Gap analysis**: Compare your current skills to the skills you identified are required to be successful in both requirements and solution analysis.

4. **Innovation application**: This is where you differentiate yourself and learn how to integrate emerging technologies *INTO* your work. Before diving into the solutions you might always go to, pause. Step back and consider what new technologies and capabilities might be applicable to this need. Go back to your SWOT analysis and identify new opportunities to build your strengths and eliminate weaknesses in both your skills and your analysis work.

The trick lies in not just analyzing yourself and your current work requirements but also pausing and looking around for what might be possible now and then creating a mini business case of what would be worth the effort to explore in your analysis work. If you want some ideas on where to start, often anything you do manually in your daily routines is a great place to look for some technological integration and application.

Now might be a good time for you to do a little exploration and learn what the emerging trends and technologies being used in your space are. This can be as simple as finding out what your organization is using. What technical tools or applications are the different departments using? Use your good elicitation techniques – from document analysis to observation and interviews – to research and see what applications different areas are using. Not just what, but why and how are they using these technological innovations? Just taking inventory of what is already being used can be a great tool in your toolkit. Also, often organizations have never looked across their departments to really know what features and capabilities they already have.

> **Tip**
> Constantly seek to deliver great value in *ALL* you do. Even when you're trying to improve yourself, do so with activities that help the business deliver greater value, and you'll always be a desired team member wherever you go!

But don't limit yourself to just walking around with a clipboard, taking inventory. Ask whether you can be a beta tester, someone who can try a new technology out to explore its applications. Even ask whether you can help the IT department with their business cases for which technologies to use. See what business justifications the various areas are using for certain application purchases. If you know *why* people are using certain apps, then you can use that to reflect whether the same scenarios appear in your work.

Then, the next step is to start exploring outside your organization. Seek out what technologies your industry is talking about and incorporating. Learn what other business analysis professionals are using in your industry, or even in other industries. Prior chapters mentioned the power of professional networks and connecting with associations. Use these resources to see what capabilities they are incorporating in their work. Just because a colleague is in a different industry, does not mean their application would be irrelevant in your industry. This research and analysis-based approach will give you ideas for your own work. All it takes is some simple brainstorming to find ways to apply these technologies in your own analysis work. It's good practice to always be a business analyst on both your business assignments *AND* your business analysis career paths and perspectives.

Table 11.2 provides a great way to help you think about ways to integrate these capabilities into your analysis work. That's the trick – first think capabilities, not technology. It is about what you can do with the technology, not which application you use. So, start by listing the business analysis activities you do, as well as those activities you discovered in your gap analysis as areas you want to develop. Then, list the technological capabilities that are available. With these activities and capabilities defined, then consider what opportunities would enhance your analysis work. *Table 11.2* gives some great examples to help you build your own listing:

Business Analysis Task/Technique	Capabilities from Emerging Technologies	Considerations for Your Analysis Work
Document analysis	Automated analysis, generated summaries, and recommendations	What areas of work are based on analyzing documentation and recorded materials?
Decision-making	Predictive analytics	Where do decision-makers need to see multiple options and the potential results of decisions made?
Prioritization	Data analysis	Where would different scenarios be helpful when making important decisions around prioritized work?
Defining design options and risk analysis	Business data analytics	Where are the risks in your analysis work where scenario planning and situational exploration could add value?

Table 11.2 – Example business analysis techniques and the considerations of emerging technologies

Constantly use and leverage *Table 11.2* whenever you are exploring and researching technologies. For that last column, it's all about asking good analysis questions. Use your current state analysis (the first two columns) to help you ask good questions to get great ideas about application. Ask questions such as the following:

- Where in our organization do we currently have this capability?

- Where in our organization do we *not* have this capability?

- What challenges are there for performing the business analysis task/technique in our organization today?

- What techniques have we done the same way for many years?

- What areas of the business are currently changing or have changed recently?

- What areas of the business have had fewer changes impacting their work over the years?

These questions are meant to help you look for strategic applications of a technology. You are seeking out those opportunities now and identifying possible threats where you can utilize advancements in technology capabilities to boost organizational value. The structured approach in *Table 11.2* helps to focus your analysis work for successful SWOT analysis when it comes to technology.

Using this format and approach, here are some common activities that have arisen at the time of writing where emerging technologies have been integrated and affected the business analysis work:

- Using AI note-taking capabilities to summarize meetings and action items

- Starting with AI chat prompts to research and generate the initial requirements listing on a topic/subject

- Leveraging ML and data analytics to generate decision trees and decision analysis results for improved and informed decision-making

- Integrating AI generation of process models into elicitation sessions

- Creating business analysis information and presentations using AI software

- Systems thinking and requirements visualization, as well as agile planning in collaborative software

These examples are changing what business analysts focus on as well as how they approach their analysis work. This shift in approach is the key to leveraging emerging technologies. Technology will affect your role, your position, and your career path. The trick is to proactively integrate it into your daily work. So, let's see how to do that and how to prepare ourselves for the next evolution, regardless of what technology evolution or business revolution emerges.

Building your analysis practice to integrate the next tech evolution

Seeing how much technology has changed is your indicator of how much more it will continue to evolve. If you plan and build your analysis practice with the thought that things are going to change, you can be flexible and nimble. This kind of mindset will keep you relevant and your skills in demand. Even by creating your own versions of the tables in the previous sections, you are helping to define the activities where your analysis skills add the most value. That focused concentration on what is needed, and *ONLY* what is needed, increases the ROI through a level of efficiency and effectiveness.

Then, the same focus on ROI is required for emerging technologies. Keep tracking what capabilities are arriving on the scene or evolving from their initial release. You might need to create a chart like the one in *Table 11.3*. It follows the same format as before, except it has more space for you to consider possibilities. In the first column, list down activities you do in your analysis work. Now, for each capability that is emerging in the evolving technology, look for a place to align it to a related analysis activity. It's okay if you are unsure of what or where the capability may align to. In these instances, write them down on their own line, like "Cryptocurrency" in *Table 11.3*. Then, do the application analysis for the last column. Ask yourself what changes are occurring in how business analysis activities are approached. For capabilities where you're unsure how they align with or support your work, consider how technology is reshaping business processes and perspectives. Identifying changes in how processes – and even entire businesses – operate is key, as these shifts are what you should apply in your analysis work. How does the technology either force you to change or give you inspiration to consider a new tactic or perspective?

Business Analysis Task/Technique	Capabilities from Emerging Technologies	Considerations for How It Changes Your Analysis Work
Visual models	Data analytics	What decisions need visual enhancement to facilitate decisions and understanding?
	Cryptocurrency	What changes are occurring in how financial transactions take place?
Status reporting		Are there tools to automate the work done each reporting period?
	Collaborative software and integration of work products	What teams need to work collaboratively on work products? Can these be evolutionary work products versus "throwaway" materials?
	Mobile technologies and integrations	How can the analysis work be done in more mobile-friendly environments?

Table 11.3 – Table for considering current and future technical capabilities

This approach builds flexibility into your work by giving you space to consider the possible applications. Vacant spots have purposely been left in this chart as evolutions like cryptocurrency not only offer new capabilities but also create new markets and change others. Do you know where this kind of capability would benefit your business analysis right now? No? That's okay! Leave space to consider it as your analysis work evolves. The same goes the opposite way. If you perform activities that are labor-intensive or seem to be of little value to your analysis work, add them to the list. Wait for a corresponding technology to emerge to address those inefficiencies. While you do not know of the capabilities available just yet, you have them on your radar to take advantage of when the right technical solution comes along. This kind of perspective is what sets you apart as an analyst, showing that you are mindful of proactively integrating the next technology that comes along. It also means you continue to always add business value to your organization.

In the same manner that organizations do not want legacy equipment or bad processes that create technical debt, your analysis work should never be stagnant or create knowledge debt. Organizations need knowledgeable staff with insights on trends in technology and business – those who are already considering the possibilities of tomorrow. Now that you are thinking about how to integrate these technological revolutions into your own work, understand that your own business models and environments are evolving too. Next, we will look at these shifts and consider what ways our business analysis work can and should evolve for maximum value delivery.

Adapting to new business environments and models

The focus on business value is what keeps business analysis professionals relevant. Yet where you do the work is changing so fast. This means you not only have to understand the changes happening in the environments that create, build, and maintain solutions but also must reflect on your business analysis work and consider how both your approach and your analysis activities have to evolve to still add value in a changed environment. A good technique used the same way in an environment that has changed will often not provide any value. Your approaches and techniques to deliver business value must adapt and evolve in the spaces in which you perform analysis work. You have to be comfortable with the fact that the way you did business analysis yesterday may not be the way you will be doing it tomorrow. The great thing is that those tasks and techniques you used yesterday *ARE* still valued tomorrow. You must just change your viewpoint to see the best way to modify and adapt those analysis practices to your solution spaces. In short, you will still elicit requirements, collaborate with stakeholders, and work in teams to create solutions with long-lasting design ideas. *HOW* you do this work is the part that changes and is what keeps this career interesting and always growing! To understand this better, consider the evolution of organizations that have and will continue to incorporate technology for their hybrid and remote workforces.

Working in remote and hybrid environments

In general, remote and hybrid working environments should be seen as just a change in the office location or style, meaning the same work still gets done. The idea is for remote and hybrid environments to add efficiency and effectiveness to delivering business value. You need to apply this same thought process to your analysis work. You still need to get business analysis work done regardless of where or how you or your teams are working. So, you will need to ensure you are comfortable enough with the technologies that you can continue to perform your analysis techniques regardless of how many (or how few) people are in the same room as you. And, as a good analyst, you will also need to understand the new and changing capabilities that hybrid-supporting technologies bring to teams and organizations. The ability to do this comes with two challenges that you are going to need to address, not just in this hybrid setting but in all your analysis work as technology evolves:

1. First, you need to learn the technologies that are enabling your organization.

    Again, you do not need to be a technologist, per se, but you need to be a good analyst and understand the technological capabilities. Simply learn what collaborative technology your organization is distributing to staff. Ask what learning options are available so that you get to know the basic business applications of the technologies.

2. Then, just like your business solutions, you have to analyze how these technological capabilities can (*and will*) affect your analysis work.

    Consider speed. For example, let's look at the shift in communication tools that has arisen in the wake of more remote and hybrid workforces. The pace of change is so fast that it almost seems like you blink, and a different platform or solution is being used by teams. This means rather than becoming an expert on how to use a virtual collaboration tool such as Zoom® (https://www.zoom.com/) or Microsoft Teams (https://www.microsoft.com/en-us/microsoft-teams/group-chat-software), focus on what the tool can do to enable meetings and workshops. Don't overwhelm yourself with trying to become an overnight expert. You need to take the approach of *just enough*. Learn the tools *just enough* to leverage their capabilities to drive some business value. In the example of these meeting tools, learn them just enough to run a simple meeting with your stakeholders. Then, when you see the differentiating value the evolving technology creates, it becomes worth asking what else the tools can do.

3. Then, you want to identify the capabilities of each technology beyond what your organization is using.

    What features are advertised for the solutions? What are other organizations and even industries using the technology for? Back to our meeting tools, realize that you are not just trying to be creative with the tool. Rather, you are focusing on what the tools can do for your meetings and workshops. *HOW* can they enable those activities you now do online that in the past you would have done in person? What benefits do they offer that might have you shifting your approach to conducting virtual meetings? That's exactly what you need to consider for the change in work environments.

4. Identify how your approach, your processes, and even your perspective need to change so that you are leveraging the capabilities now offered in your daily analysis work.

    Think about brainstorming, voting, and prioritization in hybrid environments. While the meeting software can get the group together, are there pieces of the technology that can help you do the facilitation portion? Does the remote environment actually enable greater communication among team members when they integrate collaboration tools? This is where hybrid workforces enable the use of collaboration software that many organizations already have. It might have been hard to get people to post documentation in shared spaces like Microsoft SharePoint (`https://www.microsoft.com/en-us/microsoft-365/sharepoint/collaboration`) when everyone could see each other in the same meeting room. But when your stakeholders are only able to connect digitally, the rise of collaboration tools explodes. Examples of such tools are Mural (`https://mural.co/`), Miro (`https://miro.com/`), and Lucid.app (`https://lucid.app/`), which enable teams to collaborate on their work products, often without the help of a meeting coordinator. So, that means that technology is shifting the role you play, not just your approach to the work.

5. You need to ensure you always define your value delivery approach so that you both achieve the desired business value and are able to incorporate the advancements of the technology and environments in which you do analysis work.

    So, now you must consider how to not only get people together but also how to enable them to be successful, whether it is brainstorming, voting, prioritization activities, or other change management activities. So yes, you have to learn the technology; however, you are learning how those technologies can enable you to be successful. How do these technologies help you get a list of requirements, a prioritized backlog of features, and approved design ideas that are created by your stakeholders themselves? You still need to perform those core business analysis functions, but you have to consider how to modify your approach to the changing environments that *your stakeholders* are working in. How can you use the technologies to make it easier for your stakeholders to achieve their business goals? Those analysis professionals who succeed are the ones who can align the technological capabilities with the desired outcomes of the analysis work. So, whether it is enabling digital working groups or generating data insights at lightning-fast speeds, the question becomes, "What are you going to do with these capabilities?".

There is a lot to juggle between being a facilitator, using the technology, and accomplishing business outcomes, so don't feel overwhelmed! Focus on one thing at a time. Get comfortable, then focus on the next step. If you want to dive more into hybrid working, you can check out my LinkedIn Learning course (`https://www.linkedin.com/learning/hybrid-facilitation-for-business-analysis`) to walk through how to be successful in hybrid environments as an analysis professional. With this knowledge, you will know how to use your skills to tailor your approach to each unique scenario.

Tailoring approaches and methodologies

One of the key qualities that separates business analysis professionals from senior or expert business analysis professionals is the latter's ability to tailor their work and their approach to the present as well as future situations. For example, for requirements elicitation workshops, some stakeholder analysis and prep work prior to meeting with the team will help inform you of the best approach. But if you jump into an online meeting application and start asking questions that result in little feedback, you need to be self-aware about what you are doing may not be the most effective approach. Being able to quickly pivot, especially live during a meeting, to, say, a collaboration tool or other technique that *DOES* start eliciting responses is what senior analysis professionals are great at.

There are no *bad* techniques. In this case, you just had a good technique for the wrong purpose. Pivoting to re-align your analysis goals with the stakeholders' current states by utilizing a technique that works is key to ensuring success. Even during a meeting, if one of your stakeholders is asking good questions that are getting others to share ideas and inputs, encourage them to continue. Do not be frustrated that someone else has taken on the facilitation role (in fact, I'd be ecstatic if my stakeholders took on this often-challenging role!). Rather, seek to enable it and quickly identify where and how you can still add value to the situation, such as documenting the discussion points live for a real-time visual to help others stay engaged in the conversations. What you are actually doing is focusing on the value you provide, not the role title. If the pace of evolution of the technologies you use in your analysis work is any indicator, you should *NOT* get tied to a specific technology or vendor if you can ever help it! Roles, technologies, and business needs and context are going to continue to evolve, and so should you!

This is key to your success as a business analysis professional. Organizations will change methodologies, approaches, and even business practices that will eliminate the defined business analyst role and even throw out (figuratively) entire technology stacks. Be okay with this! Remember that business analysts are simply anyone doing business analysis work. So, while the titled position does not exist, look for where there *IS* business analysis work and seek to maximize the value-delivery of that position regardless of the tools in place. Leverage your skills and capabilities, coupled with experience and adaptive approaches, and you will always find a way to add value.

Changes in not just technology but worldwide business practices are continuing to shape the role of business analysis professionals. Business analysts often found this to be the case in prior evolutions as organizations shifted to agile methodologies. The moment the product owners became overwhelmed with organizational demands, the business analysts often stepped up into pseudo-product owner roles. They did the product analysis to help the team prioritize value-based work while keeping the customer in central focus, even if they no longer had a direct line of communication with the end customer. They saw the need and used good analysis skills to align the outcomes back to business goals. That kind of attitude – stepping up to analyze and provide data-informed decision-making constructs – is what will keep you and your skills in demand no matter what changes your organization makes.

Activities to incorporate into your business analysis work

To help you adjust today to changes you may face tomorrow in your analysis work, here are a few things to think about. First, consider your digital comfort. This refers to how comfortable you are in digital spaces. Whether it is simply online communications via email and chat messages or joining remote and hybrid meetings, how comfortable are you with the different setups? The tools are going to change and evolve, but even as simple as being comfortable no matter which technology is used today will help you handle the changes of tomorrow. For example, if you are comfortable on Zoom®, would it be okay if the organization switched to Microsoft Teams tomorrow? What about Google Meet (`https://meet.google.com/`) next week? And later even Webex (`https://www.webex.com/`)? Do not worry about the application. Instead, realize that these are all online meeting applications. Each has a way to share audio, video, and screen options, even if the buttons are different. They can each accomplish the goal of meeting virtually. So, being okay with your digital environment is going to be key to being successful in a sea of technical changes.

The other superpower you need to work on right now is to enable virtual collaboration. This means being able to facilitate hybrid and remote teams. Organizations are scaling back on support staff and expecting SMEs to be just as good at running projects, holding meetings, and working with other departments as in their own area of expertise. Business analysts are often lucky enough to have an unbiased eye and a holistic view of the enterprise. This position makes you a great enabler of cross-functional teams while keeping focused on the organization's goals and, ultimately, the bottom line. But both you and your stakeholders individually do not own the solution. Solutions require more cross-functional input and ownership to be successful. Having a facilitation mindset to enable the organization to own their decisions and delivery cycles ensures greater long-term success. You need to be practicing your facilitation skills daily and building up your own competencies so that you remain relevant throughout your organization's changes.

But even the shifts in business your organization takes are an opportunity to remain relevant. How up to date are you with your organization's changes? Do you know the different departments and areas? Get to know the areas of your organization. Years ago, data teams did not exist. Now there are data analytics groups completely separate from IT or even marketing teams that look at data across the organization. How about security? This now encompasses both physical security and cybersecurity for more organizations. Are they integrated or separate divisions? How do they work together? Do you know what roles each plays? Learn what the mission and purpose of these emerging teams are and what their capabilities are. As an enterprise analyst, you can see across the departments and identify potential gaps that functional organizations may be creating. Bridging those gaps with solid analysis skills again will keep you relevant and in demand.

As pointed out, dive into learning the trends are in technology as much as you can. Consider learning types of technologies over specific applications or vendor-specific solutions. The technologies and vendors are going to change. It's what the organization does with the technology and how it can be applied to business opportunities and challenges that separates successful organizations from their competitors. Similar to our online meeting example, understanding the capabilities and features of different solutions gives you insight not just for your project-based work but in your own approach to your analysis work. The more you stay agnostic of any one solution, the more ready you will be able to adapt when (*not if!*) the technology changes again. So, let's look at some of the ways businesses have changed and how business analysis work continues to evolve as well, integrating for greater strategic business value.

The integration of business analysis with agile, DevOps, AI, and beyond

Business analysis professionals must keep up with the innovations of technology and the pace at which technology is evolving. Industries have evolved to handle this **volatility, uncertainty, complexity, and ambiguity** (**VUCA**) and are seeking out value-delivery models that welcome change. Change is the one constant that organizations have to deal with, but they are also facing even more demanding customers. Customers' interests and wants are satisfied with amazing speed thanks to digital delivery. Customers then place that same expectation on other services they are seeking. With this mindset, organizations are redesigning how fast they can incorporate feedback into solutions and deliver to their customers. Regardless of the methodology or approach, the question of how to deliver value in any environment is where the business analysis professional finds their value. So, let's walk through some adaptive approaches that welcome constant feedback and adjustment so that you can define how to build business analysis into any organizational process and value stream.

Understanding adaptive and integrated methodologies

Agile frameworks emerged to welcome the changes that were invariably happening in development, organization, and even industry environments. The goal is to focus on shorter iterations so that value can be delivered faster, even if in smaller bites, so that there is ample room for feedback and course correction. This same approach has driven business analysis professionals today to be seen more actively running interactive workshops rather than spending hours on document analysis. Remember that your goal is to understand these approaches and the reasoning behind them so that you can consider how to best apply the methodologies to your own analysis work.

Agile has introduced environments where developers work not just alongside each other but as close to the customer or end user as possible. Very little work is done behind closed doors as transparency is emphasized, coupled with a rapid turnaround time. This same approach is required of business analysis professionals today. In fact, some of the best advice for business analysts is to *NOT* take notes during meetings. But think about that. An older, often slower, process of eliciting requirements, for example, was to sit with stakeholders and ask a bunch of questions to get some feedback. Then the analyst would go back to their desk and define the requirements. Then a review meeting would be set up before the development team disappeared for months on end. They would then come back and re-engage for the user acceptance testing. Not only is this process time-consuming, but there is a huge length of time between interactions with the customer in this approach.

Now consider a requirements elicitation session, probably hybrid, but for sure leveraging collaboration and virtual meeting space tools. You, as the business analyst, still ask good questions, but you are recording the items live in the shared collaboration space. Even during the discussion, other users are adding to the shared work product. By the end of the scheduled session, you will have a list of verified and validated requirements that already have an initial prioritization set. There are no notes to type up and send out for verification. In fact, not only can the team access everything that was created, but you can already share the work with the development team for live feedback. With no "work" to follow up on from the initial session, you can perform other analysis activities while waiting for the development team's feedback. You even have time to seek feedback from participants on how best to tailor your approach for future engaging workshops, which is both constructive and reinforces your solid skills.

It is a recommendation to always do this kind of work live. Creating a process model as users walk through a process actually facilitates further discussion and insights as you are able to see the result live. But you have to get comfortable with having more direct feedback loops that actually drive greater quality in your analysis work.

DevOps is a great way to see this kind of application in even further detail. DevOps frameworks work to integrate development into daily operations. This means that changes – improvements, features, and enhancements – can be added live into the work without a full backend development cycle. Developers get to interact directly with the end users to understand their expectations and seek feedback. Analysis professionals assist in the prioritization activities, helping to holistically look at the value model being created. But in DevOps, there is a great emphasis on automation and streamlining not just the end product but also, and especially, the development and delivery processes.

These same concerns should be prevalent for business analysis professionals. What part of your process is automated? Where are you streamlining your delivery system? As organizations get comfortable with the DevOps models in their change work, they will begin to expect the same approach from you. The same is true of the transparency of your work. How transparent are you with the project team, stakeholders, and even end users and customers? This becomes an important aspect to incorporate into your analysis work. But key to these methodologies and other rapid development models is the feedback loop, which, as emphasized already, should be a core part of your business analysis processes.

Leveraging the feedback loop

The power of adaptive methodologies is in how they continuously focus on value delivery through feedback loops. The smaller increments and integrations create space for the customer to actually use the delivered product or feature and then give feedback on how it is or is not meeting their needs. This has become critical as technology itself is changing how customers interact with solutions and there are ever-decreasing delivery time frames as customers come to expect almost real-time responses to their demands. The same goes for your business analysis work. You have a goal to constantly be doing the highest-value work. To ensure this value is being delivered, you need to incorporate your own adaptive models into your analysis work. This means building in small and large feedback opportunities to give you space to course correct, adjust, and adapt. Quick feedback could include participants' comments that the session was "fun" or "engaging" or just simply a comment of "good job," as those small pieces of feedback help you know what to continue or revise. Larger efforts to seek feedback might be more formal reviews and planning sessions that you use to compare planned to actuals.

One thing the *Business Analysis Body of Knowledge® (BABOK®) Guide* does a good job of calling out is the tasks in the business analysis planning and monitoring domain (IIBA®, 2015). These tasks focus on planning your analysis approach as well as how you will assess your work, and improving the analysis work you perform. Think about that. Before you do *ANY* analysis work, have you defined a measure of success? How will you prove you delivered value? Baseline measurements need to be defined *before* you perform any actions to give you that insight. But then, do you build time into your analysis work to compare your results back to the baseline to see how well you are doing? Then, have you added to the project backlog user stories that improve the business analysis work?

Yes, retrospectives and lessons learned are for improving both the product *AND* the team, which includes anyone doing business analysis work. But see, it's the mindset that is important. Adapting to whatever methodology or process the organization uses for the business is where your own business analysis work comes in. A user story on ways to improve your elicitation workshops or user acceptance testing is valuable to both you and the business. It can be that explicit so that you are ensuring improvement in the analysis activities. But you have to have that mindset and focus to always be thinking about how to improve in your analysis work. Then, you couple this continuous improvement mindset with the consideration of how to integrate your successful analysis activities into how the business is currently, and perhaps should be, operating.

Building business analysis into the business delivery systems

Methodologies will always continue to evolve, as will the role of the business analyst. But it is the focus on value delivered to the customer where the goals of these different emerging methodologies overlap with the business analysis work. The trick to aligning the work you do as a business analysis professional is to integrate and align with the methodologies in place at your organization. *Table 11.4* shows first a list of some of these described methodologies or approaches your organization may take in its value-delivery system. The next column lists some of the value propositions that each of these methodologies or approaches brings. These help you then define what business analysis activities you can consider, do, or even tailor to incorporate the goals of each methodology or approach into your analysis work:

Methodology/Approach	Value Propositions	Business Analysis Activities
Agile project management	Short iterations of value delivery	Facilitate prioritization planning discussions
		Ensure prioritized backlog of value-based features
DevOps	Collaboration with operations and end users	Facilitate collaborative discussions and real-time discussions on features and improvements
	Speed of delivery of value-added feedback	Quality analysis of well-defined requirements
AI	Leveraging the right data sources to produce insights	Validating data sources and defining integration requirements for accurate data models
Hybrid and remote structures	Enabling cross-functional teams to work with fewer delays	Facilitating collaborative working sessions both synchronously and asynchronously
	Making teams feel connected regardless of geographical makeup	Engaging teams online as equal participants and value stakeholders with well-understood roles and responsibilities

Table 11.4 – Table aligning methodology areas of focus with business analysis activities

The ideas in *Table 11.4* are to help you consider your own environment and are not an exhaustive list. The idea is not to challenge the changes in processes that organizations take on, but rather to seek them as opportunities to leverage and build up your own analysis practice. Those who welcome new ways of working will be able to handle the future changes our environments will face. So, now let's look at how these past experiences can help you define your own requirements for a lasting and successful analysis career.

The future of business analysis: Predictions and trends

Our world is more connected than ever before, and so you have to be both technically competent as well as analytically inclined, no matter where your career finds you. There used to be a very strong differentiation between technical and non-technical analysts; however, the integration of technology in both our own lives and that of our customers has made technology a part of doing business no matter what business your organization is in. This will only continue. Regardless of the technology that emerges or the features and functionalities that become available, you *WILL* need to have a sense of digital comfort in your work. But again, the real value for organizations is when you identify the capabilities that can be applied to the business – that's where technology delivers impact. Coupling that with good analysis skills to find ways to integrate the features into not just solutions but how you bring value delivery for your organization is how the successful analysis professionals of tomorrow are identified. Each technology is going to be different. But the emergence of AI is a great model to look at and use for future technological revolutions.

Considering the impact of AI as a model for business analysis evolution

The impact of AI is a great case study to consider how business analysis activities continue to evolve as a result of technological innovations. The initial development that put generative capabilities in the hands of the average end user created almost a panicked reaction to the technology. There was a sense of dread that if you didn't "have" AI, you would lose the metaphorical race. What was actually happening was that you would not "lose" if you did not have AI tools in place. However, the real fear, actually, is that by not adopting AI, you would be beaten out by the person who knows how to use the technology.

> **The power of AI**
>
> You will not go out of business if you do not have AI technology; however, you will be outpaced, outmatched, and ultimately lose business to those who know how to leverage and integrate AI into their businesses.

For business analysis professionals work, consider the application of generative AI technologies to your elicitation sessions. Let's look at an example of how generative AI solutions are introducing opportunities to transform business analysts' approaches. Specifically, let's consider a project that aims to develop new customer-facing solutions for an organization:

1. First, the analysis professional would research the topic and context and ensure they have an understanding of business goals and purposes.
2. Next, stakeholder analysis would be required to set up the initial brainstorming sessions.

3. The analysis professional would then run the facilitated sessions, often multiple times, to focus on idea generation, designs and development plans, and feedback and next steps.

4. Finally, they would conclude with lessons learned and metrics on the solution for continuous improvement.

Considering this as the general approach for a business analysis professional, *Table 11.5* details how AI is changing the approach. The analysis work is still required, which is defined in the first column. The "traditional" approaches to analysis work, or common methods and approaches done by analysts for years now, are in the middle column. But the analysis professional of tomorrow leverages the capabilities of the AI, which are listed in the third column:

Analysis Activity	Traditional Approach	AI-Integrated Approach
Topic and context research	Document analysis. Stakeholder interviews	Ask Perplexity AI: "As a business analysis professional assigned to a project focused on [goal], what should I know about [topic]?".
Confirm business goals	Document analysis. Stakeholder interviews.	Use Copilot to summarize organizational materials and presentations to identify company metrics and measures of success.
Stakeholder analysis	Lessons learned. Document analysis. Peer support (interviews).	Ask Gemini for a list of potential stakeholders, their roles and responsibilities, and questions to ask them upon inviting them to a project kickoff for a project of type [insert project description and reference organizational documents].
Brainstorming ideas	Facilitated workshops, with multiple techniques and engagement approaches.	Brainstorm ideas with generative AI prior to the meeting to help get stakeholders going with generating ideas. Record ideas in Mural and use AI features to generate more ideas.
Generate design ideas	Facilitated workshops, with multiple techniques and engagement approaches, requiring additional stakeholders.	Ask generative AI tools to identify design ideas. Ask Copilot to identify risks and challenges with proposed design ideas. Ask a chat feature to "act as [absent stakeholder SME needed] and identify what questions they would ask and need to be addressed for their support of [proposed solution]."

Analysis Activity	Traditional Approach	AI-Integrated Approach
Create test plans	User **Requirements Traceability Matrix (RTM)** to define all requirements and a draft test plan. Review test plans with stakeholders for reviews and updates.	Ask Gemini to generate test scenarios for all identified requirements, including test steps, test data for each scenario, and expected output, grouped by SME area for distribution by SME for faster reviews.
Lessons learned	Facilitate stakeholder feedback meeting. Manually track feedback and create user stories for improvements.	Generate a survey with Copilot that records results in a collaborative spreadsheet. Ask Copilot to create user stories to address each feedback item and send a summary to the team.
Success metrics	Document analysis. Surveys.	Ask Gemini to measure results stored in Google Drive from solution usage, compare it to business goals, and generate a report.

Table 11.5 – Project tasks and business analysis activities with and without AI integration

The tools presented in *Table 11.5* are just a sampling of tools you can use. Refer to the following links for more information:

- Perplexity (`https://www.perplexity.ai/`)
- Microsoft Copilot (`https://copilot.microsoft.com/`)
- Google Gemini (`https://gemini.google.com/`)
- Mural (`https://www.mural.co/`)

If you want to dive into how to write AI chat prompts that help you ask better questions both online and offline, you can learn more in my online course on writing effective chat prompts on LinkedIn Learning (`https://www.linkedin.com/learning/ai-chat-prompts-for-business-analysis`).

Looking at *Table 11.2*, the advantages that the AI technologies provide the professional analyst include, but are not limited to, the following:

- Speed to completion of deliverables

- Accuracy checking of results and increased validation

- Less stakeholder time to participate

- Leveraging existing organizational assets

Just the speed at which the business analysis professional can operate when integrating AI is enough business justification. But the real focus is on how to leverage technological capabilities, not on how well the tool itself is used. The more you use AI, the better you are naturally going to get with it. But you have to ask how it can help enhance your analysis work and evolve your approaches. You can use this model for any technological revolution you face, and with some great analysis work, you can see how it has helped successful business analysis professionals get where they are today.

Using technology revolutions as models to position yourself for tomorrow

The emergence of AI is just as impactful as the digital transformation projects often found in an analyst's portfolio of work. Digital transformation projects are often well beyond simply taking paper-based forms and putting them in a digital format. The prospect of automations and process improvements might excite a business analysis professional, but there are also huge change management implications in helping people rethink how they service their customers and deliver business value. The technical work is often the simplest with many of these efforts. The hard part is the "people part." This means addressing challenges that emerge from questions, oppositions, and even resistance from the business users and teams who are unclear, nervous, or concerned that the new model of doing business is not going to serve them in the way the old model did.

In these projects, those who only focus on how they used to do the work are more at risk of losing their jobs if their manual work is automated. In contrast, those who ask how they can continue contributing to the service or customer journey see their roles evolve as organizations seek to maximize talent. Many actually still do some of the same work they did before but now use digital information sources versus paper. Others evolve and grow their role to analyze the data versus simply sorting and organizing it. You should adopt the same perspective for your business analysis work. Do you simply modify your work to do the same process as before with new technology? Or do you learn about the benefits of the new technology and explore what it can mean for your analysis work? Let's consider a scenario that has emerged and will continue to be relevant in helping you think about optimizing your analysis work.

Strategically shifting your business analysis work and your analysis career

Activities such as eliciting, defining, analyzing, and tracing requirements have always been core to business analysis professionals. Understanding what is needed to deliver maximum value for any stakeholders comes from the delivery of quality requirements work. Now consider that AI is introducing capabilities that can shift much of the manual requirements management work to technology. Document analysis that previously took weeks can be done in a matter of minutes. Even the initial requirements listing for a project can be generated by asking your favorite chatbot the right questions.

This massive process optimization starts to lead to the question of what the business analysis professional would actually do. However, there is a massive amount of quality work that still needs to be done. You have more time to ask the important questions, such as, "So what?" Yes, it is that simple. Sure, the data sources show a trend in customer behavior, but what are the future predictions? Or while certain prioritization criteria show a feature as more efficient for the organization, *should* the team be prioritizing more customer-centric features to maintain their brand reputation? These judgment calls based on years of experience are still relevant and applicable when working with stakeholders. It is something you should be excited about because the technology is speeding up the delivery of information so that more of your time can be spent on those important collaborative discussions with your stakeholders. Your stakeholders will be excited because you have more insights for them to make data-driven decisions than ever before. Technology is actually enabling you to shift your focus to the most value-adding activities of your analysis position – strategically looking at the value of and to an organization.

AI can optimize and even automate the duties of certain positions. If you are worried that your job will go away because of AI automation, then you are not focused on the value-adding portion of your analysis role. As much as you may be noticing what technology can now do for organizations, often the most strategic question is to ask what technology is *NOT* doing for the organization or business analysis itself. Hybrid environments are bringing more people together than ever. However, how many times have you been on a remote or hybrid meeting where cameras were off, participants were muted the whole meeting, and you felt like you and the AI note-taker were the only ones paying attention? Technology, in this case, enabled the environment to be productive, yet it still requires facilitation to achieve the business outcomes. This is exactly where you step in. You can not only enable the outcomes but also help define the best business value.

You can shift to a more strategically focused asset by simply answering the *why* of technology. The *why* is the answer to the *so what?* question. What does AI mean to your organization? Sure, everyone may appear to be using it, but what business value does it have to *your* organization? *WHY* should your organization care? *WHY* would it improve processes? *WHY* not use it? These are all strategically positioned questions that need to be asked and answered. These questions cannot be answered well with a chatbot. Your ability to see what technology is *NOT* enabling starts to become your superpower to ensure maximum value delivery of any investment. Shift your focus from how things work and even what the features and functions are to *why* these capabilities are important. Expand your horizons and look across your entire enterprise and beyond for a more global view on what trends are in the industries and what competitors and even other industries are doing. This is how you help your organization continue to leverage the maximum value, regardless of whether it's AI automation or simple business process improvement efforts. Shift the focus of your analysis work and ask your great questions.

Then, take the same approach to your career. What do these technologies mean in terms of where, when, and how you do your analysis work? Why should you care about changes in vendors, capabilities, and infrastructure? What impacts does this have on advancing your career? Answer the *so what?* questions about your role, your capabilities, and the value you provide teams and organizations now. Building these questions into each project or even quarterly assessments will strategically position you to stay relevant and constantly add the business value that your organization needs from you. It is not about how technical you are or how many applications you use to perform your analysis work. Rather, it is about how you see the impacts of technology on your organization and the way the business operates. Shifting your view to strategically look at how changes affect both your work and career is how you navigate the uncertain landscape and elevate your career to better opportunities and further horizons. Try to expand your analytical lens instead of sticking to legacy tech – stay open to what's possible tomorrow and jump in where you can make the biggest impact. The business value comes in the actions you take to ensure long-lasting value delivery in all you do.

Summary

Technology has and will continue to impact business analysis work. It will impact the solutions that are defined. It will impact the delivery methods to produce the value. And it will directly tailor the way in which business analysis activities are conducted. Those business analysis professionals who welcome these changes with curiosity and exploration will be successful in the years to come when more changes occur. The same feedback loops leveraged to increase the speed of delivery of value need to be incorporated into your analysis work.

Look at how fast you are delivering value in your business analysis work. Are there areas of improvement? Do you have feedback loops set up in your analysis work to actively seek input and ideas so that you are only focused on the most value-adding analysis activities? These are critical to your success tomorrow. In addition, you must be both digitally comfortable and relevant. The emphasis is not on becoming an SME on any one application or knowing what the cutting-edge solution is. Rather, focus on learning the capabilities of technologies and expecting them to be part of both your and your stakeholders' daily work.

Now, to help with these feedback loops, incorporate regular assessments into your analysis processes. Measuring where you are and making action plans to grow your skill sets is key to keeping your career growth on track and never letting it stagnate. The next chapter will help you measure the effectiveness of your work so that you can actively build those action plans based on the quality feedback you get.

Further reading

- International Institute for Business Analysis® (IIBA®), (2015). *The Business Analysis Body of Knowledge® (BABOK®) Guide*. International Institute of Business Analysis, Toronto, Ontario, Canada.

Unlock this book's exclusive benefits now

Scan this QR code or go to packtpub.com/unlock, then search for this book by name.

Note: Keep your purchase invoice ready before you start.

12

Assessments and Techniques for Career Success

Consider that whatever gets measured gets done. By this, I mean that if you can measure and prove your growth, you have concrete evidence to support you, in both monetary and non-monetary means, in the next evolution of your career. But it can be a challenge to prove that you are a *good* business analysis professional. How do you measure the value you provide in your analysis work? It actually is easier than you think: by simply being a good analyst and measuring how your skills and activities enable needs to be addressed. When you know not only *what* your competencies are but also *how* to assess them and how they align with both your and your organization's growth plan, you have a solid business case for your value. "Show me the money" is what you are responding to by demonstrating the value delivered by your activities against the organization's time and money spent in supporting you. And positive returns are well rewarded. But how do you measure value, especially when you are often facilitating and enabling your teams to succeed?

This chapter will walk you through some valuable assessments you can start to use immediately in your analysis career. Regardless of where you are starting from, completing the self-assessments and trying the measurement tools presented in this chapter can give you insight into where you are and how much you have already accomplished. And then, by incorporating the feedback techniques described here, you can map out and achieve your desired career goals. In this chapter, we're going to cover the following main topics:

- Utilizing self-assessment tools for analysis professionals

- Instructional guides for measuring and improving business analysis techniques

- Using feedback for improvement

Utilizing self-assessment tools for analysis professionals

In business analysis work, the joy of seeing teams connect and collaborate while still achieving project milestones and solution success is often all that is needed to fuel your next analysis initiative. Business analysis professionals enable organizations to achieve greater value. They see opportunities and areas for improvement while considering both the strengths and weaknesses of an organization. Your superpower is in doing the same for yourself and your career. Knowing your strengths and weaknesses is not enough, though, especially for the evolving analysis professional. Instead, you want to measure and analyze your own analysis work to build an *actionable* growth and improvement plan. Self-assessment tools are a great way to not only assess but even give yourself discrete measurements of both where you are and where you want to be, which is critical to knowing what to do next!

The value of evaluating your BA competencies

Self-assessment simply means measuring your own work. Measurements help evaluate the quantitative and qualitative success of your analysis work. The trick is to find the right evaluation criteria that are helpful to your career goals. Starting with an assessment from a business analysis organization, such as the **International Institute of Business Analysis® (IIBA®)** (https://www.iiba.org), means the criteria you are assessing are directly related to business analysis tasks and techniques. This is a great place to start when focused on your business analysis career, to use evaluation criteria from the international standard of the work you do.

The key with assessments is that they can give you baselines. They are objective measures back to a certain standard or level expected of different tiers of performance. Self-assessment means just that: you analyze yourself. Sure, this might feel a little biased, but assessments are really just a measurement. They are not an examination requiring a passing score. They are more of an indicator of where you are when you take them. As long as you measure your initial data in the same way you measure future data, you will always have a discrete view of your own growth. The challenge is to truly be honest with yourself and take a critical and analytical eye to what you do and how you do it. For if you know where you are, it is much easier to define where you want to go.

Utilizing the IIBA Competency Model

One of the best self-assessment tools available for business analysis professionals and those focused on careers in the business analysis space is the **Business Analysis Competency Model®** from IIBA, available at https://www.iiba.org/professional-development/business-analysis-competency-model/. This is one of the best things you can do throughout your analysis career, as it gives you proficiency levels to analyze your skills against. These range from entry-level awareness up to senior experts who work in larger, more strategic roles. Basically, it identifies the different activities an analyst would do at each of the performance levels. This is a great resource to explore the different tasks that business analysis professionals do. Anyone growing their business analysis practice, or especially managers of business analysts, should grab a copy to keep as a handy desk reference for the descriptions of what business analysis in action looks like!

Now, to use this valuable resource, first complete a self-assessment. This is not a test, but a true analysis of what level of business analysis work you are performing. Think of it as a snapshot of current skills. It is not good or bad; there is no *passing* or *failing*, but simply a measure. Look at the criteria for each task and the corresponding levels and think about what you do naturally, in day-to-day analysis work. The more honest you are and the more you go with your initial instinct, the better the ratings will truly reflect your work.

Once you have your initial baseline, compare it against the competency level definitions in the assessment. This comparison helps you identify where you do and do not align with your goals, providing critical insight for your professional gap analysis. If you know where you are and where you want to go, it can be so much easier to define the steps to get there. What those steps look like, though, can be challenging to identify and often include a lifetime of lessons learned. However, using a prebuilt competency model like the IIBA's has distinct advantages. IIBA provides the proficiency level mapping of the activities that analysts at different skill levels would be expected to apply. It not only defines what these competencies are, but it goes further and articulates *HOW* to perform them based on your desired analysis skill level.

Example application of the IIBA Business Analysis Competency Model

Let's say you review and rate yourself as "skilled" (level 3) at the task of conducting elicitation because you feel that you are able to do the following:

- Facilitate the elicitation activity

- Capture elicitation outcomes

- Adapt verbal and non-verbal communication style to the needs of the situation and the individual

- Use active listening and discovery skills to understand "real" issues/needs and build rapport

- Use facilitation skills to encourage participation from all attendees and other tasks for skilled performers

Then you set your goal to become an "expert" (level 4) at conducting elicitation because you want to do the following:

- Lead others in elicitation activities

- Consistently use meeting management skills and tools to keep discussions focused and organized

- Guide others on how to effectively use common techniques

These are specific, measurable goals you can demonstrate your understanding of, and are exactly what you need for developing an action plan with these discrete criteria. It is one thing to know where you are. It is another to know what the next level looks like so you can define that action plan to get there. So, the process to approach this great Competency Model from IIBA (and really any competency model you are considering) is to do the following:

1. Take the self-assessment. *Be honest!*

2. Review your results back to the assessment. *Fact-based comparison, no judgment!*

3. Walk through the rankings of where you are. *Are these the activities of junior analysts or senior analysts? Knowledge is power here!*

4. Identify areas where you want to improve or increase your skill sets by identifying the measures you want to see at your next assessment. *Define your goals.*

5. Identify actions you can take that will help you start performing the competencies at that desired advanced level. *Actions are what turn dreams into realities!*

Repeat this process for any assessment tool you use to maximize its value. Just make sure you pick the right assessments. Like your career decisions, you want to align your analysis work to an assessment that supports your career goals. Think about where you want to take your career. Then, look for assessment tools in those areas of work to see how your skills currently stack up. The Business Analysis Competency Model from IIBA is the most comprehensive business analysis-focused assessment. However, as your business analysis work can take your career into many areas of business as well as different industries, seeking out relevant types of assessments can help augment your career in multiple facets. Let's explore some of the other tools you might find valuable throughout your analysis journey.

Exploring other tools for self-assessment

Now, there are many types of analysis work you can do throughout your career. Equivalently, there are a number of additional business analysis self-assessment tools available to help better explore your analysis capabilities. The BA-Cube learning community has a **skills inventory** focused on business analysis and product ownership that can be great if you enjoy working in agile environments (`https://ba-cube.mn.co/spaces/14008547/page`). BrainStorm Group has an **Agile business analysis self-assessment** that is focused on agile methodologies and the analysis work that takes place (`https://www.bpminstitute.org/qsm_quiz/agile-business-analysis-aba-skills-self-assessment/`). Modern Analyst has some assessments on process modeling, such as **Unified Modeling Language** (**UML**) and creating use cases that can be insightful if you want some measurements on your tactical analysis work (`https://www.modernanalyst.com/Resources/SelfAssessment.aspx`). None of these is better than the other. They each simply list different criteria to assess yourself against. Really, the best one for you is the one that looks at the skill sets and competency areas you wish to grow in your analysis work. Yes, doing some analysis work before you dive in can ensure you continue to deliver value in your time spent on these assessments.

But even these assessments are not the only sources of work. IAG Consulting has a **requirements maturity model** (`https://www.iag.biz/about-iag/requirements-maturity-model-explained/`). Although it is focused on how well the organization meets requirements, it can be a great source for you to think about what you are enabling in your analysis role when it comes to requirements work. The same with the **Capability Maturity Model** by IEEE (`https://ieeexplore.ieee.org/document/219617`). Yes, it is focused on assessing the current maturity level of an organization, but simply asking yourself what you are doing to enable these capabilities and noticing where you spend the bulk of your time can be a great personal assessment of your analysis work. These are just a sampling, but they can help you think beyond your current work and focus on seeing where and how your work fits into the larger picture. What you are doing is seeking out ways to measure your value delivery. Each of these gives you a measurement to assess your skills. And, with a good baseline, you can clearly articulate the gaps to your own future state!

Realizing how many people skills you need in your analysis work, you might also consider some of the assessments that focus more on personality and work ethics or styles. Strength-finders and style tools, such as **Myers-Briggs Type Indicator**® (**MBTI**® `https://www.themyersbriggs.com/en-US/Products-and-Services/Myers-Briggs`) and **DISC** assessments (`https://www.everythingdisc.com/`), are great ways to get another look at your skills and strengths. They can also help you see the gaps in your professional skills and capabilities. The challenge is that this is *your* opinion. You are human, and so you naturally put your own biases on these assessments. As much as you want to be in that future state, you have to be truthful with yourself about where your skills lie today. That can be a great source of challenge and difficulty when doing self-assessment. Recognize that this is a single perspective. Asking your clients, colleagues, and team members to do the same assessments for you from *their* perspective can be a great way to get a more holistic picture.

Conducting peer reviews and assessments

Seeking peer reviews as well as getting your stakeholders' perspectives can be incredible sources of insight into the impact of your analysis work. The trick is to be focused so that it is actionable insight, which can have a direct positive impact on your career growth.

This can be as simple as asking your project stakeholders to complete an assessment on you. Use the same one that you did on yourself, as this will help you see the power of perspective. Let's take the DISC assessment. In general, this assessment looks to identify your skills and propensity toward four areas: dominance, influence, steadiness, and conscientiousness. I know I am personally very driven and action-focused on tactical items. However, it was very eye-opening that the stakeholders on my project thought I was very analytical and patient with them. That was not what I was expecting, but it was a great measurement of my analysis career work. Then, the action I made sure to incorporate into all my future project work was to explain my approach and goals clearly to my stakeholders. I now tell them that while I love to jump right in and try to help get things done, my goal in the analysis role is to listen to them and focus on understanding the challenges and opportunities at hand before helping them dive into decision-making. I would not have had this view without their help in rating my work against some predetermined criteria.

Peer reviews can be done periodically or ad hoc. Just like your personal assessment, the key is to remeasure against the same criteria after enough time has passed for you to practice and actually grow the skills. Here is a great approach to incorporating peer reviews into whatever analysis role you are playing:

1. Identify the area you want to improve on or work on more: *Doing a SWOT analysis or simply using lessons learned from a prior work effort can be great ways to focus on particular areas.*

2. Select an assessment that looks at those particular skill sets and capabilities: *An example is using the Business Analysis Competency Model.*

3. Take the assessment on yourself *BEFORE* the project or analysis work: *Get a measurement of where you currently stand with your skills.*

4. Then, as your analysis work is concluding, ask one or more of your stakeholders to complete the assessment after your work concludes: *Ensure that it is the same assessment.*

5. Compare the results:

    You are looking for both differences and similarities in the assessments:

    -   **Similarities** show alignment between your intentions and outcomes. If they reflect positive impacts, these are strengths you should continue and build upon.

    -   **Differences** highlight areas where your goals are not yet reflected in your work products or stakeholder interactions. These are valuable focus points for career growth.

6. Define the actions you will take to move you from where you are to where you want to be: *Lay these out in your career roadmaps and put them in product backlogs to commit to actively working on achieving these growth actions.*

Focusing on what you do with assessments and what actions you are taking next is how you maximize the value of your time on these career indicators. Like all your analysis work, even the simple assessments need to return value to the organization. This value could take many forms, so read on to identify where and how you can truly capture the value of these assessments and, more importantly, their insights.

Strategies for getting maximum value from assessments

Self-assessments should be repeated throughout your career, and you should also seek out updated assessments as your career grows. The industry and environments are going to continue to evolve, and so should your skill sets. Regular self-assessments are a great way to stay updated with industry standards. Use the latest versions of the assessments, as this will let you know the trending topics in each of the areas of work you explore. Also, repeating the same assessments gives you a measure of your growth.

That measure of growth is where you can course-correct your career roadmap. You want to implement a skill enhancement plan based on self-assessment results. Your assessment is for understanding your strengths and weaknesses. Doing the SWOT analysis, where you take advantage of your strengths and look for ways to mitigate weaknesses, is critical to knowing the actions required based on your assessments. Your career roadmaps, coupled with assessment results, are how you continuously strategically align your next actions with your career goals.

Application of the Competency Model

Going back to the example of improving your elicitation skills, both your self-assessment and your peer reviews articulate that you are great at facilitating elicitation activities, such as running a requirements workshop. Now, using the IIBA's Competency Model, you see that an expert would be able to lead others in elicitation activities. So, for your SWOT analysis, you might see the following opportunities as ways to leverage your strengths and eliminate weaknesses:

	Opportunities	Threats
Strengths	There is an annual server upgrade. You elicited the requirements last year. So, you then see the opportunity to help the junior BA lead this effort with your guidance.	
Weaknesses	You are quite comfortable eliciting requirements from project team members; however, the program manager needs to elicit priorities from the executive committee for the upcoming planning period. You ask to be assigned to this task so you can get more comfortable in senior-level discussions to expand your skills and be more comfortable helping other analysts.	

Table 12.1 – Example SWOT analysis using assessment

This is a great way for you to stay aware of your environment and seek out opportunities to both apply and grow your valuable analysis skill sets. Everything in your analysis world will continue to change, and so should your skill set as you aim to continue to deliver value. Now, just like your skill sets, let's take a closer look at measuring your techniques to ensure they continue to grow in value as well.

Instructional guides for measuring and improving business analysis techniques

Knowing what work needs to be done to add value in a business analysis role is the first part of growing your analysis career. Being both effective and efficient in your business analysis activities is where you begin to transition into a successful senior analyst and apply your skill sets to bigger and more complex challenges. Knowing where you are in your effectiveness will help you work to ensure you continue to both grow and strive for continued and increased value.

Measuring the success of your BA techniques

Just like your change work, knowing where you are is the first step toward improvement. With this in mind, you want to measure the usage of various BA techniques on your analysis work. Now, one of the best tools to use is the IIBA Competency Model, but you have to be a good analyst, as there is a trick to it.

The Competency Model only analyzes the tasks listed in the *Business Analysis Body of Knowledge® (BABOK®) guide*. But in each task area definition, there is a list of common techniques and their usage as applies to the respective task. Now, after you assess each of the tasks in the work, you come to the respective techniques. For tasks that you have general knowledge of and are getting more aware of, you can use the list of techniques as input and ideas to use next time you have to perform this task. For tasks you are more comfortable with, you need to assess that your usage of techniques aligns with the outcomes of that technique.

Improving the success of your BA techniques

The second part of an assessment is using the measures to build your growth steps. Again, the action is how you go from lessons *identified* to lessons *learned,* and constantly learning is key to your career success. The first part, though, is identifying the goal. What do you want or where do you want to be? Define this first. We put this in the first column in *Table 12.2.*

Then, use your assessments to define your current state. Go ahead and put this in the second column in *Table 12.2.* The current state really is as simple as where you are. Then, picturing your end goal, consider what the measurement needs to be to achieve your goal. This would be the future state that you put in the third column in *Table 12.2.* Notice how, just like your analysis work, you're defining a goal and then defining the current state and future states. Then, the *work* is in how you are going to get from the current to the future state. That action plan is the critical portion of the chart and how you deliver the value. Some examples have been put into *Table 12.2* to give you some ideas on how simple, yet focused, these elements need to be for your success. You now have the tools to build out your own action plan based on your assessment results and then incorporate industry-standard metrics. Start from the left (first column) and work your way right (the fourth column) to help ensure your success.

What is your goal?	Where are you?	Where do you want to be?	Actions to take
Obtain a senior business analysis position	Project-focused requirements	Define requirements that are more enterprise-level	Try to apply business capability analysis on the next project
Perform more formal BA assessments	Only perform annual evaluations with the manager, not BA-specific	Measurable targets and goals to work on in analysis work	Create metrics and KPIs for business analysis-specific work
Analysis expertise on non-project work (operations, process improvement)	Mostly smaller, project-related analysis requirements work	Work with operations teams on process improvement initiatives	Perform benchmarking and market analysis throughout project-based work to develop insights required for more strategic operations

Table 12.2 – Assessment action plan table

Table 12.2 shows just a few examples of what you might put in your own table. It can be difficult to come up with concrete measurements. Again, how do you prove you are a "good" analyst? Use the competency models or assessment tools for both quantitative and qualitative measures. While the example from the IIBA competency model on conducting elicitation activities feels very subjective, take a look at the techniques. Some objective measures might include things such as the following:

- Have you used brainstorming or mind mapping (or any other techniques listed) to successfully elicit requirements? *A great yes or no answer!*

- How many of the techniques have you used in your analysis work to conduct elicitation activities? *A measurable number that can be increased with experience!*

- How many stakeholders were present in each of your conducted elicitation sessions? *A tangible goal to increase your comfort level with larger and larger audiences!*

And honestly, worry less about the *measurements* and more about the *actions* you are defining to grow the skills. Actions mean implementation, and how you drive change in your skills and yourself. They are the stepping stones that allow you to not only reach that future state but also achieve your goals. Now, let's add the final component to measure and improve your analysis skills by incorporating feedback into your improvement plans.

Using feedback for improvement

Feedback is a gift. This is something that has long served business analysis professionals. Think about it. You should be less worried about negative feedback than you are about apathy. A stakeholder who tells you a design is all wrong means that they are interested enough to tell you what will or will not work. Apathy or a lack of any kind of response or feedback is the worst, as you do not know which parts are going well or could be improved. Even with negative feedback, you can be proactive and ask what didn't go as well as expected, and what the expectations were. But you must constantly be proactive and seek out this valuable information from multiple sources.

Collaborating with your stakeholders

Throughout your analysis work, always think about how you can collaborate *WITH* your stakeholders. You are never working *for* them. Rather, think that you are enabling them. Your goal is to help them achieve their organizational and business goals in the most efficient and effective manner. Asking for their input as to how you can do that can be key to your success, as they are often your customers as much as your stakeholders. Key questions to put in your own assessments at the end (and even throughout) each analysis endeavor might include the following:

- What value did the business analysis work provide, in your opinion?
- Where could there have been more business analysis support?
- Did you have any expectations of the business analysis role prior to starting?
    - If so, what were they?
    - And were they met?
- What would you like to see in future efforts?

Hearing that small things, such as a well-facilitated meeting or teaching others how to use collaborative software so you can work faster through the requirements work, can have meaningful impacts on both your current and future analysis work. But your stakeholders are not the only sources of feedback.

Working with your internal teams

Just like the feedback of your project stakeholders, your internal teams can be valuable sources of information and key stakeholders that you want to seek feedback from as you take a 360-degree view of your analysis work. Setting up regular feedback sessions with your manager, beyond the annual evaluation plans, can be a great source of both feedback and ideas. Put your professional development on your agenda. This means calling out the actions you planned and specifically making time to address your progress on your professional development growth plans. Examples of this could be as simple as the following:

- Identifying that you have only done in-person brainstorming sessions so far:

  - **Goal**: Become comfortable with facilitating online sessions

  - **Action**: Arrange training time with one of the help desk team members to learn about the features of the current set of technological tools

  - **Value**: This ensures that you can be successful in your analysis work, no matter how the environments change

- Sharing that you learned a new AI application:

  - **Goal**: Present and share how to use it with the project managers

  - **Action**: Request a meeting slot to present to the entire team and ask for your manager's support in encouraging attendance

  - **Value**: This builds a culture of knowledge-sharing and helps develop your own leadership skills

Allocate time to discuss not just where you want to be, but what is needed to get you there. Clearly articulate your requirements for what you need from your manager as a way to get support for your growth. You need to define what that growth plan is and why it is important. This means ensuring that you communicate openly with your manager, and often – at least regularly, such as a quarterly review, so that you not only stay on track, but that you work to ensure small steps are being delivered, as this is the secret recipe for larger, long-term achievement of bigger goals.

Then, expand to your peers and non-management staff. If you have colleagues doing similar analysis work or are even lucky enough to be on a business analysis team, then regular peer review sessions should be part of the team's activities. These are where you seek feedback from those who do not report to you, nor do you report to them. What do they see as your strengths? What advice would they offer to see you continue to succeed? And someone who does similar work to you, so they know the role's expectations, can have a unique view as compared to a stakeholder who is often the customer of your analysis work. These don't have to be complicated. But they *DO* need to go back to your plan.

Using the assessment action plan in *Table 12.2*, let's look at what this easy survey could be. Look at your goal, where you are now, and where you want to be. From these three columns, identify the analysis activity you do in this space. Yes, again, be a great analyst on your own work and truly think about what skill set or capability you are demonstrating in each instance. There can be multiple activities. Simply list them. This is the first column in *Table 12.3* and is labeled as **Business analysis activity**. Then, give your reviewer space to comment about what they observe. This is important as what you may feel you are doing versus what is seen and even felt by your colleagues can be quite different! Notice that you are not asking whether you do it well or not. This is not a judgment nor an assessment of whether you are a "good" or "bad" analyst! You are simply seeking objective feedback. With their consideration of your work, then ask whether there is any advice they would give for you to move forward. This is a great lesson learned that people will always give you opinions; however, advice is often more actionable and forward-thinking than personal preferences!

Business analysis activity	What do you observe?	What advice would you have going forward?
Defining requirements that apply beyond a single project		
Capturing requirements that can be easily reused by other projects and efforts		
Defining the BA performance metrics for a project		
Measuring and reporting on the actual performance back to the defined metrics		
Providing analysis of operational teams' process improvement work		
Analyzing current operations to identify improvement opportunities		

Table 12.3 – Example peer review survey format

Then, simply plan to share your surveys at different intervals. Just try to keep the same questions every time you seek feedback so that you can build up measures and compare your progress over time.

Add in other ways to get feedback from your team. Schedule informal sessions where you can share. We always called them *brown bag* sessions, where team members can share insights and highlights of what everyone has done well in their analysis work. Regardless of what you call it, giving space for teams to take turns to review business analysis artifacts and other work products, especially if scheduled regularly, is a great way to build feedback loops into your analysis practice. These sessions will give you fresh insights and allow you to share your own development work with others for that exponential value, where everyone grows.

These approaches are incredibly important if you have junior professionals working with you. It's not just you helping the next generation; even the most junior staff can give you interesting ideas. No matter how long you have worked doing analysis work, fresh perspectives can give insights into things you have missed. Actively share your own professional development plans with your teams. This will give them ideas and open up conversations to explore new techniques and approaches. Anytime you have to explain a topic to someone else, you really discover what you do and do not know. Young professionals will keep you on your toes and keep your skills sharp. But it is in seeing these opportunities for feedback and then taking the action to incorporate time for feedback that is critical to success.

Working outside your organization

Internal sources of feedback can be the easiest and most valuable to your current career track. However, if you are looking at the long-term success of your analysis work, knowing that your career could venture from more than one company and even industry, you will want other sources of feedback.

Your professional associations will continue to provide incredible value by sharing assessments, industry standards, and trends in the analysis community. Joining other associations that focus on niche areas of your work, or a particular industry will also be a great source of benchmarks for the roles you seek in the future. Even networking and getting feedback from other professionals in different arenas can be just what you need for fresh insights and ideas for your action plan. Do not discount the value an outsider's perspective can have on your analysis work, as their objectivity can be just the insight you need to look at your work from a different angle and approach! The value of your investment in membership can be returned in the following:

- Professional development events

- Hands-on and interactive training

- Facilitated sessions with experienced professionals with active feedback

- Assessments, tools, and templates written for that industry or perspective

- Career guides and examples

- Bodies of knowledge and standards defining activities and measurements

- Networking events with access to subject matter experts

- Mentorship and coaching programs

- Volunteer opportunities and even appointed or elected positions

You must seek out this feedback and ideas on how others are assessing their business analysis contributions and what they are doing for their professional development. You can even ask them about their growth plans. Just this great question could fuel the careers of others by getting them to define their own goals and opportunities. Regardless of where you seek the feedback, simply creating feedback loops into your assessments to regularly assess and measure your efforts is critical to your continued growth. Having measured where you are and defined where you will be is the foundation of the action plan that will take you there.

Summary

This chapter gave you a perspective on how to be a business analysis professional in your own analysis work. This means taking an analytical lens to the value you are providing in your business analysis activities. One of the best ways to measure your skill sets and capabilities is by using assessments. What gets measured is more meaningfully improved. If you know where you are and you define clear goals of where you want to be, it becomes easier to define the actions to get you there.

This chapter gave you many ideas and resources to actively incorporate measurements into your business analysis work and strive to achieve your goals. Practicing elicitation by seeking feedback on your own work grows your skill sets and helps you with your professional development plan. But you have to decide what that direction is. This chapter provided a great way to enhance your analysis journey as we reflect on the adventure through the chapters and conclude it in the next and final chapter. There have been a number of ideas and suggestions that can help your analysis career throughout all the chapters, and so now it is time to define those next steps and create your own roadmap of continuous professional business analysis steps.

Further reading

- International Institute for Business Analysis®, (2015). *The Business Analysis Body of Knowledge® (BABOK®) Guide. International Institute of Business Analysis*, Toronto, Ontario, Canada.

Unlock this book's exclusive benefits now

Scan this QR code or go to `packtpub.com/unlock`, then search for this book by name.

Note: Keep your purchase invoice ready before you start.

Final Thoughts and Next Steps

The world of business analysis is as dynamic as the environments in which the work can take you. Which adventure you choose in this exciting and ever-changing world is up to you! The best part is that this adventure can begin at any time. Whether it is analysis work or a titled business analyst role you seek, all are great options that will offer you a valuable career where you deliver value to others.

Now is the time to act with what you've learned about business analysis, both the practice and the profession. Like all your great analysis work, true value comes from what you do with the insights and, most importantly, what actions you are going to take.

In this chapter, we're going to cover the following main topics:

- Summary of key takeaways
- Actionable next steps
- How to engage with your business analysis community

Summary of key takeaways

The journey through these chapters has been as varied as the business analysis career paths you can take. But rather than an ending, consider this as the starting point to what comes next. Defining both the practice and profession of business analysis is meant to seed you with ideas. Then, you can cultivate and grow the ideas that take root with you the most. As you explore business analysis in your work (and your life), come back to the chapters to review topic-specific elements for more ideas and inputs on where you can go next. Remember to always think of that keyword: **VALUE**.

Whether it's to the project, the team, the organization, or (often most important!) to *YOU*, stay focused on what will deliver the most value. Think about this question with every activity you do:

What can I do that will deliver the most value?

When you are focused on this, you are at the heart of a business analysis professional. Being able to define the value is the key to success for anyone doing business analysis work!

Defining business analysis from a new perspective

Success in business analysis is often not a quantitative, explicit activity. Sure, there are metrics you can and should use, as we'll discuss later in this chapter. But success is rooted in staying true to two key concepts:

- Acknowledging both the practice and the profession of business analysis work

- The central focus on value

Everything you do should revolve around these concepts by considering the following:

- What is needed for a solution that provides the most value?

- Is the enterprise (the organization and beyond, in some cases) getting the most value for the effort?

- Are recommended solutions still providing value after their implementation and integration into daily work?

There is a special skill set in those that love to do requirements work; this value is not in how many requirements you can write but in generating artifacts that are *usable* by others. Consider the definition of requirements presented in earlier chapters; you want to think about expanding the application to *any* business work you do. When you can create materials that help others envision the same image of success, the same solution scope, and, ultimately, the same understanding, change efforts can fly to successful implementations at incredible speeds. But if others are not picturing what you are picturing, it is going to be tough work. The most efficient and effective delivery of value to an organization is a true metric of analysis success!

Now, as the business analysis job roles have become clearer throughout the chapters, with activities often found in defined job descriptions (we'll talk about this in more detail shortly), consider how business analysis professionals, especially senior business analysts, are actually trusted advisors. This is the ultimate goal you can work toward if you have passion and energy in analysis roles. You want to be seen as a trusted advisor who offers guidance and ideas such that the decision-makers can make the decisions *THEY* need to make. Even if you do the majority of the analysis work, research, interviews, and more, the work to create, change, and deliver the pieces that result in a solution rests in the hands of the SMEs under your careful watch. Business analysis professionals deliver solution ideas and options. The responsibility of the decision and execution of the resulting work rests with your stakeholders. But this is why, as you progress in your work, you will find that the most successful analysts are great at facilitation and work just as hard on their leadership skills as they do on their technical skills. Facilitation is all about making things easy. The easier you make it for your stakeholders to achieve business value, the more valued you become.

As you get comfortable with the project-based and operational process improvement efforts in your organization, challenge yourself to look for analysis everywhere.

Analysis everywhere

Successful business analysts often cannot "turn off" their analysis perspectives. They do not simply show up at an office location to do business analysis work. When they are in line at a grocery store, they are noticing the process steps that are happening to pay for groceries. When they are deciding what to order from a restaurant, they are analyzing the value of different meal options. When they are getting together with friends, they are creating mini business cases as to why they should consider one activity over another. Being a successful business analyst requires having the mindset to look for value using analysis activities, regardless of what you may call the process. So, if you are pausing right now and reflecting on how much analysis work you do daily, that is an *EXCELLENT* sign that you are well on your way to a successful career in analysis work!

If you are not sure that you are looking for analysis opportunities, the next time you have a desire to make an impulse purchase at your favorite store, stop and ask yourself these questions:

- What is the value you would get from the purchase?
- Why is it needed (or not needed) now?
- What are your alternatives?
- What are the risks of not buying it now?
- What would the impacts be if you did buy it now?

See? You just outlined a small business case by thinking about the value of your options. This is "analysis everywhere" work! Regardless of whether you call it "business analysis" or not, this perspective is exactly what is needed in your work and broader life. Broadening your perspective of where and how you can do analysis work will allow you to be successful as both a business analysis professional and a professional who does value-adding business analysis work. This is what makes it such an exciting opportunity!

Understand that the value business analysis professionals deliver is the *exact* value sought after by organizations. No matter the size, type, or even industry that the organization is in, everyone is looking for more value. Even if the titles and roles differ, the delivery of value is a capability that organizations are going to want for years to come. Business analysis is needed in every industry and every type of organization, including both for-profit and non-profit entities.

While technical areas still demand business analysis positions and skill sets, the key to success is in both your technical analysis *AND* communication skills. Your ability to work *WITH* teams and stakeholders is how you make the techniques deliver value. This is why focusing on professional growth in both your technical and non-technical capabilities leads to a long-term, successful career. The more that you focus on analysis activities rather than a job title, a location, an organization, or even an industry, the more flexibility you can build into your career to take advantage of those opportunities as they arise.

Successful business analysis professionals are constantly learning, no matter what type of work they do. From professional development training and practical skills to being able to learn the vocabulary and processes of a new area of business, the ability to adapt and adjust your analysis focus to deliver the most value is what separates successful senior analysis professionals from those just entering the field. Constantly learning, growing, and expanding your horizons is key to staying relevant. How to do this lies in your analysis activities, which we will review next, as the analysis tasks and techniques you perform are actually what give you the title of business analyst, regardless of what is listed on your business card.

Identifying business analysis tasks and techniques

Now, business analysis work is any activity that adds value to an organization or enterprise. So, the *work* that business analysts do is all the analysis tasks and techniques. This perspective brings with it both freedom and uncertainty as to what the work of a successful business analyst involves. However, certain tasks and techniques have become synonymous with business analysis work simply because they are great techniques to help define needs and recommend valuable solutions.

If you are just starting this analysis journey, then it is worthwhile to at least go through both the tasks and the techniques of the *Business Analysis Body of Knowledge® (BABOK®) Guide* by IIBA® (2015). Even if you have been doing business analysis for years, it is worth reading through it at least once to gain inspiration on new techniques or approaches to try in your next analysis session. But if you are newer to the analysis space, focus on item tracking, document analysis, observation, and estimation techniques to get you going. Regardless of where you are starting on your journey, take a two-pronged approach to building your analysis skills.

First, there is the technical execution of the analysis technique. Get comfortable with simply trying to do a technique well. Take, for example, process modeling. Get comfortable with creating a usable process model. Then, as you get confident in your technical skills, shift the focus to the soft skills you need to produce the process model. You will need to elicit ideas from your stakeholders, encourage collaboration from participants, and facilitate agreement to move forward with the resulting model. These are examples of soft skills to grow. But then, avoid stagnation by selecting another technique to explore. Perhaps data modeling might be a good next evolution. So, first focus on learning how to model data well. Then, as your skills progress, shift to growing your elicitation skills by rephrasing and acknowledging stakeholder input to articulate your understanding of their data arenas. This pattern, shown in *Figure 13.1*, enables the constant evolution of both your technical and soft skills in your analysis work.

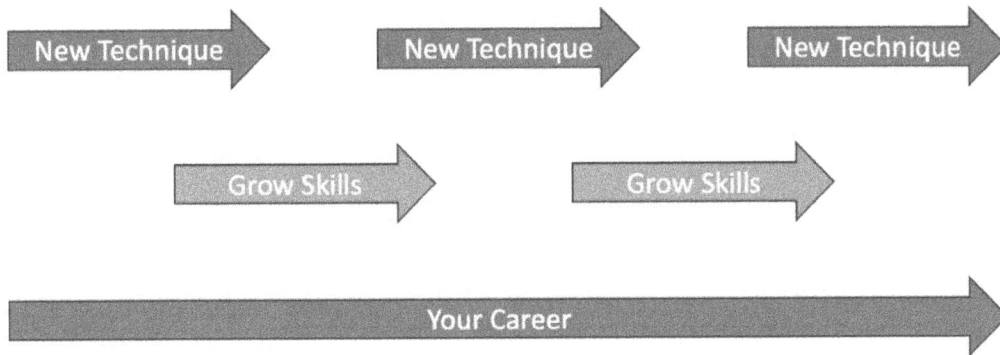

Figure 13.1 – Process of growing technical skills and soft skills in conjunction with one another

If you get comfortable with this pattern and approach, you will never have to worry about continuously growing! The challenge is to put on your roadmap what techniques and skills you want to fill this pattern with. In the previous chapter, we described goals and what you want to achieve in your career; look for how you can progress. The techniques we started off describing are very text-based. So, put some more visual techniques on your roadmap. Junior business analysts often look to others to lead, so as you grow, add more leadership skills to your growth plan. Keep in mind that successful analysis professionals live by the following motto:

See the work, say the work, do the work, and teach the work.

Now that you know what business analysts do in practice, your charge is to dive in with a growth mindset. Use more advanced techniques as you get comfortable with the basics. For example, perhaps for every project you work on, you create a context diagram. At first, you create these for your own awareness and simply include the diagrams in your requirements deliverables. Then, as projects get more complex, you start creating these context diagrams *WITH* your stakeholders. Again, start simple at first, but then build them into bigger and bigger sized workshops where you focus on facilitating the group to define the context of the change effort. Then, when you get a project that is very system or communications heavy, try building a data flow diagram in addition to the context diagram. This will have more details but will leverage the contextual analysis work you have already done. You're simply adding more and more techniques to your toolbox. But allow yourself the time to get comfortable with one technique before diving into another. The more tools you have in your toolbox, the more ways you can provide value to different business scenarios. Just keep building that bigger toolbox.

Now, what sets apart those who do analysis work well is soft skills – this is really the *magic* that those who have gotten to work with a business analysis professional love so much. Elicitation, facilitation, and collaboration (*oh my!*) are truly the definition of successful business analysis professionals. Elicitation focuses on understanding. Facilitation is all about making things easy. Collaboration focuses on others working together to deliver great results. You can see that these are all essential elements of a person aiming to help others achieve great business success. That's the definition of business analysis professionals. The tasks, techniques, and approaches used to describe analysis work in this book are not just applicable to analyzing your own career; they are also great skill sets for you to implement in daily life. That's why you want to always look beyond the current work assignment.

Going beyond the project

A number of examples and scenarios in this book emphasized that analysis work is performed as part of a project or being assigned to a project team. Some analysts love project-based work. That is a great place to keep adding value, yet dynamic enough so that every new project can be an interesting perspective or new focus area.

However, do not limit yourself to thinking that you can only do great analysis work on major projects or project-based work. Leave this book thinking that business analysis is everywhere. Defining needs and recommending solutions that deliver value is useful everywhere you look. Think about your own daily activities. From planning your day and prioritizing which activities you will and will not focus on to reflecting on how a presentation went and what you can do to enhance it for the next time, you are experiencing situations that can greatly benefit from good business analysis work. Solid analysis work that is always seeking the most value out of every effort is truly a long-term success plan that has great benefits.

But let's jump back and consider those who do like project-based work. This is a common entry point for you to start your analysis career, especially in the consulting world. Projects are a great way to get experience in different areas of business, and even industries, while providing the space to experiment, explore, and grow your skill sets. But projects are just the starting point. Know that you can easily grow into bigger and more complex areas, called *program and portfolio management*. Here, you use your experience in defining requirements and recommending solutions the same as you would on a project, but now your focus is on a much larger or expansive perspective. This includes questions such as the following:

- What is needed to deliver value for a department or even an organization?

- How does the enterprise get greater value by doing certain projects together or in a particular sequence?

- Is there a way to get greater value from combined efforts versus each individual project?

- How do we leverage the learning points and experience of prior projects to benefit future projects?

Those great questions are needed when you look beyond the project. The following are further questions that can be asked:

- What happens after the project is done?
- How do you know the product or changes the project delivered are continuing to deliver the desired value?
- Now that the products are implemented, what might be the best next initiative or project, realizing that an enhancement may or may not be a bigger priority than a new product or service?

Those pursuing more traditional analysis roles can expand into enterprise views of the organization and focus on capabilities beyond individuals or systems. All those processes you defined as part of the project work need to be leveraged for business value. *Enterprise analysts* ask questions such as the following:

- How do all those processes work together?
- What are the downstream effects of the business processes?
- What can be addressed at the beginning before those issues or impacts ever occur?

All great questions and spaces to grow your analysis career! The hardest question, though, is what do you want to do?

It is not just what types of activities you do in your analysis work but *where* you do those analysis activities. The role of business analysis professionals exists both inside and outside technology departments. The more technology gets ingrained into daily lives and activities, the more this line will get blurred. So, while you will be using technology throughout your career, do not feel confined to the technological team.

You can explore financial analysis, market analysis, and risk analysis roles. Here, you will do analysis work but within a certain area of business. You will use your analysis skills to support your respective line of business. The subject matter expertise in these roles is more focused on the area of work rather than specific business analysis capabilities and competencies. For instance, *financial analysts* will use lots of document and data analysis skills. But they are using these skills to analyze the expenditures and income.

Financial analysts often know more about finance processes such as budgeting and reporting statements than an in-depth knowledge of elicitation techniques. They just happen to use their great elicitation techniques to get the financial work done. So, no matter the area of concentration, analysis skills are valuable, impact-driven assets that any organization will be eager to have on their teams, regardless of position.

These roles can be found in different industries. You can even move your career from financial organizations to government work to the telecommunications or even healthcare industries, and then to non-profits (*just ask me – I did!*). For example, at a bank, you might need the same analysis skills and financial knowledge to be part of the finance team as you would at a job at a local government office. These same skills would be equally valued in the financial analyst role for a local hospital, which has a similar job description to a position in the local utilities team's billing department. You can thus not only easily apply for these jobs but also be wildly successful at them! Every position you hold at each of those organizations can be different in name and even focus. But any of these positions is an incredible place to grow your analysis skills and learn to adapt and adjust your abilities to your context to continuously add value!

Technology is, of course, shaping not only your world but your organizations' and customers' worlds as well. So, if you love technology, diving into specialization in cybersecurity, artificial intelligence, or even Internet 3.0 or beyond will make you an incredible resource when you can articulate not just what these technologies are but, more importantly, what value they can bring to companies and their business value propositions. With technology changing so rapidly, don't stress about having to stay up to date with the latest technology and all its details. Focus on knowing the *what* and the *why* of these innovations. The general understanding that will often come from your own natural curiosity can be very helpful to organizational teams that have no knowledge of current trends and expanding capabilities. Remember, you want to approach your organizations from the perspective of a valued partnership where you are all working toward the same goals. The more knowledge you equip yourself with, the more valuable a partner you will be! Learn what the different systems are capable of doing. What kinds of processes and functions do they perform that are being done manually today or with more than one system having to be integrated? Know the capabilities of the technology so you can consider what they can mean to your organization or enterprise. When you can articulate the *why* of any technology, you aren't just giving that needed value; you are standing out from the crowd! Knowing the business value of any opportunity is part of the elite qualities and reasons why organizations don't want to be without their precious business analysis teams! So, let's explore what you can do now that you have this insight into the business analysis profession.

Actionable next steps

Your business analysis work fulfills the value proposition through actions driven by the insights you provide. Basically, your analysis work is only as good as what others can *do* with it. So, now that you have done great analysis work on what the profession and practice of business analysis looks like, a great question is: *What are you going to do with this knowledge?* This is the part where you actually get to implement those great recommendations.

Now, the best action plans articulate where you are and where you want to be. The actions are then easy to define as they are simply the steps of getting from the current state to the desired future state. And you can take the same approach with your career. This is where your item tracking, prioritization, and backlog techniques come into play for your personal goals.

Specific, measurable outcomes are more likely to be attained because you can articulate a definition of *done*. Do not be afraid to get very specific and detailed in your career roadmaps. The better the expectations are articulated, the easier it is to know whether you have achieved the desired outcome and to measure your success against the goal.

But then, also, understand that you work in a world of change. Using agility techniques, build a backlog of ideas that you can constantly reprioritize based on environmental context, lessons learned, and even your stakeholder analysis. **Rolling-wave planning** is a great technique to incorporate into your career planning methods. Think of this as planning the details for your immediate goals, then only planning high-level milestones for further-out goals. Essentially, the farther the due date, the fewer details or specifics you define at this current moment. The closer the due date moves to today, the more details and specifics you want to define. This way, you can always correct the course and reprioritize your goals. Use the career roadmaps from the previous chapter and group your goals into immediate timeframes, near-term, and farther out (use the **Now**, **Next**, **Later** roadmaps of *Chapter 10*). The environment you start your career in will not be the same environment you end it in. So, your goals should evolve just like your roles do. Let's start with what the areas you can put on your growth roadmap are and then jump into how you can define success.

Building your capabilities

Knowing the full spectrum of business analysis career adventures, the question then turns to where to go with your career. But like our business analysis work, it can be most helpful knowing where we are starting. That means doing the assessments and analyzing your competencies. Make sure to go beyond the business analysis tasks and techniques; include leadership and facilitation skills coupled with your interests in technology, business, and industry terms and themes. Refer to those in the previous chapter to help you get started! This can be a great activity to do on an annual, if not bi-annual, basis. Set aside time in your calendar to analyze your skill sets and what value you provide the stakeholders you get to work with. Assessments and even personality quizzes can be very insightful and just what you need to get motivated, but you have to make time for this personal analysis work. One of the best things you can consider is what is often referred to as **360-degree evaluations** or assessments. This refers to a more holistic assessment of your skills beyond your personal bias. Pick an assessment or criteria you want to evaluate and the rating/ranking system you will use. **Surveys and questionnaires** are the business analysis techniques you are using here, so if you need more help in defining your specific questions, there are lots of resources available online focused on using these techniques. The value of your own assessment is in *WHO* you ask these questions of. This is where the 360-degree view comes into play. Consider asking the same questions (an important part of any survey) to the following stakeholders:

- Your manager

- A peer analyst professional

- A project stakeholder, especially an SME

- The last project manager you worked with

- An end user or customer

- A colleague or other coworker not on the same team

These varied perspectives will give you a more complete picture of the impact of your analysis work. This insight can be very powerful in driving what areas you consider for the future. For example, you might think you need to work on your communication skills, particularly in writing and sharing information with a large group of stakeholders. But then your stakeholders share in their assessment that you are very good at communicating the expectations and next steps clearly. With this insight, perhaps working on your communication skills is not the best use of your energy, and you should consider another skill to focus on in the immediate future. But it's best to get this insight first to make informed decisions about future work.

Use these kinds of assessments or the ones in the previous chapters, but once you have some understanding of your analysis success, think about where you want to be, not just in your analysis career but even with your own personal interests. You are more likely to get more involved and dive deeper into the subject matter if you are passionate or at least curious about the subject matter. For example, by doing analysis work in a major graphics design organization, even if you feel like you are not an artistically inclined person, you might find the processes of designing and communicating brands and customer desires very fascinating. So, you have an interest to learn more about the industry while doing analysis work that adds value.

The challenge, of course, is thinking about what you want to do. *Just because you can, doesn't mean you should* is a great mantra to use in your analysis work, but it can also apply here. What this means is that you do not need to limit yourself to what you are currently good at today. Exploring interests in domains where you have to learn and grow fast to be successful is a great opportunity! You just have to be a good business analyst and build the business case for any direction you want to take your career in. There needs to be a full-value proposition of any efforts you put into your career. For example, say you find the legal profession fascinating; does pursuing a law degree return value for the time, money, and energy you will put into earning that degree? If it doesn't result in long-term career value, that is, you never plan to become a lawyer, judge, or even legal analyst, then you need to reconsider the business case for this action. However, job shadowing some of the legal team members at your organization to understand how they work, and their priorities might be incredibly valuable as you work on major regulatory projects at a financial institution or even a non-profit. Your small investment in time to understand that area of business will often yield significant returns, as well as time savings and smarter solutions. No matter what aspect of the career you pursue, there should be business value to your organization, context, and yourself in every action you take. It is this practice of being focused on value delivery that is the ultimate key to success.

But you have to know what you want. Knowing both where you are and where you want to go is key to making a plan that works. So, with the current state analyzed and the future state defined, pull out your SWOT analysis and layer in what opportunities and threats are on the horizon that you can act on now. In *Table 13.1*, you can put in your current and future competency measurements. Then, brainstorm the actions to get to your future state. Feel free to jump back to *Chapter 4* for help with doing assessments and then thinking through the action items. Once you have some specific actions, though, it is time to lay out the opportunities and threats. What external elements can help support or might challenge your efforts?

Current Competency	Future (Desired) Competency	Actions to Get to the Future State	Opportunities	Threats
Take notes and build process models at your desk	Be able to build process models live with stakeholders for immediate feedback and validation	Try process modeling live with just one stakeholder	Vested product owner on current project	No standards for organizational modeling
			Assigned a project that is changing how the business operates	Tight deadlines and the desire to deliver fast on a product
		Attend a process modeling training course	Manager who is very supportive of professional development plans	Budgets for administrative and non-project-related activities have been reduced

Table 13.1 – Example SWOT identification table for business analyst competencies

Table 13.1 shows an example of looking at one's ability to build process models live during stakeholder discussions, with the current state and future state. A few simple yet impactful ideas of how to try performing the technique, as well as resources, are brainstormed in the **Actions to Get to the Future State** column. Again, brainstorm the opportunities and threats that are happening in the enterprise right now. You can then layer the SWOT analysis on top and get some great insights. The value is that you can now ask those two important career-driving questions:

- What opportunities can you take advantage of to move those actions forward?

- What threats are out there to which you might have to tailor your actions to still be successful?

Now, you are using your great business analysis skills to strategically drive your career forward! So, let's think about the ways that you can improve your analysis techniques to give you an actionable career roadmap.

Improving your analysis techniques

The best way to improve the techniques is to do them. Do more of the analysis tasks that require you to apply these techniques. Sure, there are techniques you will use very often simply because they work. But one of the best ways to grow is to try something new. Think of a workshop or facilitated session that you plan to run. Pick a session where you know the stakeholders well, they all work together well, and the topic is easy enough that most people can contribute, or again, have a good understanding of what needs to be done by whom. Then, use that opportunity to try to achieve your goal, say, elicit prioritization, by trying a technique that you do not normally incorporate. Perhaps this time you try some **Kano analysis** to see whether you can get your stakeholders to look at the features at hand from another perspective. What you are doing is looking for *safe spaces* to practice alternative and advanced techniques so that you can truly learn (through experience) what it takes to be successful with each tool you add to your toolbox.

But also, think about how many techniques you can do daily. Every email you write should be a mini business case. Think of how actionable your email would be when you need information from someone else if your email included the following, and *ONLY* the following, information:

- **Goal**: Why are you sending the email?

- **Current situation**: What is happening or changed to surface this need at this point in time?

- **Desired situation or outcome**: What needs to happen or be achieved?

- **Recommended approach**: What are you asking for in your email? Consider the costs, risks, and impacts of this ask.

- **Alternative approaches**: What other options could be considered and what are their respective costs, risks, and impacts, including doing nothing?

- **Restate and define the recommended approach**: Clearly restate the ask of the email and what will come next.

This should seem familiar as it is the same format for a great business case! But that is what each ask should be. It should give enough information to perform the requested action without having to email back and forth. Again, consider the value to your organization where you can save people valuable time and money!

Example email written as a business case

Subject: Need response on requirements for new website by Friday

Hello,

Thank you for your support for the new website design, as the goal to convert more leads into clients will help us grow our market share.

To accomplish this, we need your confirmation that the attached list of defined features is the comprehensive list that you want to use for our prioritization working session coming up.

We want to prioritize those elements that will give the most value as we are working with a constrained timeline and budgetary fluctuations.

Of course, please provide additional ideas you want on the long-term plan, but understand that more advanced or intricate features will have to be balanced within our constraints and developer capabilities.

Please let me know if you have any questions. We would appreciate your response by Friday. We will be bringing the confirmed list to next week's prioritization meeting where we will confirm the first few sprints for development.

Thank you.

The preceding example is a little longer than you might even need, but it addresses all aspects of your work while forcing you to think about what a good business case looks like. The more you do these techniques in your daily work, the easier they will be to incorporate as part of your analysis activities. How about one more trick? Use the user story format to create your value proposition statement or your elevator pitch! Remember that a **user story** explains the following:

As a WHO, I need a/to do WHAT so that WHY.

Think of your introduction to the project team as follows:

> "**As** *the person responsible for the requirements on this project,* **I will need** *your participation and input as to your current business needs and product expectations,* **so that** *there is clarity in the work for the developers to accurately build what you are looking for within the time constraints of our current project.*"

This might seem a little wordy for a quick introduction, but you have answered way more than simply saying, "I'm the business analyst." Not to mention, what if you just say your title or position and the stakeholders have no clue what a business analysis professional even does? This user story intro gives context and focus to not only what you are doing but also what you need from them and why. It is really this simple to start practicing business analysis techniques. Just analyze your day-to-day activities and look for where you can leverage your knowledge of the techniques you have practiced.

This is the first step: take the techniques you use most frequently in your business analysis work and perform them in everyday scenarios. Techniques might include things such as the following:

- Document analysis
- Observation
- Interviews

These are techniques junior analysis professionals perform frequently in their project-based work. Once you become comfortable in these assigned business analysis roles, you want to practice them as much as possible in daily activities. This simply extrapolates your value to well beyond any assigned project and makes you valuable to the overall organization.

Once you feel comfortable with these entry-level techniques, expand your project and initiative focus to doing more advanced techniques in your work. The natural progression in your roles is to evolve from simple analysis projects to more complex, varied, and diverse projects in scope and deliverables. So, your techniques should be expanding in the same fashion. Use the IIBA (2015) *BABOK Guide* to learn new techniques for your next initiative or assignment. A **balanced scorecard** or a **business model canvas technique** might be the unique perspective the team needs on a new project. Even in team or department discussions that are exploring new ideas, perhaps you use a new technique to facilitate the discussion. Be okay with feeling uncomfortable the first time you try a new technique or something you have hardly used before, as you will learn from the experience. That is what this stage is all about. You have to analyze your own experience and approach and define the activities to do next. Using new techniques means there is no current state. You have to try different techniques to get an idea of your comfort level and ability to handle different contexts and stakeholders. This will give a baseline for a current state analysis. From there, you can then make improvements. Is there something about the technique you need to practice more? Or is the technique great and fun, but it highlighted the need to have solid skills and expertise when dealing with different stakeholders?

Exploring advanced techniques is what gets you qualified to apply for senior analyst positions. You need that measurement to help you define the path between your current and desired position. Of course, what is often the case here is that you realize how valuable the skill sets are – the capabilities of being able to work with others, run successful meetings and workshops, and handle personalities – and why they set successful business analysis professionals apart from the rest! But you will not realize this until you try. Know that you never have to tell your stakeholders you tried a technique and it did not work. Simply course correct in your session with a new technique and focus on the outcomes you produced.

As you practice analysis work in everyday activities, ensure you get some baseline metrics. Use the assessments in *Chapter 12* to get a good, objective (if possible) measure of your skill set. This becomes the most important metric to help you define where you want to take your career next. It also points out the almost more important aspect of business analysis work, and that is your skill set. Think about what it takes to work *WITH* stakeholders. They can be opinionated, particular, and even moody. So, the successful business analysis professional of both today and tomorrow is the one who is constantly growing their skills as their techniques evolve.

Improving your skills

Your skills will grow in the same way you build your techniques' competencies. The more you integrate leadership, facilitation, and good business-focused practices into your daily routines, the stronger these skills will get. Just keep it simple. Take, for instance, *asking good questions*. At your next meeting, before you explain something or chime in with why you did or did not take a particular action, ask a question. It can be as simple as, "What information would help you the most?" or "What (*or why!*) do you need the information for?" Being open and seeking clarity helps build the context for not only you but everyone else present at that time. And context is always needed to solve problems. These questions are helping to shift your role from an order-taker to a collaborator. This means evolving your work from intense, independent analysis to collaborative, engaging sessions where the work is actually "done," or at least built and drafted, live with everyone. You want your stakeholders to do as much of the work as possible. Ask good questions that *THEY* have to answer. Redirect questions that come to you to the other team members for THEM to answer. Get stakeholders talking to each other as much as possible. *Elicitation, facilitation, and collaboration* is not just a mouthful of syllables, but rather where the real business value lies in business analysis skills. Enabling others to succeed is the real business value. The way you do that is through these **soft skills**. But just like your analysis techniques, you have to measure and evolve them to be able to keep growing and succeeding in the varied environments you'll face.

Take digital notetakers such as Fathom (`https://fathom.video/`) as an example. This tool will record your conversation and highlight when you are speaking more than other participants. That is, it will break down how much of the discussion within the session was done by you. If you are in the role of *facilitator*, then you probably want to do as little talking as possible. You should speak just enough to get the team members to collaborate with each other and then step back and let *THEIR* creative ideas fly! Use the tool to help give you the data points. But then it is on you to leverage this lesson learned in your retrospective of how you will grow from this knowledge and expand your skills. Just aiming to speak less at the next meeting is a great goal. This means you have to ask great facilitating questions that get the teams involved and diving into the topic at hand almost without you being needed (don't worry, you will still be needed to articulate the needs, not just the wants!). But you need to take the same approach with your skill sets that you adopted for your techniques. Measure where you are and define where you want to be. Then, lay out the action plan of where and how you will build these skill sets. It is the practice and application in real-world environments where you will find out just how comfortable you are with the techniques, stakeholders, and more.

Consider the following. Regardless of whether you are pursuing technical-focused roles or not, aim to grow your *digital comfort* skills. Take, for example, software you use to build process models. Sure, you can become an expert at Microsoft Visio® and be able to create multiple process models. But are you comfortable with using a comparable tool on a Macintosh operating system? For example, if you were given Lucidchart (`https://www.lucidchart.com/`) to build your process model, could you still facilitate a live discussion and capture the process model in Lucidchart? You want to be comfortable with the processes and the general features and functionality to do the analysis work. Technology is going to keep changing, so are you comfortable with whatever the tool of choice is? The comfort is not in just switching technology, but in achieving your analysis objectives regardless of the tool. This is where you are improving your skill set. You are building agility, learning, and strategic leadership by facilitating teams to achieve their outcomes.

But this comfort only comes with practice. It can be as simple as having an online meeting with a vendor or external party. Ask them which meeting tool *THEY* prefer. Sure, it may not be the one you love using, but if it makes it easier for your stakeholders to participate and get that necessary information elicited or confirmed, then it is the right choice for the challenge at hand. See, this is where you turn technology into the means to the outcome, not the product. Analysts are going to work in worlds that are not just dominated by technology but evolve and will ultimately be competitively driven by the ways in which technology is applied successfully. That is your trick – learn to apply the technology regardless of your focus or context.

You'll notice that this work is less about defining *success* for yourself and more about how you apply that knowledge. Learning is a key skill for business analysis professionals and requires you to constantly be applying what you learn. Your future success lies in the action plan. If you can articulate some metric or measure of what you are currently doing today, it is both easier to plan the future and celebrate your amazing achievements, as we will talk about next.

Measuring your success

Just like your requirements, tracking your growth helps you visualize, measure, and simply realize how much amazing growth you have achieved.

Measures of success for a business analysis professional might include the following:

- Stakeholders who are engaged and excited to come to the next meeting you are hosting.

- Stakeholders who come with "requirements" already defined or "process maps" that the team created for your meetings.*

  The use of the quotes ("") around these terms is for the positivity in seeing your stakeholders start to use business analysis terminology, though you will often have to do a lot of review and revision of requirements and other artifacts to get them to their "usable" position needed for the effort.

- Minimal or no review sessions to confirm elicitation results from prior requirements workshops or sessions.

- Test cases passing on first pass or first attempt.

- Solutions put into production perform with minimal user-reported issues in the first X months of deployment.

It's not just about what you did or didn't achieve – that is not the end goal. Success is a continuous road where true analysts use measurements to continue to propel themselves beyond where they are now. Continuous improvement needs to be a key element of your career, no matter whether you are pursuing business analysis-related work or not. Every effort you are assigned, every project you support, and every daily task is an opportunity to learn. It is also an opportunity to grow. Remember: It is one thing to measure how well you are doing. It is another thing, and the differentiator to long-term success, to define your future actions based on those measures.

Incorporating feedback into your work

How do you know you are successful? What is the measure of success? As much as you might have goals for yourself, remember that most of your work is geared toward enabling others to be wildly successful. You are actually successful when *THEY* are successful. So, where are those measurements in your analysis work? Those continuous improvements come from actively seeking and passively receiving the inputs of the stakeholders you work with.

Trust, like many other skill sets, is not unique to business analysis work. However, those who can build rapport *WITH* their stakeholders will be more successful than those who do not. Think about how many successful working relationships you have had with your stakeholders. Now, this measurement can be just like trying to measure your business analysis success – the measure is really about whether things worked. Did you achieve your outcomes, both your technical change work and your application of soft skills? So, in addition to your business outcomes, consider some of the following things stakeholders exhibit as a means of measuring business analysis success:

Quantitative Measures	Qualitative Measures
Attend meetings that they are invited to	Share openly and honestly with you
Give you feedback when asked	Give constructive (often critical) feedback
Provide positive survey responses	Speak positively of you to others
Ask questions for clarity	Seek an understanding of your business analysis processes
Deliver information on requested due dates	Share that they enjoy working with you

Table 13.2 – Quantitative and qualitative measures of success

These are some ideas to measure whether you are working well with your stakeholders. When they want to work with you, that is a great sign of success. If you are seeing these things in your analysis work, then you want to find ways to ensure these kinds of feedback and actions continue to happen. If you are not seeing this in your analysis work, then you want to consider how to *MAKE* it happen in your future endeavors.

Actively incorporating stakeholder feedback

You must still actively plan out how to ensure stakeholder feedback is incorporated into your business analysis processes.

If there is positive feedback from stakeholders or the engagement activities feel good and fun, then ask the following:

- What worked well that I need to keep doing on the next initiative?

- How do I tailor my tasks, techniques, or even templates to ensure/make that reaction happen again?

- What can I do to ensure this becomes a consistent response?

If there is negative feedback or you are not seeing these measurements of success, then you need to ask:

- What did or did not happen that led to this result? What can I do to avoid this on future initiatives?

- What was missing from the technique or approach that resulted in this response? What can I do to adjust my actions to avoid this response in the future?

Regardless of what happened, know that the actions you do or do not take become your true measure of success!

Your skills and techniques assessments can be quite insightful to help you assess how well you are performing as a business analyst. How are you measuring your repeated value delivery? For example, say you are worried about how to deliver even more value for whatever the next initiative is. Yes, always do the best you can, focusing on how to deliver maximum value. But remember that often, the maximum value comes from the templates, lessons learned, and teachings you share with others for THEIR success in future efforts. Think about that: if everyone tried to make it easier for the next person in whatever they were doing, the world, or at least your business, would run a little smoother. But you must answer the *so what?* question. Sure, you did a good job on this project – so what? So, what are you going to do next time? What are you *NOT* going to do next time? Answering these questions with a focus on how to make both yours and your team's next effort even more successful is the true measure of success. The way you get there is by defining the actions you plan to take on this career journey!

Building and using a career roadmap

Now, while your soft skills might be harder to measure, you can create a concrete plan for the actions you will take to ensure your growth and continued success. Like any good plan, consider the near term, mid term, and long term. This is as simple as asking yourself the following:

- **One-year goals**: What do you want to achieve in one year?

- **Three-year opportunities**: What do you need to learn, explore, and experience to understand the value of those opportunities over the next three years?

- **Five-year direction**: What lessons learned, feedback, and outcomes are you taking from each initiative that are helping you define what you do (and do not!) love about analysis work? Those ideas should guide the direction of your five-year lens.

These are your KPIs for career success. They are tangible measurements to help you show that you have achieved success in the intended direction.

Now, the most important part is in *defining what actions you are going to take to achieve these success metrics*. Just like a roadmap, the near-term items should be extremely detailed and even include due dates and other tangible numbers and metrics. The farther the distance for your KPIs, the less detail, so that you can welcome changing perspectives and directions that are going to happen (*not if!*). This is, in fact, the exact same rolling-wave planning you help others do in your analysis work to keep you focused yet flexible. See *Table 13.3*, which shows some examples of discrete to broader actionable goals:

One Year	Three Years	Five Years
Specific, measurable	Defined, yet high-level	Larger goals, aspirations
Run a workshop with more than 40 participants	Perform a training session on a business analysis technique	Manage a project
Lead the UAT effort	Achieve IIBA® certification	Be a mentor or manager to a team of business analysts

Table 13.3 – Example actions to achieve roadmap goals

Go ahead and create your own roadmap of goals. Just brainstorm ideas of what you want your career to look like in one year, three years, and five years. Then, turn the items in the **One Year** column into actionable items, with due dates and dependencies. It is the action that will turn you from a good analyst into a successful business analysis professional. For three-year goals, put a timeframe in which they should be completed so you hold yourself to those ideas. But don't be afraid to generalize, such as "next quarter" or "on the next project." For the five-year items, you just want to add some adjectives to them and review and update those definitions every time you are reviewing and revising the plan.

This way, they will continuously get more tangible and be easier to achieve as they move into three-year and eventually one-year goals.

As you work so hard within your organization, your success will truly blossom when you seek external support. So now, let's explore the power of coupling your hard work for whatever organization or industry you work for with an association and resources that are committed to the full success of business analysis professionals.

How to engage with your business analysis community

You may be a team of one or be lucky enough to be part of a business analysis team. But these people, as well as your managers and stakeholders you work with, are not the only ones rooting for your success. There are entire communities around the world that aim to propel the business analysis profession into long-term value. Successful business analysts are always observing and analyzing documentation and trends. What others are doing in other industries, and even other parts of the world, and team compositions can be just the insight or fresh ideas you need to be wildly successful in your own position. But, like your analysis work, you get out of these associations what you put into them. That effort is such a precious commodity that you want to analyze the options and pick those resources that will give you the maximum value for the minimum investment. Yes, just like you try to help your stakeholders, now you need to help yourself with this value-focused perspective.

Leveraging the investment of professional associations

Think of the time and money you spend to join professional associations as a true investment in your career. The more you invest, the more you will get out of it. The most successful long-term career analysts are often deeply invested in their professional associations. Pull out your career roadmaps and see where business analysis professional growth, leadership, and community activity are on your plan. As you brainstorm ways to achieve your goals, consider the power of IIBA (www.iiba.org). They have a huge amount of resources that you can use to explore business analysis work. Even more importantly, they have a network of professionals you can engage with to collaborate and explore the various facets of business analysis work. Whether online, with local chapters, or even introducing you to other associations and organizations related to business analysis, there are ways to immerse yourself in all kinds of business analysis approaches.

If your goal is certification, then first seek out what certifications IIBA offers as your first source. Yes, do your analysis work and compare the requirements for the different options, assess their value, and analyze both your prior experience and future career goals. Then, seek out local resources such as study groups and chapter meetings, where you can engage with other professionals to learn from their certification experiences and the value they've gained. Elicit understanding and knowledge that become inputs back into your roadmap and validate your direction or open up opportunities. Use these feedback loops, continuous analysis, and re-evaluation of decisions from your external sources to adapt and adjust your plan. Having a second (or third, or fourth) opinion in any decision-making is always a good idea!

Now, membership in these organizations can quickly have a positive ROI if you approach it with your questions ready and focus areas defined. Attend events ready to ask: *Who knows about [your topic/goal]?* Or ask the chapter presidents or membership chairs: *Who can help me with [career goal]?* Whether it's a business analysis association such as IIBA or an industry trade or other professional group, walk in ready with your elicitation questions. These are the professionals who have tried and done things you may have yet to experience. And what a great way to learn lessons without having to do the work! You have to approach the association events and connection opportunities with the same fervor you do your elicitation sessions or requirements workshops. Analyze the stakeholders. Understand their wants, needs, and desires (and your own!). Ask great questions that elicit conversations and collaborations. Seek to explore new ideas and opportunities *WITH* others. Think about how much you can gain with this approach. The more you commit to your network, the more you will actually become the valued resource others will seek out!

Giving back to the profession

As your career and comfort level grow, it is time to shift beyond your own bubble and start to look around you. In the beginning, we learn as much as we can. As we learn, we work with others to explore unique ways to apply analysis techniques and deliver value. If you love to continuously climb and reach higher with your work and abilities, you will notice that others will start to look up to *YOU*. Your experience, learning, and judgment earned from years of application become the fuel for the next generation. Here is where you find some of the best growth opportunities no matter where you are in your career: the opportunity to help others. But this does not need to be formal. Those same informal events where you found inspiration and ideas from others are where you can start to share your knowledge.

Presenting at conferences

Conferences and professional events will continue to be the place where business analysis leaders share ideas and explore new opportunities. These are often the largest and most diverse gatherings of professionals in any industry. There are topic-specific conferences, as well as industry-agnostic and industry-specific conferences and events. The challenge is finding one that aligns with your roadmap. Look for events that are going to address the maximum number of questions or insights you are looking for in your career.

But in that same respect, realize that you too will have a lot to offer as you get more experience in your career. It does not need to be anything fancy or "professionally" done. Most conferences prioritize case studies – where you simply share what you did, why you did it, and what you learned. Remember, the best lessons learned are learning from someone else, so you don't have to go through their pain. Others want to know what you did so they can learn what to do (and not to do!) in their own efforts. Just share! That's all you have to do. But when you share, you realize how much you do know about your work. It does not always have to involve speaking. It can be as simple as writing an article or submitting a paper on your own experiences. Case study papers, and even blog articles and interviews or podcast discussions, are constantly being sought after by professional communities. There will be great questions, and you can see just how deeply your experience is helping you. The more you have to explain your actions to others, the more insight you get about yourself and can grow your career successfully!

While speakers may present a topic or novel idea, it is the conversations that happen afterward where the real learning and growth take place. Getting inspired by what others are doing and asking questions in a venue that provides analytical feedback only leaves you feeling charged and ready to go and conquer the world. Think of conferences, especially business analysis conferences, as one big mastermind event with different groups. You can ask questions, seek feedback, and inspire others all day long.

But again, you get what you put into it. The more effort you put into sharing, connecting, and learning, the more you will get out of these efforts. And hey, a free conference pass is a pretty good business case to the boss, right? Definitely put both conferences and speaking on your roadmap for professional growth. IIBA and other professional associations' conferences and events will always seek great professionals to inspire their membership. Why not let it be you and learn in the process?!

Volunteering your business analysis skills

While you may work for an employer who pays you to do quality analysis, there are many organizations and individuals out there who would love to learn from you and get your insights on how they can achieve value in their own work. It can be as simple as volunteering to speak at a business analysis chapter event. Or you can coordinate a panel of analysis professionals or simply a networking event with others working on project-based work. Even outside the realm of business analysis, getting involved in organizations and associations that share knowledge, facilitate networking opportunities, and provide professional development activities can be one of the greatest ways to learn while helping others.

Finding ways to give back is also where you see the mentorship circle come to completeness. Looking at your career roadmap, you want to seek out mentors or people working in areas that have the experience or success you desire. Surrounding yourself with those who have achieved more and operate on a faster, more complex scale will give you insight into what you can look forward to and even provide learning opportunities without suffering the hard lessons many of them will have experienced.

But as your career grows, realize that you will now become that person with the experience. *YOU* will be the one with certifications, experience in technical or non-technical teams, project-level or enterprise-level work, and more! Others will naturally want to be around you to hear your stories and learn what information they should elicit for their own career success. This is where you begin to evolve into the role of a mentor and coach.

Mentoring others is like teaching. You realize what you do and do not know… and fast! You can share your own experience, while your mentee brings fresh ideas and asks questions from perspectives you may not have considered. This is why so many people love helping others – they get inspired to analyze their own work. It also makes you an even better analysis professional when you have to explain *why* to someone:

- Why did you approach a project, job, or position in a certain way?

- Why did you take (or not take) an action for a given situation or scenario?

- Why does your own roadmap look the way it does?

You elicit bountiful ideas for your own career when you help others with their careers. The trick is in finding the right audiences where you enjoy giving to others and sharing your talents. Again, look back at your roadmap and see what gaps you have or areas you wish to grow into. Then, find the organizations and groups that talk about those topics and seek out events where you can share, learn, and grow with others. Regardless of where you share your talents, keeping that focus on delivering maximum value in anything you do – including helping others achieve great value – is what brings you success in business analysis!

Summary

Whether you hold the title of a business analysis professional or are excited about pursuing a new adventure, I hope you put down this book thinking about *value*. Business analysis professionals maximize value delivery in all they do and all they influence and inspire. There is not only the value you provide to an organization or even your team but also the value you provide to yourself. The challenge is to look for the opportunity and develop your growth plans. But this is only the beginning!

Yes, that means being a business analyst on yourself as much as, if not more, than your employed profession:

- What do you want and why?

- Where are you and where do you want to be?

- What opportunities are changing your roadmap of tomorrow, yet driving your actions of today?

The years in front of you should be an exciting time filled with opportunity and ideas of what's possible. Your biggest challenge should not be worrying about whether you want to be a business analysis professional or not. Rather, it should be selecting where and how you want to grow, live, and apply your valuable analysis skills for a career full of success, knowing you have given great value to this incredible world! Good luck!

Further reading

- International Institute for Business Analysis® (IIBA®), (2015). *The Business Analysis Body of Knowledge® (BABOK®) Guide*. International Institute of Business Analysis, Toronto, Ontario, Canada.

Unlock this book's exclusive benefits now

Scan this QR code or go to `packtpub.com/unlock`, then search for this book by name.

Note: Keep your purchase invoice ready before you start.

Index

‹packt›

`packtpub.com`

Subscribe to our online digital library for full access to over 7,000 books and videos, as well as industry leading tools to help you plan your personal development and advance your career. For more information, please visit our website.

Why subscribe?

- Spend less time learning and more time coding with practical eBooks and Videos from over 4,000 industry professionals

- Improve your learning with Skill Plans built especially for you

- Get a free eBook or video every month

- Fully searchable for easy access to vital information

- Copy and paste, print, and bookmark content

Did you know that Packt offers eBook versions of every book published, with PDF and ePub files available? You can upgrade to the eBook version at `packtpub.com` and as a print book customer, you are entitled to a discount on the eBook copy. Get in touch with us at `customercare@packtpub.com` for more details.

At `www.packtpub.com`, you can also read a collection of free technical articles, sign up for a range of free newsletters, and receive exclusive discounts and offers on Packt books and eBooks.

Other Books You May Enjoy

If you enjoyed this book, you may be interested in these other books by Packt:

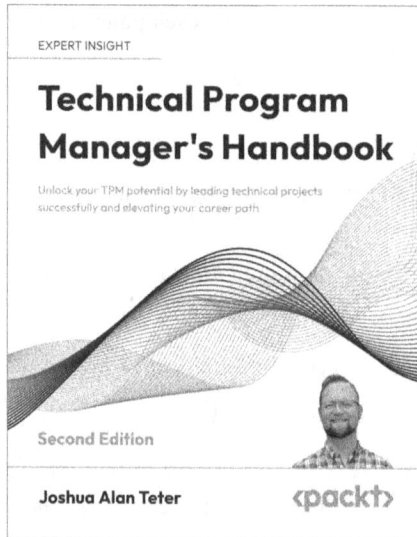

Technical Program Manager's Handbook, Second Edition

Joshua Alan Teter

ISBN: 978-1-83620-047-5

- Uncover the critical importance of the TPM role in the tech industry
- Understand and leverage the unique aspects of the TPM role
- Discover what makes a successful TPM through real-world case studies
- Master project management with advanced technical skills and AI tools
- Apply EI to enhance leadership and team management
- Explore careers and paths for TPMs in the Big Five tech companies

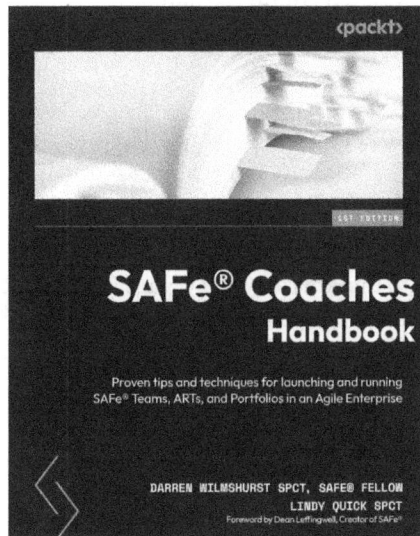

SAFe® Coaches Handbook

Darren Wilmshurst, Lindy Quick

ISBN: 978-1-83921-045-7

- Discover how to set up Agile Teams to attain maximum effectiveness
- Avoid common mistakes organizations make with SAFe®
- Find out how to set up the Agile Release Train
- Discover common mistakes enterprises make that affect the success of the ART
- Understand the importance of Value Streams and learn how to work with them successfully
- Start using the best ways to measure the progress of Teams and ARTs at an Enterprise level
- Recognize the impact of successful SAFe® adoption on Enterprise strategy and organizational structure

Packt is searching for authors like you

If you're interested in becoming an author for Packt, please visit `authors.packtpub.com` and apply today. We have worked with thousands of developers and tech professionals, just like you, to help them share their insight with the global tech community. You can make a general application, apply for a specific hot topic that we are recruiting an author for, or submit your own idea.

Share Your Thoughts

Now you've finished *The Business Analyst's Career Master Plan*, we'd love to hear your thoughts! Scan the QR code below to go straight to the Amazon review page for this book and share your feedback or leave a review on the site that you purchased it from.

`https://packt.link/r/1-836-20685-2`

Your review is important to us and the tech community and will help us make sure we're delivering excellent quality content.

www.ingramcontent.com/pod-product-compliance
Lightning Source LLC
Chambersburg PA
CBHW061803210326
41599CB00034B/6860